SHADOW OF THE
SULTAN'S REALM

SHADOW OF THE
SULTAN'S REALM

The Destruction of the Ottoman Empire and the Creation of the Modern Middle East

Daniel Allen Butler

Potomac Books
Washington, D.C.

Library of Congress Cataloging-in-Publication Data
Butler, Daniel Allen.
  Shadow of the sultan's realm : the destruction of the Ottoman Empire and
the creation of the modern Middle East / Daniel Allen Butler. — 1st ed.
     p. cm.
  Includes bibliographical references and index.
  ISBN 978-1-59797-496-7 (hardcover)
  ISBN 978-1-59797-584-1 (electronic edition)
  1. Turkey—History—Mehmed V, 1909–1918. 2. World War, 1914–1918—Turkey.
  3. Middle East—History—1914–1923. I. Title.
  DR583.B87 2011
  956'.02—dc22

                                                    2011005409

Printed in the United States of America on acid-free paper that meets the American National Standards Institute Z39-48 Standard.

Potomac Books
22841 Quicksilver Drive
Dulles, Virginia 20166

First Edition

10 9 8 7 6 5 4 3 2 1

To Emily Korf

It's amazing how far ten years of friendship can take you.

CONTENTS

MAPS

INTRODUCTION

It was the cataclysm that nobody knew had occurred.

Just as the world had kept its attention riveted to the four-year-long carnage of the Western Front during the Great War, so, also, it focused on the drama unfolding in the palace of Versailles as the victorious Allies dictated terms of peace to the defeated Germans. And so hardly anyone noticed that along with the Houses of Romanov, Hapsburg, and Hohenzollern, another imperial throne had vanished in the dust and rubble that were postwar Europe. It was a realm far older than any of the others, one with a history as rich, colorful, tumultuous, and bloody as any of them—an empire that, at the height of its glory, had stretched from the eastern shore of the Black Sea to the Pillars of Hercules: the House of Osman and the Ottoman Empire.

And yet, in its passing, the Ottoman Empire determined much of how the next century would unfold, not only in the Middle East, but for the larger part of the civilized world as well. It was both the fortune and the curse of the Ottoman Empire and the sultans who ruled it to have been at the center of world events for most of its fourteen hundred–year history. Geography had placed the Ottoman Turks at what would become a crossroads between the Occident and the Orient at a time when those terms were still valid; history dictated that their empire would still have a place in the political and military calculus of the Great Powers even after the Ottomans' power had irrecoverably waned.

Nor did the influence of the Sultan's realm end with its collapse. The destruction of the Ottoman Empire would lead to the creation of one of the greatest superpowers of the twentieth century—the Union of the Soviet Socialist Republics, and with it, a half-century of international tension that became known as the Cold War. At the same time, as the Allies dismembered the empire and created the patchwork of nation-states that became the modern Middle East, they sowed the wind that would be the whirlwind of terror and warfare reaped in the opening decade of the twenty-first century.

And because they were looking elsewhere, fascinated first by the negotiations in Versailles' Hall of Mirrors, then turning their attention inward as they began to confront their own grief over the sacrifices of blood and treasure that had been made during the Great War, nobody really knew it had happened.

The Ottoman Empire would be destroyed through a combination of battles, blunders, bureaucrats, and buffoons. Campaigns such as Gallipoli, battles with names like Kut and Beersheba. Monarchs such as Sultan Abdul-Hamid and Kaiser Wilhelm II of Germany and ambitious politicians like Ismail Enver, Mehmed Talaat, David Lloyd George, and Arthur Balfour. Diplomatic ciphers like Sir Mark Sykes and François Georges-Picot. The empire would be brought down by men such as Gen. Sir Frederick Maude, Gen. Sir Edmund Allenby, and Lt. Col. T. E. Lawrence. And as it finally fell, the empire would introduce to the world the towering figure of Middle Eastern history in the twentieth century, Mustafa Kemal Atatürk.

While much of the narrative that follows is, of necessity, military in content, this is not a military history in the conventional sense of being a "battle narrative." It is an accounting of who, how, and why, not a recapitulation of carnage and combat; it is an examination of how the Ottoman Empire essentially destroyed itself. For the Ottoman Turks did not passively stand aside while greedy and ambitious politicians in London and Paris plotted and schemed over how they would dismember the corpse of what had been called "the Sick Man of Europe." That Sick Man showed a remarkable vigor in what were supposed to be his final days and, for a few brief astonishing moments, actually stood on the threshold of triumphing over the combined naval and military power of France and the British Empire. That the Turks failed in so doing was not the result of the brilliant and ruthless execution of policies by the Allies or any glorious feat of Allied arms; the Turks failed because of their own acts of commission and omission, which combined to bring down the edifice of the Ottoman Empire. In the end, it was brought down so low that all what remained, when the dust had finally settled in the Middle East, was just the shadow of the Sultan's realm.

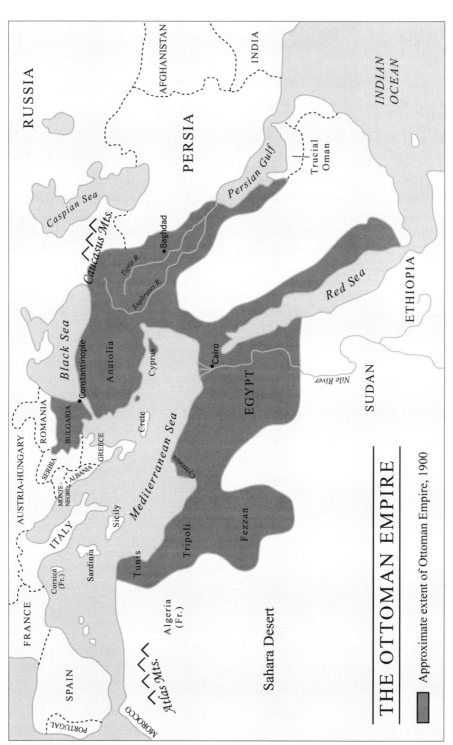

THE OTTOMAN EMPIRE

■ Approximate extent of Ottoman Empire, 1900

Chad Blevins

CHAPTER ONE
THE SULTAN'S REALM

Embedded in one of the walls of the nave of St. Stephen's Cathedral in Vienna is a Turkish cannonball. A relic from the Siege of 1683, it marks the flood tide of the last great surge of the Ottoman Empire into Europe, the farthest point of the Turkish assault on Christendom. The Austrian-Polish Army, led by the Polish warrior-king Jan Sobieski, reached Vienna, with only days to spare before the beleaguered city fell, and immediately attacked the Turks. From September 11 to September 13 the two armies fought, a struggle marked by merciless ferocity and astonishing courage on both sides, before the Turks, already nearly exhausted by the siege, withdrew from Vienna, never to return. Although more than three centuries would pass before the Ottoman Empire ceased to exist, the retreat of the Ottoman Army from the walls of Vienna signaled the beginning of the empire's irreversible decline and eventual collapse. Lost in the shadows of the Great War, it was a fall to which much of the world paid scant attention, yet as it died, the Ottoman Empire would give shape to the next century.

The origins of the Ottoman Turks can be traced back to the Turkic peoples who had migrated from the steppes of Central Asia to the central and eastern parts of the old Roman province of Anatolia, what is today modern Turkey, sometime between 300 and 400 A.D. In the eighth century these seminomadic tribes had given up their somewhat amorphous animistic religion in exchange for the new dynamic creed of Islam, which was then surging out of the Arabian Peninsula, its faithful bringing conversion on the edge of their swords. Called Beyliks, as early as

1

the sixth century A.D., these settlements became small emirates nominally subject to the authority of the Seljuk Turks of Mesopotamia, their responsibility being the protection of the border that the Seljuk realm shared with the Byzantine Empire.

The first turning point in the Ottoman Turks' history came in 1071, when the Seljuk Sultanate of Rûm won a decisive victory over the Byzantines at the Battle of Manzikert. No sooner had the Seljuk Empire defeated the Byzantines than it became embroiled in a struggle for dominance of the Moslem world with the Arab Fatimids in Egypt and southern Syria. Taking advantage of the Seljuks' distraction, the Beyliks were able to permanently establish themselves, asserting their independence from the Seljuks as they carved out a homeland for themselves in western and central Anatolia, in what had once been the heart of the Byzantine Empire.

The first collision between Christian Byzantium and Islam had come in 636 A.D., when Arab Moslems surged out of Arabia and ran headlong into the Byzantine Empire. The last remnant of the ancient Roman Empire, ruled from Constantinople (originally known as "Byzantium" and still often called that centuries later, the city gave the empire its name), it had been a separate entity since 395 A.D. When Christianity and Islam first clashed, the Byzantine Empire covered much of present-day Turkey, Armenia, Jordan, Syria, Israel, and Egypt. When they first met the Moslems, the Byzantines had just concluded a long and costly war with the Persians, who themselves were exhausted and would soon fall to advancing Islamic armies. The Byzantine Empire, however, would prove more difficult for the Arab Moslems to overwhelm—even in her weakened state Byzantium was very strong. Only a combination of unrelenting pressure from without, coupled with disorder and discord within the empire, would finally topple the Byzantines, a process that would take almost four hundred years.

Because the Ottoman Turks would eventually bring down the Byzantine Empire—and the Byzantines would exert such a powerful influence on the Ottomans—it is worth taking note of the edifice they would supplant. In 330 A.D. Emperor Constantine, concluding that the Roman Empire had grown too large to be effectively ruled from Rome alone, divided the empire into eastern and western halves, establishing the capital of the eastern empire in the Greek port of Byzantium—a city strategically situated on the European side of the Bosporus at its entrance to the Sea of Marmara, where the Black Sea flows into the Mediterranean. For almost twelve hundred years this city, which Constantine had modestly renamed Constantinople, would rule the Byzantine Empire, the last bastion of Roman glory and a formidable power unto itself.

The language and the culture of the Byzantine Empire were Greek, while its laws and governance were Roman; this gave the empire a distinctly cosmopolitan attitude toward the rest of the world. For most of its history the Byzantine Empire was remarkably tolerant of non-Christian religious beliefs—such as the cults and mystery religions from Egypt and Persia—although Christianity was the "official" state religion. Emulating the glory days of Rome, the Byzantine emperors aggressively expanded their realm during the fifth and sixth centuries until the empire included not only Greece and Anatolia, but Syria, Egypt, Sicily, most of Italy, and the Balkans, with outposts across North Africa as far as Morocco.

Anatolia (modern-day Turkey and northwest Iraq) was the heart of the empire, and when Syria fell to the Moslems in the seventh century, it became the frontier as well. Byzantium's absolute power reached its zenith under Emperor Basil II (976–1025), who extended the empire's boundaries eastward to the Euphrates and made considerable inroads north into Bulgaria. Yet conquest was achieved at the cost of overextending the empire's economy, and as a consequence decline soon set in. By the end of the eleventh century, Byzantine power in Mesopotamia would be broken, the defenses of Anatolia breached by the rising tide of the Islamic Empire.

Of course, the "Islamic Empire" was not an empire in the traditional sense—a vast collection of lands ruled by a central authority. It was a far different creature, for there was no single seat of supreme authority from which all power flowed and which ruled over the territories conquered by the Moslem armies. Rather, it was a confederation of principalities along with their conquered territories, loosely bound together, driven in equal part by a desire to conquer and by the missionary imperative in Islam to spread the True Faith—by force if necessary.

Among those principalities was a tribe of Turks called the Söğüt, after the village where they lived. Having for the most part avoided any involvement in the Crusades during the twelfth and thirteenth centuries, they were gathered together under a chieftain by the name of Ertugrul and had settled in the valley of the Sakarya River. When Ertugrul died in 1281, he was succeeded by his son Osman (or Othman, as the name is sometimes spelled), who was intelligent, ambitious, carefully aggressive, and a conscientious ruler as he expanded his realm. As other Beyliks busied themselves with intertribal bickering, Osman, once he was certain his base of power was secure, began moving against these smaller, weaker Turkish princelings. By the end of the thirteenth century, Osman had absorbed, through either conquest or political maneuver, all of the petty Turkish states in Anatolia. He now ruled a territory that encompassed more than 10,000 square miles (16,000 square kilometers). It was Osman who would give a name to this new Turkish state: "Osman," distorted by Europeans who could never master the Turkish pronunciation, became "Ottoman," and his people became the "Ottoman" Turks.

Osman also bequeathed his successors a remarkably well-organized government system that would endure for nearly four centuries. Unlike most of its contemporaries, including the Arab states, the Ottoman bureaucracy was not a strictly military form of government. The viability of the Ottoman state was not dependent on a continuous policy of aggression. Undeniably expansionist, the empire was nonetheless never predisposed to wars of unbridled rapine and plunder—conquest for its own sake—which had been the method of the Mongols. Instead, the military campaigns of the Turks were carefully thought-out preludes to Ottoman settlement in the areas that had been attacked.

In 1299 Osman declared himself a sultan, Osman I; originally, "sultan" was an abstract Arabic noun that meant "sovereign authority," but before long it had evolved into a title that was soon being bestowed upon—or assumed by—ruling nobles, princes, and magistrates. Osman's assumption of the rank of sultan marked the beginning of the Ottoman Dynasty. He also set a remarkable precedent for his heirs: the twenty-five years of his reign were marked by such ability and wisdom that it became a proverb among the Turks on the accession of a new sultan to say, "May he rule as well as Osman."

Following Osman's death in 1324, his son Orhan I continued his policy of expansion. As clever a military leader as his father, Orhan also played the political game with a high degree of skill. His marriage to Theodora, the daughter of John Cantacuzenus, a Byzantine prince who had designs on the imperial throne in Constantinople, was a carefully calculated dynastic alliance. When Cantacuzenus revolted against the Emperor John V Palaeologus in 1346, Orhan openly supported him. His reward, once Cantacuzenus was safely ensconced as co-emperor, was to be allowed the privilege of raiding the Gallipoli Peninsula at the southern end of the Dardanelles, thus giving the Ottomans their first stronghold in Europe. It would serve as a springboard for Ottoman invasion and colonization throughout Thrace and parts of Bulgaria and give the Turks strategic control over the land routes that connected Byzantium with the rest of Europe, or Christendom, as it was called then.

Orhan also set about refining the structure of the Turkish bureaucracy. Osman himself had created its basic organization, and it was a work of genius, for it was able to function with an admirable degree of efficiency for nearly five hundred years. Only when the world around the Ottoman Empire changed economically, socially, and scientifically beyond anything that Osman would have recognized did the system of government administration he created finally begin to break down.

That administration was known as the "millet system." It divided the empire into a collection of semiautonomous principalities, also known as "millets" or *muqata'ah*, with their boundaries being drawn along either ethnic or religious lines, whichever was more effective and efficient. Each muqata'ah was ruled by its own religious or secular leader, usually known as the *hidiv* (a Turkish word meaning "governor," taken from the Persian *khidew*), or *pasha* (sometimes rendered *bashaw*, meaning "lord"), and was allowed to retain its own laws and customs in exchange for a pledge of ultimate fealty to the Sultan. The hidiv, granted viceroylike authority, almost always answered directly to the Sultan, only rarely to an intermediary or a representative, and was charged with maintaining order within his muqata'ah by collecting taxes and levying troops in time of war. In return, the hidiv was allowed to keep a specified portion of the revenues collected, which would be his to spend as he saw fit. Some lower-level administrators or minor governors were given similar privileges in place of salaries. Although it was a system that seemed tailor-made for graft and corruption, on balance the majority of the hidiv were reasonably honest; even in the cases where they were more avaricious than usual, the system ensured a regular collection of revenues and eliminated the need for large numbers of bureaucrats.

By allowing nominally subject peoples to retain the larger measure of their ethnic and religious identities while at the same time ruling with a relatively light hand, the Ottomans eliminated most potential sources of discontent and rebellion. There were also institutions that united the peoples ruled by the Ottoman Turks. Foremost among these were the artisans' guilds, which usually took no note of religion or ethnicity but simply recognized skilled artistry. Another unifying influence was trade, both within the empire and without: at this point in time, all of the trade routes from Europe to the Far East—India and China—passed through Ottoman lands. Tolls and taxes were exacted for these passages, while supplying the traders with animals, fodder, and provisions became one of the foundations of the Ottoman economy.

Together Osman and Orhan set the precedents for ability by which all subsequent sultans would be judged. When Orhan died in 1360, he bequeathed an empire to his heirs that was militarily strong, financially stable, and well organized. For the next two hundred years their successors lived up to those standards with admirable competence, culminating in the reign of the aptly named Suleiman the Magnificent. Eight generations of sultans would oversee the ongoing expansion of the Ottoman Empire by whatever means was available to them.

It was not a steady expansion, nor was it uninterrupted. The Turks lost as many battles as they won, as Serbs, Bulgars, Albanians, Greeks, Venetians, Walachians, Hungarians, and Poles, in diverse combinations at various times, fought bitterly to oppose Turkish expansion into the Balkans or throw them out of lands they had already conquered. In 1400 a Mongol horde led by Tamerlane (or Timur Leng) appeared in eastern Anatolia, and the Mongols quickly subjugated the Ottoman Turks for almost a decade, a period known in Ottoman history as the Interregnum. A bitter, bloody civil war followed: for ten years Sultan Bezayid I's four surviving sons fought one another for the throne (Bezayid himself died in captivity at the hands of the Mongols). Nevertheless, by 1451, through a combination of military skill, political adroitness, and pure good fortune, the Ottoman Turks gradually regained their cohesion and their realm. The Turkish position in the Balkans was finally secure, and the Sultan, by then Mehmed II, turned his attention to the most glittering prize of all—Constantinople.

In the fifteenth century, the magic conjured up by the name "Constantinople" was immense, powerful, heady stuff indeed—and totally devoid of reality. The blunt truth was that by 1451, the city was a mere shadow of its former self—a feeble, desiccated, old dowager clinging fitfully to its faded glory and the scraps of its once-sprawling power. The Byzantine Empire had been reduced to little more than the city of Constantinople itself, along with a few small patches of land on either side of the Straits of Bosporus. The city had been viciously sacked by a Crusader Army in 1204, the culmination of a conspiracy by the Venetians who sought to break the economic power of their chief rival for the lucrative merchant trade from India and

China. Byzantium never fully recovered from the disaster, and after two centuries of poverty large sections of the city had fallen into disrepair while its population had steadily dwindled.

Yet Constantinople retained a mystique that it would never lose. Heir to ancient Rome's mantle of glory, the city was imbued with a sentimental nimbus of the unity and direction lost a millennium earlier when Rome fell to the Visigoths; it was a moral touchstone for the nations of Europe that were only beginning to shape their own national identities. The strength of the city's defenses and the skill and courage of the Byzantine *cataphractarii* (heavy cavalry) were legendary. Despite the schism between the Roman Catholic and Eastern Orthodox churches, Constantinople was recognized by all of Christendom as one of Christianity's two epicenters (Rome being the other) of spiritual authority, learning, and instruction. Finally, despite the truth of the poverty into which Constantinople had fallen, in the minds of nearly everyone in Europe the legends and the myths of Byzantium's fabulous wealth persisted. All in all, the sway exerted by Byzantium—Constantinople—was so powerful that although the city's importance had become more symbolic than substantive, having it fall into the hands of the "infidel" Turks would shake the morale of Christendom to its foundations.

Mehmed II spent two years in meticulous preparation for the siege. He ordered the construction of a fleet of galleys powerful enough to cut off the Byzantine capital from any chance of support or reinforcement from the maritime cities of Italy. The Rumeli Fortress was built on the Bosporus to serve as a base of operations for the siege, as well as a training ground for the army that would assault the city. An enormous siege train of very heavy cannons was procured from Hungarian gunsmiths. Finally, Mehmed gauged his moment carefully, choosing to begin the siege in April 1453, as springtime was when most of the Christian powers of Europe would be preoccupied with their own political and dynastic squabbles.

The Siege of Constantinople became the stuff of legends. The city had no realistic chance of successfully resisting the Turks—an eventuality that assumed the Italian city-states could cease their bickering and unite in the effort to raise the siege. Yet Constantinople's defenders, led by the emperor, Constantine XI Palaiologos, and Giovanni Giustiniani, a Venetian mercenary general, fought with a determination that bordered on the fanatical. In the end, however, the once-impregnable walls of the city were breached after a relentless bombardment, and on May 29, 1453, after fifty-three days of fighting before the walls of Constantinople, the Turks stormed the city.

Mehmed renamed the city "Istanbul," although for most of the rest of the world—and many of the Ottoman Turks as well—it continued to be known as "Constantinople." It became the imperial capital in 1462 when the Topkapi Palace was completed. Mehmed fell victim to the city's imperial mystique when he began to style himself "Kaiser-i-Rum," or "Roman Caesar," and attempted to restructure his bureaucracy along the lines of the old Byzantine state. His little fantasies and pretensions did nothing to dilute his energies or vision, however. Emissaries were sent to the four corners of the empire with orders to attract as many emigrants to the new capital as possible, particularly skilled artisans, craftsmen, and traders, in an effort to repopulate the city and protect its commerce. Among the enticements were choice bits of property within the city, as well as guarantees to Jews and Christians that they would be allowed to practice their own religions without fear of repression or reprisal. Within a generation of its fall to the Turks, Constantinople was growing and thriving—multiethnic and multicultural, it quickly became the economic, cultural, and political heart of the Sultan's realm.

Mehmed II, who also began to style himself "the Conqueror," devoted considerable energy to codifying Ottoman law and establishing several outstanding centers of learning, but he would continue to fight wars of expansion and consolidation for the remaining twenty-eight years of his life. In this he became the exemplar for the next several generations, who found themselves obliged to quell rebellions among the empire's Slavic vassals in the Balkans, as well as intermittent incursions of varying severity by foreign powers to the east and west. In a little more than a century and a half, the Ottomans had evolved from being just one more petty state among the remnants of the Great Seljuk Empire to the overlords of what had been the last and perhaps grandest legatee of the Roman Empire. Weakness and a frequent lack of unity on the part of their foes had played no small part in their spectacular rise, but it was the Turks' distinctive combination of a remarkable talent for war coupled with a gift for administration that allowed them not only to create their empire but to maintain their hold on it. It is a military maxim that conquest is easy; keeping that which was conquered is difficult. The Ottomans' superior military and civil organization gave them the ability to do both.

The power, splendor, and size of the Ottoman Empire reached their peak in the sixteenth century, under a sultan who has been known throughout Western history by the justly deserved title "Suleiman the Magnificent." Ruling for forty-six years, from 1520 to 1566, the Turks know him as Suleiman the Law-Giver. No matter what name he is called, his reign would become the embodiment of the popular conception of the Ottoman Empire. Born in 1494, Suleiman was the tenth Ottoman sultan—a contemporary to Charles V, the Holy Roman Emperor; Francis I of France; and England's Henry VIII. It is no overstatement to say that his accomplishments far outshine those of any of them.

Suleiman was a fighting monarch, a warrior as well as a ruler, and he personally led Ottoman armies in some of their most stunning conquests. Suleiman defeated the Mamelukes of Egypt and Syria and took Cairo in 1517. He defeated Algiers in 1518, and Ottoman fleets dominated the eastern Mediterranean Sea, the Black Sea, the Red Sea, and the Persian Gulf; most of the Greek islands that had been held by the Venetians fell to the Turks. The Hungarians were defeated at Mohács in 1526, which left the fortress of Buda vulnerable—it would fall in 1541, along with most of the rest of Hungary. Transylvania, Walachia, and Moldavia all became tributaries of Constantinople—even Vienna was briefly besieged in 1529. When the last Abbasid caliph in Damascus abdicated in 1534, Suleiman annexed all of Mesopotamia and Persia to the empire and at the same time reduced Baghdad, hitherto the secular center of Islam, to little more than a provincial city. He imposed Ottoman rule over most of the Levant and what is today Saudi Arabia and annexed vast stretches of Arab territory in North Africa as far west as Morocco.

This tremendous expansion would ultimately carry deeper and more lasting consequences for the conquerors than for the conquered. For the most part, the newly subject Arabs continued to simply maintain allegiance to a tribal chieftain or caliph, who in turn pledged fealty to an imperial governor and the Sultan; for the Ottomans, however, it opened an entirely unexpected chapter in their history. With an empire that stretched from India to Europe, holding absolute sway over the trade routes to the Far East, as well as a dominant position in the Mediterranean Sea, the Ottomans were no longer merely a regional power but were now compelled to assume the mantle of a world empire.

It was a task to which Suleiman was equal. In 1535 he initiated what would become a long-standing friendship with France, one built on their mutual interest in containing the growing power of Hapsburg Austria and Spain. Wisely, Suleiman declined to formalize the relationship as an alliance, allowing the empire to avoid becoming entangled in the factionalism of Europe's religious wars that followed the Reformation.

Suleiman's chief legacy to his subjects was his recognition of the need for genuine justice—the rule of law—and his intolerance of corruption. He was fascinated by law, and, working with some of the finest legal minds, he oversaw a complete reconstruction of the Turkish legal system, bringing uniformity and rationalism to what had been an often-contradictory muddle of tradition and Moslem doctrine. While the Sultan's power was absolute in theory, in practice his prerogatives were limited by the spirit of Moslem canonical law, and he usually shared his authority with the leading clerical authority, as well as with his Grand Vizier, an office much akin to a European prime minister. Suleiman's genius was in codifying these relationships so that the laws could be consistently applied throughout the empire, an accomplishment that earned his legacy among Moslems as "The Lawgiver."

Suleiman was also a keen patron of science and the arts, filling his court with poets, architects, artists, and philosophers; he is justifiably remembered as one of Islam's great poets and was noted for his talent as a goldsmith. Science—it was called "natural philosophy" in those days—reached a pinnacle within the empire under Suleiman was well. Patronage of scholars had actually begun a century earlier, under Muhammed II, owing in no small part to his personal interest in science and education, which led to his establishment of several schools of higher learning in Constantinople after its capture. Muhammed had taken an interest in European culture long before he became sultan and was taught Roman and European history while still a prince by a group of Italian scholars led by the humanist Ciriaco d'Ancona. Showing the same cosmopolitan outlook that characterized Ottoman attitudes toward religion and culture, Muhammed became the sponsor of numerous Islamic, Greek, and Italian scholars, philosophers, astronomers, mathematicians, and mapmakers. During Suleiman's reign, scientific, philosophical, and religious debate took place in his court without fear of censure or retribution; this was at a time when scientific inquiry was, in most of Europe, still being regarded as borderline heresy, if not outright blasphemy.

The grand tradition of Ottoman architecture also peaked in the sixteenth century under Suleiman. As befitting the imperial capital, Constantinople was the most glittering jewel in the Ottoman crown of cities. A visitor sailing up the Sea of Marmara and into the narrows of the Bosporus would be struck by the bustle of the city's waterfront. Here, ships from every corner of the Mediterranean world, from the Black Sea, and from as far as India, emptied their cargoes of rice, sugar, pepper, spices, saffron, salt, silk, cotton, coffee, tea, and a thousand other sundries. These cargoes would make their way to Constantinople's bazaars and markets, where the centuries-old ritual of haggling would continue from sunrise to sunset. Next the visitor would notice how green was the city: cypresses and fruit trees grew everywhere, every dwelling had its garden. The impression created was that of a vast pleasure garden.

Rising through the canopy of foliage would be the towers, domes, and spires of the city's mosques, libraries, and palaces. Ottoman architecture achieved its grandest expression in the series of mosques that still dominate the horizon of modern Istanbul—the Fatih, built between 1463 and 1470; the Bayazid Mosque, completed in 1491; the Selim Mosque, finished in 1522; and the Sehzade and Suleiman *külliyes*, built in the 1540s. These masterpieces of Ottoman style were the ultimate fusion of two aesthetic traditions, Byzantine and Islamic. The style also extended to public baths, caravansaries, and in particular the elaborate pavilions, halls, and fountains of the huge palace complex of the Topkapi, which still sits in unrivaled splendor over the skyline of modern Istanbul.

The Topkapi perches on a rocky promontory that in part forms the Golden Horn, the strait that separates the Sea of Marmara from the Bosporus. Here, in the Sultan's seraglio, the ultimate seat of Ottoman power reposed. More than five thousand men and woman lived and worked here solely to fulfill the Sultan's every need and wish. Virtually a city within a city, the seraglio was home to an etiquette and a protocol even more formal, stylized, and ritualistic than that which Louis XIV would inflict upon the court of Versailles a century later. There were whole companies of servants assigned to the imperial wardrobe, the imperial laundry, and the imperial bath. There were servants responsible for lighting the imperial pipe, others for serving the needs of the imperial toilet, still others for opening and closing specific doors. One servant was charged solely with the duty of properly folding the Sultan's turban; another was responsible for the placement and adjustment of the imperial napkin at mealtimes. He would carry out his duties in between the ministrations of the Pickle Server, the Fruit Server, the Water Server, or one of a platoon of Tray Servers. The whole of the Sultan's court was organized to ensure that the Sultan did not have to exert himself in even a single effort he did not wish to make.

Within the realm of the seraglio was yet another realm, one that was never seen by the outside world and whose occupants were barely aware that there *was* a world outside the walls confining them: the harem. The word comes from the Arabic *harim*, which means "forbidden," and it was perfectly descriptive—only the Sultan, his privileged guests, and the women who lived in the harem, along with their eunuch guards, were ever allowed to be inside the harem. The women inside were never permitted to leave.

The popular concept of the Ottoman harem is that of a world of limitless luxury, sex, and intrigue, yet what is startling about this perception is its overall accuracy. The harem's origins lay in the reign of Suleiman the Magnificent. His wife, Roxelana, was an intelligent, strong-willed Russian woman possessed of fiery red hair and a temperament to match, who continually sought to interfere in the affairs of the Ottoman government. Doing so, she created so many problems for Suleiman's ministers that after his death, it became the custom for sultans never to formally marry but merely to take concubines for the dual purposes of producing heirs and obtaining sensual satisfaction.

Inevitably, this resulted in life becoming rigidly stratified among the women confined within the harem. The only way a woman could gain influence or power in the court at Constantinople was through a male, beginning with the Sultan himself and then, in descending order of importance, through the potential heirs to the throne, from eldest to youngest. In practice this meant that the mother of the reigning sultan essentially ruled the harem, with the mothers of the other potential heirs vying and scrambling for position below her.

When Osman founded the empire, no rule of primogeniture—the right of the firstborn to inherit the throne—existed under Ottoman custom or Islamic sharia law. If a sultan died without a son or, as usually happened, he left several sons without designating an heir to the throne, the question of succession was usually settled by violence—poison, strangulation, or the assassin's dagger were the order of the day within the harem. It quickly became the custom, once a successor had been crowned, to eliminate potential rivals by executing all of his male relatives—a custom formalized in 1413 by Mehmed I after a power struggle of the Interregnum and the civil war that followed in the wake of the Mongol invasion by Tamerlane in 1400. This ruthless policy was adhered to for nearly three hundred years before being repealed in the early seventeenth century and replaced with the rule of primogeniture. In the meantime, the knowledge that failure to succeed to the throne was tantamount to a death sentence led to endless scheming among the head wives and the concubines, each striving to gain preference for their sons, while the princes themselves became proficient in the art of lethal palace intrigues—hardly the proper training for sultans-to-be—which did nothing to make them fit to rule.

Throughout the seventeenth and eighteenth centuries, the sultans grew weaker, cocooned as they were in a life of luxury and with the distractions of the harem continually at hand, and the Office of Grand Vizier accrued more and more real power unto itself. The power of the Sultan flowed through the Grand Vizier, who served as a sort of prime minister, confidant, and imperial majordomo. The actual administration of the imperial bureaucracy, the judiciary, and the army was his responsibility; consequently, it is easy to see how the authority of the office grew. Such authority was not without its perils: until well into the nineteenth century, most Grand Viziers died in office, strangled by an imperial executioner who, acting on the Sultan's instructions, was exacting payment for some failure in the performance of their duties. Nevertheless, the power inherent in the office was an almost-irresistible allure to men of talent and ambition, and there was rarely a scarcity of candidates for the office.

The open, or public, court of the Sultan, which was overseen by the Grand Vizier, was known as the Sublime Porte. The original "porte" was the gate, the Bab-i Ali, or "Lofty Gate," which led to the Office of Grand Vizier in the Topkapi Palace. According to an ancient Persian tradition that the Ottomans freely borrowed, the gates of cities and royal palaces were places of meeting and assembly. So it was at this gate where the Sultan traditionally greeted and met with foreign ambassadors. "Sublime Porte" is a French translation of "Lofty Gate," and given France's unique (at that time) relationship with the Ottoman Empire, the choice of language was hardly surprising. Nor was it startling that the name was widely viewed as an acknowledgment of the empire's position as the gateway between Europe and Asia.

Yet with Suleiman's death in 1566, the first faint cracks began to appear in the grand façade of the empire, although more than two hundred years would pass before they became visible to the rest of the world. The empire had suffered its first serious setback in 1571 off the western coast of Greece in the Gulf of Lepanto, where a Turkish galley fleet was attempting to expand Ottoman dominance along the Adriatic coast. Met by a combined Spanish and Venetian fleet led by Don John of Austria, the Turks were defeated at the Battle of Lepanto, and their advance up the Adriatic, which would have threatened the whole of northern Italy, as well as the heart of Hapsburg Austria, was stopped cold. It was a significant reverse, for Turkish naval power had long played a vital part in Ottoman expansion. When Capt. Alfred Thayer Mahan, the nineteenth-century American naval historian and theorist, defined sea power as the ability to use the oceans and the seas to move men, materiel, and goods at will, where and when they were needed, while denying an enemy the opportunity to do the same, he was articulating a concept that the Ottomans had instinctively understood as early as the thirteenth century.

Unlike the Romans and the Byzantines, who usually viewed the sea as a vast barrier and an obstacle to be overcome, the Turks emulated the Greeks and the Phoenicians, who had seen the sea as an opportunity and who had used it as an unobstructed pathway to prosperity. Turkish naval policy was never one of simple raiding for plunder and loot, like that of the Barbary pirates of the Mediterranean or the Scythians of the Black Sea. Instead, it played a vital role in the empire's expansion, coastal raids and landing parties serving as the vanguard for permanent Turkish settlements along the coasts of the eastern Mediterranean, Aegean, Adriatic, and Black Seas. Turkish power would then spread inland from these settlements, whose lines of communication were secure and protected by the Turkish galleys. Turkish sea power would be the decisive factor in containing Russia's southward expansion in the seventeenth and eighteenth centuries, turning back Peter the Great as he tried to wrest control of the Crimea and the northern coast of the Black Sea from the Sublime Porte. The Ottoman Turks would always remain conscious of the importance of sea power, and the empire would continue to be the dominant naval power in the Middle East until the nineteenth century. Eventually, the Turks' desire to reassert their maritime authority in the Aegean and Black Seas would have decisive consequences for the fate of the empire.

Although it temporarily eclipsed Turkish sea power, the defeat at Lepanto was regarded as merely a temporary setback, although by this time the Ottomans were facing enemies along every frontier. Venice, Austria, Poland, Russia, and Persia were all making war on the Turks, often in combination with one another. In the first half of the seventeenth century, Sultan Murad IV restored a large measure of Turkish military prestige when he defeated a resurgent Persia in 1638, and wrested Crete from the Venetians. In 1683 a huge Turkish army under Grand Vizier Kara

Mustafa lunged westward out of Hungary into Austria and surrounded the Hapsburg capital of Vienna. The city would have been taken if not for the last-minute
arrival of a relieving army led by King Jan Sobieski of Poland. Then a series of campaigns by the Polish king, along with those led by Charles V of Lorraine, Louis of
Baden, and the great Prince Eugene of Savoy, drove the Turks back deep into their
own territory, a retreat that ended only when the Treaty of Karlowitz was signed
in 1699.

The treaty cost the Ottomans dearly—they surrendered the whole of Hungary to the House of Hapsburg and were forced to abandon large sections of their Balkan territories. Karlowitz was the real, tangible beginning of the empire's decline,
as the next two hundred years would be marked by constant compromise, concilia-
tion, and concession, with Ottoman power and authority steadily diminishing.

A form of stagnation began to take hold of Ottoman affairs and institutions.
Rather than growing and evolving to keep pace with the rest of the Mediterranean
world, the Ottoman Empire froze in time, held in the thrall of Suleiman's great-
ness. As happens all too often when a monarch of the stature of Suleiman passes,
those who succeed him are seen by comparison as being lesser men, which, inevitably, they are. Seventeen sultans would ascend to the Ottoman throne in the
years between Suleiman's death in 1566 and 1789, and for the most part—there
were few exceptions—they were an admittedly indifferent lot: men of limited ability, with little or no education or training in the responsibilities and duties of rule.
When Muhammed III died in 1605, his two minor sons were the only direct male
heirs. The elder, Ahmet I, spared his brother Mustafa's life but locked him away in
a secluded apartment in the harem of Topkapi Palace. Ahmet's decision, though
unusually merciful, marked the beginning of the pernicious influence the harem
would exert on the affairs of the empire. It was also a mistake, for Mustafa in turn
would lead a palace revolt in 1617 in which he would overthrow his brother and
take his place on the throne, in turn banishing Ahmet to the harem for the remainder of his life.

At the same time, other gradual but profound shifts in power began. In the
Topkapi Palace, as the sultans spent less and less time in the actual exercising of
their authority in ruling the empire, the Grand Viziers began to fill the power void.
In the provinces, the long-standing Turkish tradition of promotion by merit began
to give way to bribery, corruption, and nepotism. The millet system began to fail

as ambitious officials exploited it shamelessly, buying their offices, then imposing ever-harsher taxes on the people in order to pay for them.

The history of the Ottoman Empire in the years between 1566 and 1789 has sometimes been described as "The Decline of Faith and State," but to Western ears the phrase can be misleading, for the cultural meaning of the terminology was different. In the parlance of the Ottoman world, "decline" did not necessarily imply "decay"; rather, it meant "change"—that the traditional order had in some way been disrupted or displaced. Reforms enacted to halt or reverse the decline, then, were not efforts at producing workable solutions within the context of the problems, but rather attempts to restore the old order that had produced the Golden Age of Suleiman. Consequently, the term "reform" became increasingly reactionary. While the rest of the world (particularly Europe) was slowly—or sometimes rapidly—evolving, the Sultan and his court continually sought to drag the Ottoman Empire back into a time and a place that, with each passing decade, were less and less attuned to the reality of the world developing outside its borders. It was a situation guaranteed to institutionalize imperial stagnation.

The causes of the Ottoman "decline" can be summed up in fairly swift order. Europe entered the Age of Exploration in the late fifteenth and early sixteenth centuries, and by opening direct seagoing trade routes to the Far East, the nations of Western Europe no longer needed the overland routes that had passed through the Levant for more than a millennia. As the overland trade declined, with it went the revenues that maintaining and servicing those routes had provided, hamstringing the economy of the empire just at the time when Europe's economy began to grow at an unprecedented rate. Gold that had been flowing into Ottoman purses was now filling European treasuries.

The explosion of scientific and artistic genius that marked the Renaissance in Italy was paralleled by a quieter but more profound flowering of practical science in much of the rest of Europe. In particular, European farmers were discovering the beginnings of scientific agriculture, which led to larger crop yields and in turn produced larger populations, bigger labor forces, and increased demands for skilled trades and services. Reform, meanwhile, stifled what had once been the world's outstanding scientific and academic community, all in the name of preserving Suleiman's Golden Age. Just as Europe's scientists, engineers, and philosophers were stepping across the threshold of one of the greatest sustained periods of creativity and innovation in the history of the world, the scholars of the Ottoman Empire fell into the embrace of conservative thinking, resisting new ideas and denouncing unorthodox thinking as heretical. Taking for granted the superiority of Moslem and Ottoman civilization, the empire's intellectual community refused to study or even acknowledge the advances being made by the "infidels." Ottoman scholars—and the Moslem clerics who increasingly made up the majority of the Ottomans' intellectual "elite"—would recognize the superiority of a particular "infidel" innovation or practice only when compelled to do so by circumstances. Even then, such recognition would be made only for specific applications of such innovations, because the reactionary Moslem clergy refused to exploit them or the thinking that created them, denouncing such practices as "blasphemous" and "heretical."

Hand in hand with the atrophy of learning and scholarship within the Ottoman Empire came the erosion of imperial authority. With the Sultan often reduced to little more than a figurehead, corrupt and incompetent governors, no longer fearing imperial retribution should they fail to administer their provinces efficiently, turned increasingly to maintaining and enhancing their own personal power, position, and prestige at the expense of the regions for which they were responsible. This occurred at a time when the monarchs of Europe were consolidating their own positions and emplacing strong centralized government structures and bureaucracies of their own to administer the rising power of their nations.

An unexpected by-product of those governments and bureaucracies was the rise of a mercantile class that had no equivalent in the Ottoman Empire. With stable governments came stable societies in which businesses and industries could grow and flourish. The emerging middle classes of the European nations, though small, quickly became national bulwarks at the same time that they were leading their countries into entirely new directions of growth. None of this was happening in the Ottoman Empire, where the mercantile classes resisted change and growth as departures from the idea of the Golden Age. By the end of the eighteenth century, the "traditional" ways of doing business and conducting the affairs of the empire had become so well entrenched that it would take an extraordinary individual to effect any change at all. Yet changes had to come if the empire was to survive.

The extraordinary individual appeared in the person of Sultan Mahmud II, who rose to the throne of the Sublime Porte in 1808. He was determined to carry through the plans for genuine reform and innovation that had been implemented by Sultan Selim III as far back as 1789. Called the New Order, or *Nizam-i Cedid*, Selim's plans had emphasized military and fiscal reform aimed at modernizing the Turkish Army and bringing to account the nobles and the governors who barely acknowledged the authority of the Sultan. On his orders, new military and naval schools were opened, and the Turkish Army was completely reorganized, trained, and equipped along European lines. The traditionally superb Ottoman cavalry forces were retained, but for the first time "infantry" units, as understood by the European powers, were introduced. Selim found new ways of increasing imperial revenues by instituting taxes on liquor, tobacco, and coffee, and Levantine and Greek merchants, who enjoyed enormous prosperity and influence but had paid little in the way of taxes, were stripped of many of their privileges. Ottoman embassies were opened in the major European capitals to provide for direct contact with the West.

The reforms begun by Selim III were left incomplete as he was distracted by wars with Russia and France; the two sultans who succeeded him displayed little interest in continuing Selim's efforts. They were taken up again by Mahmud II in 1808. For more than twenty years, in what later Turks would call the *Tanzimat*, a blizzard of *firmans* (imperial decrees) descended from the Topkapi, abolishing corrupt administration, curbing the sometimes arbitrary authority of the hidivs and the pashas, revising the legal system to make it more evenhanded, and revising the imperial tax code to make it more difficult for governors to find opportunities for graft and corruption. At the same time Mahmud began to regularly attend the meetings of the *divan*, or "state council," driving home the point that he intended to take a personal interest in the affairs of the empire.

Mahmud extended his reforms to the Ottoman Army as well, most notably in his abolition of the Janissary Corps in 1826. The Janissaries had been exerting a baleful influence on the empire for more than a century: forgetting their tradition of being the Sultan's personal bondservants, they increasingly became a law unto themselves. In the provinces, the Janissaries acted like semiautonomous local rulers, while in Constantinople they were a constant source of disruption, often acting in combination with the city's artisans, craftsmen, and students. Echoing the role played by the Praetorian Guard in the declining years of the Roman Empire, they influenced (and sometimes openly decided) the appointment and replacement of governors and other officials and, on occasion, even determined who would succeed to the Sultanate. It was an intolerable state of affairs—clearly, the Janissaries had to go. Here, technology provided Mahmud with an unanswerable argument: the introduction of the musket and with it the disciplined, trained, professional, firepower-based armies of Europe reduced the Janissaries to a colorful anachronism. The Janissaries were summarily disbanded; in their place Mahmud brought in German advisers to restructure the Turkish Army along modern European lines. At the same time he began an ambitious modernization program—constructing roads, aqueducts, and public buildings and improving the education of his subjects—in an attempt to make the imperial bureaucracy more efficient and effective.

Encouraged by their father's example, Mahmud's sons continued his efforts at reform and modernization after his death in 1839. But the rot had gone far and deep: many of the "reforms" of Mahmud's successors were thinly disguised concessions to the four Great Powers of Europe—Great Britain, France, Austria, and Russia—because by now the empire's military strength was only a shadow of its former glory, as it no longer possessed the power of open defiance backed by force of arms. The most humiliating of these reforms by far would be the Ottoman Public Debt Administration (OPDA), created in 1881 for the purpose of collecting taxes in order to pay off the empire's debts owed to European business interests. Staffed entirely by Europeans, with more than five thousand officials posted all across the empire, the OPDA was an independent bureaucracy within the Ottoman bureaucracy. Particularly galling for the Turks was that in addition to its own efforts, the administration had first call on any funds collected by Ottoman tax officials. The Turks grievously resented the implication that they were working to fill foreigners' collection boxes.

By the middle of the nineteenth century, Ottoman foreign policy was increasingly one of merely reacting to the moves and maneuvers of those foreign powers. When European intervention compelled Constantinople to grant Greece her independence, it introduced what would become one of the great issues of European politics for the rest of the century, what was euphemistically termed the "Eastern Question"—that is, how should the spoils be divided when the Ottoman Empire collapsed, and who would do the dividing? Although it could not reasonably be said that the empire was on its last legs, clearly it was weakening with each passing decade. No amount of palliatives could permanently stem the loss of territory and prestige through rebellion or foreign intervention.

Perhaps the best illustration of Turkish weakness was made during the Crimean War. A dispute had arisen between Russia and France over which nation was the rightful "protector" of the various sites in Palestine that were sacred to Christianity. Nominally Ottoman territory, these holy places were traditionally defended by one of Europe's Christian powers. In 1852 France challenged Russia's claim to guardianship and wrested a number of concessions in access and occupation of parts of Palestine and Syria from the Turks. Russia demanded equal consideration, and when it was turned down, it advanced into the province of Bulgaria and down the coast of the Black Sea in October 1853. The Ottomans promptly declared war, and in March 1854 England and France, in truth more concerned with preventing Russia from seizing the Bosporus and Constantinople than with defending Ottoman sovereignty, decided to make common cause against the tsar of Russia and declared war on Russia as well.

The British and the French determined that the Russians were particularly vulnerable to an assault against the Crimean Peninsula: the strategic focus of the campaign would be the fortified port of Sebastopol, Russia's main naval base on the Black Sea. A naval force of British and French warships blockaded the port while a force of 26,000 British and 30,000 French troops were landed at the mouth of the Balaklava Valley. The Ottomans, whose grievances were the ostensible cause of the war, were unable to send a single warship to join the blockading force, and a paltry 5,000 Turkish troops were assembled with the landing force.

Even this pathetic effort nearly exhausted the Turks economically, and although the Ottomans were "victorious" in the Crimean War, the Congress of Paris, which brought the war to an end in 1856, found it necessary to formally recognize the independence and integrity of the Ottoman Empire. It was a humiliating development for the Sublime Porte—despite its diplomatic courtesies and eloquent circumlocutions, the congress had given formal confirmation that the empire's existence now depended on the tolerance of the European powers, rather than on its ability to assert its own sovereignty.

Events that were bringing the empire closer to dissolution now began to acquire a momentum of their own. In 1875 a rebellion in the provinces of Bosnia and Herzegovina triggered the Russo-Turkish War of 1877–78. Despite a surprisingly strong showing by the Turkish Army, the Russians marched almost to the gates of Constantinople, only to be halted by diplomatic pressure from Great Britain and France. The peace settlement, imposed by the Congress of Berlin, saw Romania (formerly, Walachia and Moldavia), Serbia, and Montenegro declared fully independent, while Bosnia and Herzegovina were placed under Austrian administration. Bulgaria, though still nominally an Ottoman principality, became an all-but-autonomous kingdom and asserted its position in 1885, when Bulgar troops occupied the province of Eastern Rumelia with impunity.

There was still hope for the empire: Midhat Pasha succeeded in introducing a liberal constitution in late 1876, and under it, the first Turkish parliament was seated early in the following year. The assembly was short-lived. The new sultan, Abdul-Hamid II, ordered it dissolved in fewer than two years, suspended the constitution, and began to rule as an absolute autocrat. Only by asserting such authority, he believed, could the empire avoid the upheaval that he feared would begin the process by which it would begin to break up. Dissolution was Abdul-Hamid's worst nightmare. It appeared to be coming true in the wake of the Russo-Turkish War of 1877–78, when the Treaty of San Stefano stripped the Sultan of most of his European provinces. It was only because the British, the French, and the Austrians feared that imperial Russia would dominate the states newly formed from the former Ottoman provinces that the Congress of Berlin rewrote the treaty a few months later, softening most of its harshest terms and reducing much of the damage done to the Ottoman Empire. Yet such assistance came at a price: Cyprus was "rented" to Britain in 1878, and when the British occupied Egypt in 1882 after a revolt by the Egyptian Army, Constantinople was forced to accept Egypt's status as a de facto British colony. In 1885 Bulgaria annexed the province of Eastern Rumelia, and the Turks were helpless to prevent it.

Meanwhile, word of the first Armenian massacres reached the outside world, and Western opinion turned sharply against the Sultan and his realm, relegating them to the status of little more than international pariahs. The slaughter of frightful numbers of Armenians living within the bounds of the Ottoman Empire is argued in some circles to be the first documented "holocaust," and there would be a sickening recurrence in the last decades of the Sultan's realm. It also earned Abdul-Hamid his enduring nickname of "Abdul the Damned." At the time some two million Armenians, all nominally Christians, were subjects of the empire, living primarily in northern and eastern Anatolia. The vast majority of them held to the Armenian Apostolic Church; the rest were mostly divided between the Catholic and Protestant faiths. An unassuming, industrious people, the Armenians rarely came into conflict with their neighbors, although they quietly held to a dream of independence. Yet they also had a reputation of unbroken loyalty to their Ottoman overlords right through to the last decade of the nineteenth century, so the Armenians were regarded as *millet-i sadika* (a loyal nation).

Like other minorities, the Armenians were subject to laws that gave them fewer legal rights than the empire's Moslem population; along with Greeks and Jews, they were barred from military service and were taxed twice as much as Moslems. When the Ottomans were defeated in the Russo-Turkish War of 1877–78, imperial Russia announced that it was assuming the role of "protector" of the Christian peoples of the Ottoman Empire, an act of unnecessary bombast that had two completely unforeseen consequences. The first was that the Turks regarded it as a veiled threat, believing that the Russians would use their "protectorate" as a pretext for further incursions into Turkish territory. At the same time the Armenians believed that it was an implied declaration of Russian support, should they seek independence from the Ottomans.

The trigger for the first wave of massacres was a minor Armenian uprising in Bitlis Province in 1894. The local Turkish authorities reacted with unexpected ferocity, fearing Russian intervention should the uprising grow into an open revolt, and they ruthlessly suppressed it, beginning a cycle of brutal attacks on Armenian communities during the next three years. Reliable reports reaching Europe indicated that as many as 300,000 Armenians were killed between 1894 and 1897. Although there was no evidence that directly linked the attacks to Constantinople, perhaps more damning was that neither was there much to indicate that the Sultan had made any effort to prevent the slaughter. In the capitals of Europe the assumption was quickly reached that Abdul-Hamid, like his local magistrates fearing a widespread Armenian uprising, had given tacit permission for the massacres. Whatever the truth may have been, the perception would taint relationships between Constantinople and most of the Great Powers for the few remaining years of the empire.

There were, however, some positive accomplishments under Abdul-Hamid, most notably the construction of the Hejaz Railway and the promotion of the Berlin-to-Baghdad Railway, which brought the Ottoman Turks and imperial Germany into a particularly close diplomatic relationship. Construction of the Hejaz

Railway was begun in 1900, part of Abdul-Hamid's "Pan-Islamic" vision for reviving and reunifying the empire. Completed in 1908, it permitted thousands of Moslems to make the traditional Islamic pilgrimage to Mecca (the *hajj*) in relative comfort and safety. At the same time it also helped reinforce Ottoman control over the chronically troublesome territories in western Arabia.

Yet the blunt truth was that as the nineteenth century was passing into the twentieth century, the "Sick Man of Europe" was clearly in critical condition. Civil rights as they were understood in Western Europe simply did not exist—people were arrested, detained, and oftentimes executed simply on the whim of the Sultan or one of his favored subordinates; even Russian *muzhiks* had more protection under the law than the typical Turkish peasant did. Corruption was rampant once more, there was little industry or technical infrastructure—in 1901 there were barely 1,600 miles (3,000 kilometers) of railroad in the whole of the empire—and what little existed was owned by foreigners, primarily Germans.

Foreigners had become a particular problem, for they were in many ways unraveling the fabric of the empire. By the time Abdul-Hamid assumed the throne, the "concessions" being made to the European powers were literally that: the Turks were conceding their rights and sovereignty to the Westerners. Perhaps the most telling example of the decline of Ottoman authority was a diplomatic convention concluded in 1887 that held Europeans living within the empire from being subject to imperial legality. Instead, when accused of a breach of the empire's laws, the European in question would be tried in Constantinople before a court constituted of fellow Europeans, who judged the accused according to their appropriate national legal code.

Germany was particularly aggressive in seeking a favorable position within the empire, sponsoring the Berlin-to-Baghdad Railway, which was intended to rival France's legendary Orient Express and Great Britain's dream of a Cape-Town-to-Cairo Railway in Africa, as well as providing the technical expertise to build the rest of the empire's railways. Germans managed all of Constantinople's electricity generating plants, its gasworks, its munitions factory, and its arsenal, and the Kaiser's subjects occupied almost all of the skilled technical positions. Not surprisingly, the Ottoman Army was trained and equipped by the Germans. Increasingly, the feeling among educated Turks, who were becoming a shrinking minority within the empire, was that the Sultan's realm was being given away piecemeal by the very men who were charged with maintaining its integrity.

The typical Turkish peasant, meanwhile, eked out an existence from the soil of Anatolia, lived in ignorance, and was usually functionally illiterate. The once-vaunted Ottoman scholarship had been overtaken by the reactionary Moslem clergy, who were most concerned that the Ottoman peasantry faithfully adhere to the teachings of Mohammed—as interpreted by the clerics. It seemed far better to them that those peasants stoically accept their lot and blindly and unquestioningly embrace the teachings of their imams and mullahs, rather than risk overburdening their intellects with such basic skills as reading, writing, or mathematics. Among the empire's Arab population the situation was even worse, as the vast majority of the Arabs lived as seminomads, their lives little different than those of their ancestors in the Middle Ages. All the while the presence of the all-pervasive secret police and its accompanying network of informers loomed over the population, Turk and Arab alike, and kept it in a constant state of near-terror.

It was a situation that could not last long, and in 1908 the Ottoman Empire underwent a convulsion the likes of which it had never before experienced. All of Europe—even the entire world—could see that "the Sick Man of Europe" was living on borrowed time. The empire had been in decline for nearly two centuries, for it had far to fall. Indeed, the "fall" of the Ottoman Empire lasted longer than the span of years that many other empires had existed. In 1908, however, a group of semirevolutionary idealists who called themselves the Young Turks sought to arrest that fall, leading a near-bloodless coup that stripped Abdul-Hamid of much of his power and forced the restoration of the 1876 constitution that Abdul had suspended more than thirty years earlier.

For better or worse, the Ottoman Empire was entering what would be its last chapter. In whatever form it emerged from the reforms and ambitions of the Young Turks, the empire would never be the same. At once reformist and strongly nationalist, the Young Turks were determined to drag the Ottoman Empire out of its quasi-Orientalism and somnolence and transform the nation into a modern, strong, stable European-style state. What they did not anticipate—indeed, what they could never have anticipated—was that in doing so, they would be helping to write the final chapter to the fourteen-centuries-old saga of the Ottoman Empire.

CHAPTER TWO
THE EVE OF WAR

Ironically, the burden of responsibility for the empire's demise fell most heavily on the shoulders of the same men who had set out to save it—the Young Turks. That they would ultimately bring down the empire should, in retrospect, come as no great surprise, for they were remarkably inept. There was something reminiscent of a comic opera about them almost from the moment they stripped the Sultan of his absolute authority and their handpicked parliament took up the reins of power. Yet it had not started that way: the Turkish Revolution of 1908 was one of the swiftest and most successful revolts in modern history. Unlike the convulsions that would sweep across Russia in 1917, shatter Austria-Hungary in 1918, and shake imperial Germany off her foundations that same year (during which time the peasantry, the workers, and the middle class would join together to topple the tsar, the emperor, and the Kaiser from their thrones), the Turkish revolt was led by the Ottoman upper and middle classes to radically reform the Sultanate, rather than abolish it. The Sultan was carefully preserved in his position, while at the same time methodically stripped of his autocratic power, and the Midhat Constitution was restored with the intent of returning the empire to a parliamentary government.

The Midhat Constitution—so named after Midhat Pasha, the Turkish legal scholar who drafted it—had originally been promulgated by Abdul-Hamid on December 23, 1876. By establishing a parliament modeled vaguely along British lines, the Sultan's subjects would, for the first time in the empire's history, have a voice in the formulation of its laws and policies. At least in theory, that was how it was supposed to work. In practice it was something of a failure, for there was very little sense of a genuine need for the document and its institutions among the Turkish ruling caste. Many regarded it, with some justification, as nothing more than a sop to Western liberal sentiment, an expedient to make the Turks appear more "acceptable" and enlightened, particularly to the French and the British. Most did not mourn when Abdul-Hamid suspended the constitution barely six months after it was adopted. For their part, the empire's peasants were indifferent to the document's fate, if they even knew of its existence. Yet the subsequent thirty years of an increasingly erratic monarchy, rising corruption, an oppressive and increasingly pervasive secret police, the assassination or exile of anyone who appeared to oppose the regime in any way, and the loss of territory and prestige through even further "concessions" to the Europeans wrought a profound change in the attitude of the Turkish aristocracy. The realization began to grow that Abdul-Hamid's sole focus was maintaining his position and power. He felt little compulsion to do anything to improve the lives of his subjects, whatever their class, and equally little interest in preserving, strengthening, or reviving the empire. Consequently, educated Turks of every class and political perspective began to view responsible government as embodied in the Midhat Constitution the Ottoman Empire's only hope of salvation.

Organized opposition to Abdul-Hamid began to gain coherence in 1889 within the ranks of university students and military cadets in Constantinople but soon spread beyond such stereotypical idealists. Artists, teachers, scientists, bankers, and mid-level government officials discovered common cause in their opposition to Abdul-Hamid's regime in the last years of the nineteenth century. It didn't take long for them to establish ties with a collection of like-minded liberal exiles living in France. It was a journal published by these Parisian exiles, *Young Turkey* (*La Jeune Turquie*), that gave the would-be revolutionaries their popular name—"the Young Turks." Another publication, this one smuggled into Ottoman Turkey with the connivance of various foreign post offices, bore the subtitle "Order and Progress," which was soon modified to "Union and Progress," and gave its name to the revolutionary organization in Paris, the Committee of Union and Progress (CUP). It was neither the first nor the most prominent of the factions opposed to the Sultan, but the apparent willingness of its leadership to work through cooperation and compromise caused its numbers to grow rapidly.

By the autumn of 1896 the committee felt that it was sufficiently strong to attempt to topple Abdul-Hamid, but the coup proved to be a damp squib because an informer within the CUP ranks alerted the Sublime Porte. The response by the Sultan's secret police was sharp and prolonged repression of anyone who was suspected of liberal sympathies. The result was that the Young Turks' most vocal and energetic leaders were driven to live abroad for their own safety. Inevitably, they settled in the perpetual epicenter of revolution, Paris, where in 1902 they held a congress of Turkish opposition movements in the hope of forming an ideological alliance that would further the actual revolution. The congress was remarkable for the fact that almost all of the ethnic groups of the empire who felt themselves in some way oppressed by the Sultan's regime were present—Albanians, Serbs, Bulgars, Greeks, Arabs, and Armenians, as well as Turks, were represented.

Soon the major factions coalesced. The constitutionalists, led by Ahmed Riza, advocated curbing the power of the Sultan and for the return of the Midhat Constitution in a parliamentary framework, all with a minimum of foreign intervention; a collection of high-ranking, liberal-minded statesmen under the leadership of Sabahheddin Bey proposed to create an advisory council to the Sultan, much like a Western Cabinet, which would limit his authority while providing for better accountability; the medical students and the military cadets had no clear agenda but were merely enthralled with the romanticism of revolution; there was also a small but vocal (and sometimes annoying) collection of anarchists; and, finally, Khachatur Maloumian's Armenian Revolutionary Federation joined in. It was the factions led by Ahmed Riza and Sabahheddin Bey, however, that quickly dominated the congress—factions that, while agreeing that the empire had to be saved from further disgrace and depredation by Abdul-Hamid, were fundamentally in opposition to each other as to what shape Ottoman society and the empire's government should take.

Riza was a scientist who would later become the minister of education under the Young Turks. Essentially an authoritarian and something of a cynic where human nature was concerned, he advocated a strong central government with sweeping agricultural reform and massive economic redress within the empire to be the focus of any new government's responsibility. Born a commoner, he was understandably vehemently opposed to privilege based merely on social class; he was also passionately opposed to any form of foreign intervention or influence within the empire. At the same time he openly believed that the Turks were "superior" to Arabs, Armenians, and Jews; consequently, Turks should be given a preeminent and preferential position in any new government. It was an argument that went far beyond mere nationalism or the idea of Turks as *primus inter pares* and became the core of the doctrine of "Ottomanism." While Ottomanism nominally paid lip service to the concept that all subjects of the empire were equal before the law, in practice the preference it gave the Turks led to understandable resentment by the empire's non-Turkish majority.

While Riza was a commoner, Sabahheddin, who would become better known to history as Behaeddin Shakir, was an aristocrat. It should come as no surprise, then, that he held to a political view almost totally opposite that of Riza. Most profoundly, Sabahheddin's party was strongly opposed to any further centralization of the Ottoman government; instead, it was firmly committed to maintaining the traditional class and social privileges. Although Sabahheddin's party was hardly "liberal" by Western European standards, it was far more ethnically tolerant and inclusive than Riza's. Sabahheddin also welcomed foreign investment in the empire and was committed to the belief that only by encouraging foreign experts and technicians to come to work in the empire and help build a modern infrastructure could the Sultan's realm have any hope of rejoining the community of Great Powers. Despite their deep ideological differences, between 1902 and 1908 the two groups managed to work together in order to further the cause of the revolution, gradually bringing the other factions under the umbrella of the CUP, although no permanent working solutions to their fundamental disagreements were ever found. Contacts throughout the empire, particularly within the units of the Ottoman Army, as well as among the students in Constantinople's secular universities, kept the Parisian exiles very accurately informed as to the mood of the empire's peoples.

The revolution itself was unintentionally put into motion by the tensions raised by an issue that came to be known as the Macedonian Question, a quarrel that sprang up in the Balkans in the latter part of the nineteenth century as Turkish authority declined in that turbulent peninsula. Various powers and would-be powers in the region, among them Bulgaria, Russia, Austria-Hungary, and the Ottoman Empire, as well as Serbia, Bulgaria, and Greece, had been squabbling over possession of the territory of Macedonia for nearly three decades. In 1878 a semi-autonomous Bulgaria had attempted an outright annexation of the region, only to find itself blocked by the Great Powers of Europe. Serbs, Greeks, Bulgars, and Turks subsequently sought to assert their authority over Macedonia, leading to a state of near anarchy, as each nation soon posted "garrisons" of "soldiers" in the territory, ostensibly to protect their ethnic brethren living in Macedonia but in truth acting as little more than sanctioned bandits, waging nocturnal campaigns against other ethnic groups—pillaging, burning, and murdering in a manner reminiscent of the "ethnic cleansing" that would plague the same region a century later.

Finally, Tsar Nicholas II of Russia and Emperor Franz Joseph of Austria-Hungary, both fearing that the violence in Macedonia would spill over into their own empires, intervened. In 1903 diplomatic discussions began, which led to the imposition of Russian and Austrian advisory commissions that exerted administrative control over Macedonia. The Ottomans could do nothing against the combined strength of the two Great Powers and so were forced to accept this solution as a fait accompli, although they did all they could to subsequently subvert the commissions' authority.

Meanwhile, the near chaos in Macedonia had prompted the Sultan to post increasingly larger garrisons there, a move that proved to be his undoing. With little to do apart from a seemingly endless routine of patrols, the Turkish soldiers soon became restive and discipline began to erode; frequently, their officers were disaffected themselves. Particularly galling were the omnipresent foreign military advisers, mostly Germans, who were a constant reminder that the days of the empire's strength and glory had passed. For many, the final straw seemed to be an announcement made in Vienna in February 1908 regarding a railroad that would be built, in effect, to bring all of the western Balkans, including Macedonia, under Austrian control and influence. Though the railway would be built through what was unquestionably Ottoman territory, Constantinople had not even been consulted about its construction, a final humiliating illustration of Ottoman impotence.

The revolutionaries in Paris sensed an opportunity, and the reaction was swift. On May 13, 1908, the Committee of Union and Progress sent word to the Sultan that "the dynasty will be in danger" unless the 1877 constitution was brought back. Meanwhile, emissaries sent out among the Turkish troops found ready and receptive audiences. When word of the troops' increasing discontent and their open welcome of the committee's representatives reached the Sublime Porte, Abdul-Hamid, alarmed by the CUP's brazen warning, decided to send out an investigating committee to determine how far the disaffection had spread and how deep it ran.

This was the trigger that set off the revolt. It began among the soldiers of the Third Army Corps in Macedonia. One Maj. Ahmed Niyazi had thrown in his lot with the Committee of Union and Progress and feared the Sultan's investigators, who had been granted Inquisition-like powers of arrest and interrogation. On July 3, 1908, taking two hundred loyal soldiers, Niyazi set out for Constantinople, where he was prepared to demand by force the restoration of the 1877 constitution. In a scenario reminiscent of other revolutions, the troops that had been sent out to arrest Major Niyazi joined the rebellion, and the revolution was openly proclaimed on July 6, 1908.

Meanwhile, the Sultan's investigators, who arrived in Salonika on June 20, discovered that another popular young officer, Maj. Ismail Enver Bey (who happened to be Niyazi's brother-in-law), was a principal ringleader of the revolutionary movement among the Macedonian garrisons. Enver was ordered to report to Constantinople, ostensibly to receive some unspecified decoration and be promoted. Not fooled for an instant by these blandishments, Enver immediately went into hiding, began gathering loyal troops—particularly deserters from the garrison of Tikvesh—and within a fortnight was setting off for Constantinople in support of Major Niyazi.

By the standards of European revolutions, there was a remarkable lack of violence. Troops from garrisons throughout the Balkans mobilized and began moving on Constantinople when word reached them that Niyazi and Enver were marching. At the same time the handful of units within the city loyal to the Sultan quickly realized that not only were they badly outnumbered, but the populace was hostile to them as well. After some desultory exchanges of gunfire with the rebel troops, which produced very little actual bloodshed, they quickly melted away. A proclamation drafted in Paris by the CUP and published in Constantinople announced that the Midhat Constitution was to be restored, political and economic restrictions on Christians and Jews would be lifted, and a general amnesty declared for political prisoners and exiles. The proclamation also affirmed the safety of foreigners and their interests within the empire. The CUP quickly turned discontent with the Sultan's rule into popular support for the revolution.

Like every similarly cornered autocrat, Abdul-Hamid fought to delay the inevitable with gestures and posturing. He dismissed his Grand Vizier and the minister of war on July 22. The next day, at a loud, long, and acrimonious meeting of the Council of Ministers at the palace, Abdul-Hamid groped for a way to crush the growing revolt. When it was explained to him in no uncertain terms that there weren't enough loyal troops left to stop the advancing revolutionaries, the debate turned to what sort of reform—short of the restoration of the constitution—might be acceptable. The new Grand Vizier, Said Pasha, made it clear to the Sultan that the time for such transparent gestures had passed. Bowing to the inevitable, Abdul-Hamid then resorted to hypocrisy, announcing that he would be pleased to re-establish the Midhat Constitution, which, he piously claimed, had been granted by him in the first place and which had never been abrogated. Wrapping himself further in this cloak of self-righteous fiction, Abdul-Hamid declared that when the parliament had been suspended in 1878, it had been done as a temporary mea-sure (any mention that "temporary" in this case had stretched into thirty years was scrupulously avoided). The following morning, July 24, all of the newspapers in Constantinople carried a short paragraph, usually buried on one of the inner pages, announcing that the Sultan had decided to call for national elections and the seat-ing of a parliament.

The new National Assembly, to be styled the "divan," was seated on August 5, 1908, despite the inevitable allegations of electoral fraud and hints of racial trou-bles. Inevitably, the CUP was the single largest party, with sixty seats, and it was quickly able to engineer the election of Ahmed Riza as the National Assembly's first speaker. Great things were expected of this new parliament, not least because its membership so accurately reflected the ethnically cosmopolitan nature of the empire itself: when it was seated, there were 142 Turks, 60 Arabs, 25 Albanians, 23 Greeks, 12 Armenians, 5 Jews, 4 Bulgars, 3 Serbs, and 1 Walach in the new parliament.

It *was* a promising start, holding out the prospect of truly representative gov-ernment, and in the rosy afterglow of success the various factions continued to work in some semblance of harmony for a brief time, but the habits that the Young Turks had learned in the long years of exile began to bear fruit that was neither expected nor welcome. The CUP in particular had long since come to rely on co-ercion as a means of inducing cooperation in its activities and agitation in the Bal-kans and now began employing similar tactics in the new parliament. Cooperation was demanded, rather than encouraged or earned.

No matter what else followed, to their everlasting credit the members of the new divan kept their promise that the first substantial action they would undertake would be a revision of the Midhat Constitution, which became known as the *Kanûn Esâsî*, or "Basic Law." The most far-reaching revision was the one that denied the Sultan any genuine powers, reducing him to little more than a figurehead who reigned but did not rule; the National Assembly was now the sole seat of Ottoman authority.

Significantly, the new constitution rendered Moslem sharia (holy or clerical law) subordinate to secular law. This did not sit well with large segments of the empire's population, especially the Arabs; it also raised the ire of the Moslem clergy, who correctly saw it as an attempt to erode their deep-seated power base within the empire. At the same time, in a deliberate attempt to place the whole of the bureaucracy in the hands of ethnic Turks, almost every Arab official was summarily removed from office, their singular fault being that they were Arabs and had been appointed by the Sultan. It was a move that would later bear bitter fruit for the Young Turks and the empire.

It was here that the Young Turks first stumbled, and badly: competent, experienced replacements for those officials who were dismissed simply did not exist—especially at the highest levels. Simultaneously, the army was being purged of any officers suspected of having an excess of loyalty to the Sultan. The void left by these purges was soon felt by the new regime, leading one Cabinet member to begin advocating the employment of "honest foreign advisers" in the Ottoman civil service.

The Young Turks also promised to undertake sweeping initiatives that would modernize Ottoman society, including industrial and commercial reforms, along with measures designed to first minimize, then gradually exclude foreign influences in the government. Among the most profound social changes brought about by the CUP were the establishment of subsidies for the education of women and a fundamental restructuring of the administration responsible for state-run primary schools, decisions that further angered the already offended Arab population, as well as much of the Moslem clergy.

Just as they were in the middle of such sweeping reforms, the efforts of the Young Turks began to founder. Lacking any experience in or traditions of the day-to-day workings of parliamentary politics and having no understanding of the mechanisms of deal-making that allowed Western republics and democracies to function, the various factions simply made demands and, when they were not met in full by their colleagues, refused to negotiate or compromise. The British ambassador Gerald Fitzmaurice wrote in a report to London that "the Turkish people, after their thirty years of despotism, are like a two-year-old infant that can't walk firmly and is somewhat inarticulate. They are very raw and the Government as such is none too strong." His successor, Sir Gerard Lowther, echoed Fitzmaurice when he informed the Foreign Office that the new government "lacked responsible leaders of position," and that they were about as competent as "a collection of good-intentioned children."

The housecleaning of the corruption and the deadwood among the old regime's functionaries in the bureaucracy resembled nothing so much as a purge. The CUP pressed for the dismissal of any government official believed to have had close connections with the palace, despite knowing that there were very few competent replacements who were "untainted" by association with the old regime. This led to a game of musical chairs among the remaining senior administrators, as they were constantly shuffled and shifted between posts in a vain effort to find people who could competently run the government's offices and departments.

Abdul-Hamid himself was untouchable: ironically, he enjoyed a degree of popularity for having "restored" the Midhat Constitution. As Sultan-caliph he was still venerated by a vast majority of the empire's common people, particularly the Arabs, who had been deeply offended by the Young Turks' assertion of the supremacy of secular law over sharia and the dismissal of the Grand Sharif of Mecca.

Nor was the army immune from the attentions of the CUP, despite its almost uniform support for the revolution. Hundreds of officers who owed their promotions to the Sultan's patronage—as opposed to most of the officers in the ranks of the Young Turks, who were graduates of academies—were dismissed or reduced in grade. This was one of the CUP's more carefully calculated moves, for had these officers as a body been even reasonably competent, they could have posed a serious threat to the life of the new regime. (As it was, when these cashiered officers eventually moved against the committee and the divan, their incompetence would prove to be their undoing.)

In an effort to make administrative positions in the new government attractive to talented, competent Turks, the CUP announced in September 1908 that it was launching a program of decentralization, giving wider authority to provincial officials than they had enjoyed under Abdul-Hamid's despotism, while at the same time enforcing a stricter accountability. There was a calculated measure of political expedience in this project, for it took some wind out the sails of Sabahheddin, who led the opposition to the CUP within the divan and who had just announced the formation of the Liberal (Ahrar) Party, which had decentralization of the imperial government as one of its founding policies.

In the immediate aftermath of the revolution, although the Sultan was allowed to retain his throne, the restored constitution sharply curtailed his actual authority. The newly created Cabinet and the Grand Vizier immediately began scrambling to seize whatever power they could grab. Over the centuries, the Office of Grand Vizier had evolved from a merely advisory role (the word "adviser" is a Western corruption of "vizier") into something akin to that of a prime minister. Originally, because the Grand Vizier served at the pleasure of the Sultan, the throne was expected to be the sole object of his loyalty. Now, however, he was required to guide the new government, with his loyalty pledged to the National Assembly but not to any particular party.

The most serious flaw in the Midhat Constitution was that it made no provision for clearly defined separations of power between the Grand Vizier and the parliament, which would have defined the roles and boundaries of each. The result was political instability as each entity tried to assert itself over the others. Aggravating the situation, the CUP suffered from a distinct sense of insecurity as, typical of most successful revolutionary movements, it questioned its own legitimacy and sought to reinforce it by extending its authority as far as possible. It was hardly surprising, then, that a succession of political upheavals began once the new government's initial burst of activity had passed: in the first year following the revolution, there were five changes of government, a counterrevolutionary uprising, and the beginnings of organized opposition to the Young Turks within the divan.

The instability began when the committee chose to demonstrate an ascendancy over both Sultan and Vizier by orchestrating the dismissal of Said Pasha, the first Grand Vizier of the new era, barely two weeks after his appointment. Said and his Cabinet were, it was claimed, too closely identified with the old regime. The only individual competent enough to hold the post and be acceptable to both Cabinet and Divan was an elderly statesman who had twice earlier served as Grand Vizier, Kibrisli Mehmed Kiamil Pasha.

Kiamil Pasha is one of the most tantalizing figures of the empire, the great "might have been" of Ottoman Turkey. Had he been a man of slightly less integrity but greater ambition, the history of the Ottoman Empire, Europe, indeed the whole of the twentieth century, would have been vastly different. As it was, Mehmed Kiamil Pasha would still be remembered as the most distinguished Ottoman statesman of the late nineteenth and early twentieth centuries. He was born in 1833 in the village of Lefkosia in northern Cyprus, the son of an Ottoman army officer. Intriguingly, he was Jewish by birth (through his mother) but was raised in the Islamic faith. He would remain a dedicated Moslem his whole life. Early in his schooling, his intellect and academic excellence set him apart as a young man with a bright future, destined for service in the imperial administration. His first such appointment, at the age of eighteen, was a minor posting in the household of Mohammed Abbas, the khedive of Egypt, who by this time barely acknowledged the authority of the Sultan. In the summer of 1851 Kiamil was given charge of one of the khedive's sons, who was being sent to Great Britain to visit the Great Exhibition in London. It would prove to be a turning point for Kiamil, for the months he spent in England left him with an admiration for the British people and their social and political institutions that would last for the rest of his life. His respect for the British Royal Family (he was presented to Queen Victoria, then later King Edward VII and Queen Alexandra a number of times during the course of his career) bordered on reverence, and he never made any effort to disguise the fact that he was an Anglophile. It was during this time that he acquired the habit of reading the *London Times* every morning, something he would continue to do every day for the rest of his life. He even went to the length of having the paper delivered to his offices wherever he might be serving within the empire; late in life he remarked to a friend that he had never missed a single issue.

Returning to Egypt, Kiamil would remain there until 1860, when he began serving a succession of postings as regional and provincial governor. In the span of the next nineteen years he would be given administrative appointments in every part of the Sultan's realm, which arguably made him the single best-informed official in regard to the true state of the Ottoman Empire. His rise through the bureaucratic ranks was due entirely to his talents: unique among his colleagues, he was neither venal nor personally ambitious, and everyone knew him as a scrupulously honest man. Above all, he was a patriot.

The effectiveness of his provincial administration and the depth of his patriotism combined to bring him to the attention of the Sultan, who appointed Kiamil to the Ministry of the Interior in 1881. For the next three decades he would hold a succession of Cabinet posts, ultimately serving as Grand Vizier on four different occasions—the first time in 1884, the last in 1913. When confronted with Said's dismissal, Abdul-Hamid, though he shared little of Kiamil's Anglophilia and none of his moderate political views, recognized that Kiamil was the only man in the Ottoman service who had the confidence of both the Sublime Porte and the National Assembly. On August 5, 1908, Abdul-Hamid named him the new Grand Vizier.

Kiamil's dream was to see the Ottoman divan evolve into a respected and effective institution like the British House of Commons. His Anglophilia caused him to envision the Ottoman Empire recreating itself as a constitutional monarchy much as the British Empire had become. He did his best to work with the divan; Sabahheddin announced that he was forming the Liberal Party (Ahrar), which would in effect become the main opposition party to the CUP and the pillar of Kiamil's support within the National Assembly. It was hardly enough, though. As news of the revolution and the restoration of the constitution spread through the empire, challenges were thrown down to local authorities. Acts of civil and sometimes armed disobedience began to occur with alarming frequency, as peasants and tribes in the countryside staged revolts of their own. In Beirut there were strikes in the gas company and among the dockworkers and the stevedores along the waterfront, butchers in Damascus and Beirut protested the slaughter tax, workers of the Damascus-Hama railroad struck for wage increases and improved working conditions.

By February 14, 1909, with the CUP becoming increasingly obstructive and uncooperative, Kiamil decided he had had enough and resigned. Bulgaria had just announced that it was throwing off the last vestiges of Ottoman suzerainty and assuming full independence—and the Young Turks were helpless to prevent this latest humiliation. Hüseyin Hilmi Pasha, a diplomat and an administrator, replacedKiamil; he had also held the post of inspector-general of Rumelia. Like Kiamil he was an "Old Turk," but he lacked his predecessor's political stature. The Bulgar declaration, coupled with the CUP's inability to maintain a working majority of its own in the National Assembly, as well as its ineptitude in working with the other political parties and factions, gave Hilmi's new regime a distinct aura of incompetence and weakness. It was a perception that led Abdul-Hamid and his supporters—particularly among the Moslem clergy, who had refused to become resigned to the permanence of the revolution—to contemplate a countercoup that would restore the Sultan's lost power.

Army units that had not taken part in the 1908 revolution were quietly brought from the southern reaches of the empire into Constantinople, where they were carefully indoctrinated by the Sultan's loyalists and Moslem clergymen. On April 13, 1909 (March 31 in the old-style Orthodox calendar then in use—yet another Ottoman quirk), they revolted, in what became known as the Countercoup, seizing key government buildings and intersections throughout the capital. They were quickly joined by large numbers of theological students, predominantly Arabs, and turbaned clerics shouting, "We want sharia!" and announcing the Sultan's return to power.

The Countercoup served as a catalyst for the disparate elements in the divan for once to act in concert: troops loyal to the revolution were immediately called up from Macedonia to suppress the revolt. Constantinople was taken back from the Sultan's loyalists by April 24; three days later Abdul-Hamid was deposed, and his brother, who had promised to be more pliant and tractable to the divan's wishes, ascended the throne as Mehmed V. Because the strongest support for the Countercoup had come from the empire's Arab subjects, the repression that followed the Countercoup's failure drove an immovable wedge between the Turks and the already alienated Arabs. Arab societies and organizations that worked to empower Arab interests within Ottoman society were swiftly outlawed—including the Society of Arab-Ottoman Brotherhood—and several Arab-language journals and newspapers were banned from publication. This political repression of the empire's Arab population had the additional effect of promoting the Young Turks' program of "Ottomanism," which gave preference to ethnic Ottoman Turks over any of the empire's other subject peoples, effectively excluding Arabs from government service at all but the lowest levels of the bureaucracy.

At first, the Great Powers of Europe paid scant attention to the revolution in July 1908, believing that it was little more than one of the empire's dying convulsions and expecting that when the "Sick Man" finally expired, they could move in at their convenience to pick over the corpse. But after the Countercoup was suppressed and the 1877 constitution was once again restored, the Great Powers began to take notice. Not surprisingly, perhaps, Kaiser Wilhelm II of Germany had been a staunch supporter of Abdul-Hamid's regime, even though the Armenian massacres had outraged the rest of Europe. Wilhelm's stance was dictated by a solitary, overarching objective: to make Germany's political, financial, and social inroads run so deep into the empire as to reduce it to a semicolonial dependency. Wilhelm little cared what form the regime in Constantinople took, as long as it continued to be favorably disposed toward Berlin, so when the Young Turks seized power, he shifted his support to them without so much as batting an eye. The people of France and Great Britain, however, had naturally turned against the Sultan, and with them, their governments. Consequently, the revolution and its promises of liberty, tolerance, and enlightenment proved immensely popular in both countries, although the Young Turks did little to take advantage of this goodwill.

Predictably, some foreign powers did their best to take advantage of the inevitable period of instability that followed the Young Turks' assumption of power. Bulgaria, of course, declared her complete independence from Constantinople with almost obscene haste, an announcement that was quickly followed by the occupation of Crete by Greece and Austria-Hungary's annexation of Bosnia and Herzegovina. Later that same year, the Bulgars, feeling their oats and seeking to emphasize their newly minted autonomy, forced Constantinople into a prolonged series of negotiations to settle the question of Turkish railway access to Europe across Bulgar territory—yet another embarrassment for the new regime.

Worse was to come. Italy, pretending to possess a Great Power status she had neither earned nor deserved, carefully chose the moment when the Turkish government was most distracted to launch a blatant campaign of aggression and territorial conquest, bent on seizing the Ottoman provinces of Tripolitania and Cyrenaica (modern Libya), along with the island of Rhodes and the Dodecanese archipelago just off the Anatolian shoreline. Though little remembered today, the Italo-Turkish War set the stage for the Balkan Wars by triggering a wave of nationalism among the Balkan states, all of which saw an opportunity to take advantage of the Ottomans' obvious weakness for their own benefit.

Italy's rather shaky claims to the two African provinces rested on a couple of shady diplomatic deals done with France in the last quarter of the nineteenth century, agreements that were never formally ratified. By the end of the first decade of the twentieth century, however, the Italian government began to cast covetous eyes on North Africa. Italy was caving in to pressure from the popular press decrying Italy's lack of overseas colonies and the way in which she had been denied her "place in the sun" by France and Great Britain (much the way Germany had complained a quarter-century earlier). As the Italian press grew more strident, Italy's foreign minister, the Marchese di San Giuliano, made an effort to allay Ottoman suspicions and publicly declared before the Italian legislature in December 1910, "We desire the integrity of the Ottoman Empire and we wish Tripoli always to remain Turkish." Yet even as he was uttering this pronouncement, his government was planning a war of expansion at the Turks' expense. It was believed in Rome that the undertaking would be little more than a training exercise conducted with live ammunition.

Prime Minister Giovanni Giolitti's government sent an ultimatum to the Ottoman Turks on the night of September 26, 1911, demanding that Constantinople cede to Italy outright the province Cyrenaica (modern Libya) and the islands of Rhodes and the Dodecanese. The Turks replied by offering to transfer the actual control of these territories to Italy, while maintaining the fiction of nominal Ottoman suzerainty, with no need to resort to open conflict. Giolitti refused the offer, and the Italian parliament declared war on September 29, 1911.

Despite having almost four months to prepare, the Italian military was far from ready, with no definitive plan of campaign drawn up and its supply arrangements incomplete. At first this seemed to matter little, as the Italian Army met with minimal resistance, seizing a string of cities and towns along the Libyan coast in the first week of October. Fewer than three weeks later, however, careless deployment allowed almost three-quarters of the Italian forces to be surrounded and captured near the port of Tripoli by a mixed force of Arab cavalry and Ottoman infantry.

Stunned by this defeat, the Italians quickly expanded the expeditionary force, sending reinforcements to Libya until more than a hundred thousand Italian soldiers—nearly one-half of the entire Italian Army—were deployed against fewer than one-third of that number of Turks and Arabs. The Turks quickly learned that all they need do was simply dig in around key positions in Cyrenaica and Tripolitania and hold on, for while the Italian infantrymen were competent fighters, their officers showed neither enthusiasm nor aptitude for offensive actions. When the new year arrived, the Ottoman forces were still the de facto masters of the disputed provinces.

By spring 1912 the Italians were desperately looking for a way to force an end to what had become a bloody, drawn-out affair. Austria-Hungary had emphatically vetoed any Italian action in the Balkans, fearing, with some justification, that the whole peninsula would explode into open war. The Italians turned to the Imam of Sana (modern Sana'a) in Yemen, at the southern end of the Arabian Peninsula, who had been leading a sputtering rebellion there since 1910. Weapons and equipment were sent across the Red Sea from Eritrea and Somaliland (known today as Somalia) to Sana in the expectation that the Turks would be forced to withdraw forces from Libya to confront this revived revolt, but it proved a vain hope, as the regional governors were able to contain the imam's forces with the garrisons at hand. Italy had a modern and fairly large navy, however, which was able to gain control of the whole of the Libyan coast during the spring and summer of 1912, depriving the Turks of any opportunity to reinforce their Libyan garrison, and a stalemate ensued. (Although Egypt was still theoretically an Ottoman province, Great Britain, which had established a protectorate over the country in 1882, forbade the passage of Turkish troops through the country. There was genuine concern that the presence, however transitory, of large numbers of Turkish troops might lead to a violent reaction among the Egyptian Arabs, who despised the Ottomans.) That summer Italy occupied the Dodecanese and the island of Rhodes, which the Turks, lacking an effective navy of their own, were unable to prevent. By this time the other Great Powers began to exert increasing pressure on Italy to bring the war to an end, sensing that one or more of the Balkan states was about to exploit the Turks' weak and overstretched position.

It was not a mistaken perception. As autumn set in, Bulgaria, Serbia, and Greece mobilized their armies. On October 8 Montenegro declared war against the Ottomans in what was the beginning of the First Balkan War. It came as a relief to the Italian government, frustrated as it had been by rising casualties and stubborn Turkish resistance in Libya, which chose to take advantage of the situation in its own way, offering to negotiate a peace settlement with Constantinople. The Treaty of Ouchy was signed on October 18, 1912, in a small town near Lausanne, Switzerland. Ironically, it did little more than formalize the terms of the offer made by the Turks before the war began: Italy would have control of Libya and the Aegean islands it had occupied, while maintaining the legal fiction that they were still subject to Ottoman authority. This allowed the Italian government to maintain, with a perfectly straight face, that it had honored the Marchese di San Giuliano's claim that Italy desired Tripoli and Cyrenaica to remain part of the Ottoman Empire forever.

For the Turks, such a settlement was more than they had hoped for, and more than welcome—they were being too sorely pressed in the Balkans to have much time or energy to devote to the war in Libya. Almost from the moment Montenegro had declared war, things began going badly on the Balkan front for Turkey.

The Balkan Wars were a direct consequence of the greed among the patchwork of nation-states that coalesced in the Balkan Peninsula in the nineteenth century. The first to emerge had been Greece, which had actually been independent since 1823 and had wrested the province of Thessaly away from the Turks in 1881; next came Serbia, an independent kingdom after the Russo-Turkish War of 1877–78 that coveted sections of Macedonia; while Bulgaria, which became an autonomous principality in 1878, forcibly incorporated the province of Eastern Rumelia into her borders in 1885. Like carrion birds circling a dying animal, these three kingdoms were waiting with mounting impatience for the final collapse of the Ottoman regime in order to pick the Balkan carcass bare.

During the wars, these three minor nations were serving as pawns and cats' paws of the Great Powers, each of which had very specific, if divergent, objectives in mind for the fate of the Ottoman Empire. Russia hoped to gain control of Constantinople herself, in part for religious reasons—the city was the traditional seat of the Orthodox Church—but also because possession of the Ottoman capital would give Russia her long desired "warm water" port. It was only natural, then, that she supported the ambitions of the Slavic kingdoms of Serbia and Bulgaria. Great Britain, conversely, had no desire to see the imperial Russian navy's Black Sea Fleet gain access to the Mediterranean. British policy was thus directed toward maintaining the integrity of the Ottoman Empire, as long as such maintenance was consistent with continued British power and prestige in the eastern Mediterranean. France, maintaining that she had long-standing interests in the Middle East dating back to the time of Bonaparte's expedition to Egypt, as well as a centuries-old friendship with the Turks, sought to strengthen her position in the region, especially in the Levant—something that could be accomplished only at the empire's expense. Austria-Hungary, in turn, despite the traditional antipathy between Constantinople and Vienna, had no desire to see the Ottoman regime further weakened, allowing Serbia to expand. It would not do for the ethnic minorities in the Dual Monarchy to watch as another multiethnic power ruled by a small elite was slowly dismantled—it might give them ideas. Germany, of course, had her own designs on the empire, and there was no desire in Berlin to see the regime in Constantinople collapse before it could be properly reduced to a vassal state, effectively ruled from Berlin.

The result was a constantly shifting tide of diplomatic influence continually washing across the Balkans, as each of the Great Powers sought to advance its interests. As the Ottoman Empire grew increasingly weaker, however, the smaller states began to develop designs of their own. A complex skein of diplomatic negotiations and agreements between Serbia, Bulgaria, Montenegro, and Greece, to which none of the Great Powers were party, was the prelude to the war. The resulting loosely knit alliance became known as the Balkan League, and its existence was anathema to all of the Great Powers.

The first move was a treaty signed by Serbia and Bulgaria in March 1912 that formalized how the partition of Macedonia would be carried out between them after a victorious war against the Turks. Next came a strategic agreement along similar lines between the Serbs and the Greeks in May 1912. As long as the Turks could draw on reinforcements from the Levant and Arabia, the Balkan states would be unable to amass the numbers of troops necessary to ensure victory. Yet the deplorable state of the Ottoman railways meant that the only reliable means of bringing those reinforcements to the Balkans was by sea, and the Greeks possessed a fairly modern navy of sufficient size and power to prevent the passage of any troop convoys through the Aegean Sea. The Greek government delayed the start of hostilities a number of times, however, as it was working to first complete an ambitious construction program for its navy. The fuse was actually lit when Montenegro subsequently concluded her own agreements with Serbia and Bulgaria, formalizing the further division of Turkish territories on October 5, 1912, just three days before war was declared.

Despite the extraordinary degree of diplomatic cooperation that precluded the war, there was no formal plan of campaign against the Ottomans drawn up among the four Balkan "Allies." The war has been described, not inaccurately, as four separate wars being fought against the same enemy, at the same time, in the same region. The Montenegrin forces attacked to the north, the Serbs battled in the south, the Bulgars struck to the south and the east, the Greeks thrust first northward and then to the west. At sea the Greek navy quickly swept up most of those Turkish possessions in the Aegean Sea that the Italians had not already occupied. As could be expected, since there was no unified plan of campaign, none of these attacks were mutually supporting, and in the case of the Serbs, the Montenegrins, and the Greeks, at times those on the same side actually got in one another's way, but for the Turks the effect was the same as if it had all been carefully thought out in advance. Outnumbered and outgunned, Ottoman defenses collapsed and Turkish troops fled north, east, south—whichever direction led away from the enemy.

Within weeks, most of southern Macedonia had fallen to the Greeks (who also carved off a piece of Albania in the process), while the Serbs took the northern section of the province, and the Bulgars drove to the Aegean and pushed the Turks far beyond Adrianople—they were stopped only when they were almost within sight of Constantinople itself. The situation deteriorated so rapidly that by the end of October, Mehmed V felt compelled to recall Kiamil Pasha to the Office of Grand Vizier, believing that only he possessed the stature and authority to be able to establish some order out of the chaos. But so complete was the Turkish collapse in the Balkans that not even a month would pass before the Kiamil's government felt compelled to call for an armistice. What was immediately apparent to everyone, even to the commoners, within the empire as well as outside, was that in the three years that it had been in power, the new parliament—and specifically the CUP-dominated conservatives—had done little to revive the empire's waning strength. The Turks were weaker than ever.

A peace conference was convened in London, with delegates from all of the warring powers in attendance, along with a Conference of Ambassadors from all of the Great Powers, chaired by the British foreign secretary Sir Edward Grey. The first meetings were held on December 16, 1912. Feeling that they were dealing from a position of unassailable strength, the Balkan Allies made severe and strident demands. Each of the Balkan states expected the Turks to pay a war indemnity, and their collective territorial demands amounted to the cession of all European Ottoman territory, including the province of Albania, as well as the island of Crete and the remaining Turkish possessions in the Aegean Sea. A small strip of territory barely larger than the limits of Constantinople was all that would remain of the Ottomans' once-vast European conquests.

At first, though they were willing to concede on all other terms, the Turks were utterly unwilling to allow Adrianople to remain in the hands of the Bulgars. The city had tremendous symbolic significance to the Ottoman Empire, having been the imperial capital before the fall of Constantinople in 1453. To their dismay, the overall strategic situation was so bad that the National Assembly ultimately had no choice but to concede, and Grand Vizier Kiamil Pasha cabled the Ottoman representatives in London to accept all of the Balkan Allies' terms. The message was sent in the early evening of January 22, 1913; no one could have imagined the consequences it would produce.

As the Cabinet was at its usual morning meeting the next day, a handful of armed army officers led by Lt. Col. Ismail Enver burst into the Cabinet Room within the Sublime Porte and brusquely announced that because of the capitulation to the Balkan Allies, the government was dissolved and Kiamil Pasha was no longer the Grand Vizier. When Minister of War Nazim Pasha began to protest, Maj. Yakub Kemil (*not* Enver, as legend would soon tell the tale) drew his service revolver and shot Nazim in the head, killing him instantly.

Literally staring down the barrel of a gun, Kiamil offered no resistance, immediately agreed to resign, and was replaced by Mahmud Sekvet Pasha. (Sekvet would in turn be assassinated fewer than five months later, on June 11, 1913—a reprisal, it was said in the streets of Constantinople, for the murder of Nazim Pasha, who was succeeded by Said Halim Pasha. By then, however, the Office of Grand Vizier had been reduced to a figurehead.) When the word of this coup d'état reached the peace conference in London, it was made instantly clear that further negotiations were pointless and the war would resume. Another eight weeks of fighting followed before the Turks once again sought an armistice, while petty bickering among the Balkan Allies prevented them from agreeing to a cease-fire before the end of April. A second conference was convened in London, and this time a peace treaty was actually drawn up and signed on May 17, 1913.

Ironically, the men who had led the coup in January had acted as they did because they believed that the abysmal performance of the Ottoman forces in the Balkans had been due to incompetent and apathetic leadership in Constantinople. Yet when they gathered up the reins of power, they performed no better than their deposed predecessors, so poor was the condition of the Turkish Army, as well as its overall strategic position. With the coup of January 23, 1913, however, as the men who had seized power predictably refused to let it go, the Ottoman Empire entered its terminal stage of existence. Circumstances—the pathetic state of the imperial bureaucracy, the growing hostility of the Arab population, the questionable quality of the armed forces, and the shaky condition of the empire's finances—conspired to force them into adopting the same old ways of government that they had initially so deeply despised, as graft, favoritism, nepotism, and corruption soon returned as the status quo in imperial affairs.

The triumvirate that replaced Kiamil's last Cabinet became known as the "Rule of the Three Pashas." The government was completely dominated by the trio of Ismail Enver Bey, the new minister of war; Ahmed Djemal Pasha, the minister of the navy; and the minister of the interior, Mehmed Talaat Pasha. All other Cabinet ministers and even the Grand Vizier himself were marginalized. Together, these three men (but above all Enver, who now styled himself Enver Pasha) would control the destiny of the Ottoman Empire for the last seven years of its existence.

If Kiamil Pasha was the Ottoman Empire's great "might have been," Enver Bey would prove to be its greatest misfortune. A deep-running current of opportunism in his character, coupled with some early minor successes, would lead him to vastly overestimate his abilities, and his ambition and a taste for brinkmanship would compel him to continually reach for more and more power. All the while his personal charisma (which concealed the psychopath lurking beneath) led others to feel more confidence in him than he genuinely deserved. Underlying these character traits was an enduring fascination with intrigue and with it an equally strong love of danger, all mixed with extreme vanity. (In another time and place, he would have made for a magnificent pirate.) When combined with Enver's poor judgment in diplomacy, however, particularly in deciding who were the Turks' friends, it was a perilous mixture, for soon Enver would be the single most powerful man in the whole of the empire—but also most assuredly the wrong man in the wrong place at the wrong time.

Much of Ismail Enver's personal history is, like the man himself, elusive, vague, contradictory, and of questionable credibility. Enver was born on November 22, 1881, the eldest of six children, that much is certain. Yet other details are somewhat clouded. His place of birth has been given as Constantinople by some sources; others say the village of Adano, on the Black Sea coast. Likewise, some sources say that his family was one of relatively humble means from Monastir; others claim that he was born into relative wealth and privilege. His father, Ahmet, was an ethnic Turk, and it is believed that at one point in his life he worked as a railway porter, although there is some evidence in existing records that indicates that he was actually a minor administrative official in the Turkish state railroad.

Enver's mother, Aisha, is an even more elusive figure. She is variously described as a Christian Armenian (which would be astonishing if true, given later events), a Moslem Circassian, or an ethnic Albanian who held the lowliest occupation in the empire—that of laying out the dead. In any event, Enver's father somehow came to the attention of the Sultan, Abdul-Hamid, who appointed Ahmet to the imperial entourage, promoting him to the position of Bey, then later to Pasha. The family moved to Constantinople, where Enver grew up and was educated.

Enver, in an effort to burnish his image as a man born of the common people, would later tell the tale that he had been educated at home by his grandmother, but records show that he was a product of Constantinople's secular public schools; at the age of eighteen he enrolled in the Military Academy of Istanbul. He graduated in 1902, ranked second in his class, and was assigned to the Third Army headquarters in Thessaloniki, Macedonia. By 1906 he was a major—his rise through the ranks was absurdly fast, almost certainly the product of his connections at court coupled with his opportunism, for Enver had a knack for knowing how to ingratiate himself with almost anyone, while at the same time seizing the main chance and following the sharp practice.

Over a two-year period, he led several successful operations against Serb, Bulgar, and Greek guerrillas in Macedonia. It was during this posting that officers who had already decided to throw in their lot with the Committee of Union and Progress approached him; Enver took up the revolutionary cause. Exactly why he did so remains a mystery, because the patronage of Abdul-Hamid was as much responsible for his current position as any inherent ability he possessed. Given Enver's love of intrigue, it is quite possible he saw an opportunity to play off both sides against each other. An equally plausible explanation is the opportunities that revolutionary agitation offered for exercising his remarkable gift for demagoguery, a gift that would within a few years make Enver the de facto dictator of the Ottoman realm.

Whatever his motives, he indeed proved to be a skilled subversive leader. By 1908 CUP operations in his section of Macedonia were fully under Enver's control. Rumor of his activities reached the Sublime Porte, and the Sultan's secret police soon began looking closely at Major Enver. On Enver's orders, the lead investigator was murdered, and rather than obey the Sultan's summons to Constantinople, Enver fled into the mountains of Macedonia. Though he would later try to give his flight a romantic gloss, with a sympathetic countryside aiding and abetting his movements and hiding him from the secret police until he could raise the banner of revolution, in truth he was little more than a common fugitive. It was his brother-in-law, Maj. Niyazi Bey, who actually proclaimed the revolution and marched on Constantinople. Because Niyazi had guns, ammunition, cash, and more than two hundred followers, it was he who became the focus of the revolt. Only once he was sure that it was safe did Enver come down from the hills and join Niyazi.

Having taken great pains nonetheless to make known his association with Niyazi, Enver was rewarded by the new government with a posting to Berlin, where he served as the military attaché at the Turkish embassy from 1909 to 1911. It was a turning point for him, for during his tenure in Berlin he became thoroughly besotted with all things part and parcel of the German Army, and he made a particular effort to become fluent in German. When Italy declared war on the Ottoman Turks in September 1911, Enver was recalled from Berlin and sent to Libya, where, it was hoped, he might be as successful against the Italians as he had been against the guerrillas in Macedonia.

The Ottoman Army, determined to hold on to Libya even as the government dithered and seemed resigned to losing the North African provinces, sent two groups of officers into Cyrenaica and Tripolitania to help organize Libyan resistance to the Italian invasion, the first led by Enver himself. For nearly a year Enver led some sixteen thousand Arab irregulars on frequent, sporadic raids, endlessly harassing the regular Italian forces. Materially, these raids had little practical value, but they served to erode the Italians' already sagging morale.

For his efforts, Enver was appointed governor of Benghazi, although his tenure there would be short: he returned to Constantinople in October 1912 once the Treaty of Lausanne had been signed. He then led a vain effort to prevent Adrianople from falling to the Bulgars. Returning again to the capital, he found the city rife with discontent after the capitulation in Libya and the succession of defeats and retreats in the Balkans. He soon gave his penchant for intrigue free rein. It was at this point that Enver began to form a political alliance with Ahmed Djemal and Mehmed Talaat. Precisely what brought the three of them together is unknown; certainly Enver's love of scheming and conspiracy would have eventually drawn him into some radical faction or another. There was something of the compulsive gambler in Enver—he had an insatiable need to take risks. And it may be that although Djemal and Talaat were strong personalities in themselves, they found themselves simply overawed and overwhelmed by Enver and so allowed themselves to be manipulated by him.

Enver was unquestionably a compelling figure in those days: photographs show a neat and handsome young man, barely into his thirties, of slightly smaller-than-average build, with flashing eyes, a long, straight nose, his mouth firmly set, and the points of his mustaches waxed and turned upward in conscious imitation of the German Kaiser, Wilhelm II. He was charming, dynamic, remorseless, cold-blooded, and determined; he was often referred to as "Napoleonlik"—the little Napoleon, a comparison he eventually began to take to heart. He definitely possessed no low opinion of himself or his abilities: visitors to Enver's study would find hanging on the wall behind him two portraits, one of Bonaparte and the other of Frederick the Great—Enver's desk chair was carefully situated between them. Confronted with such a supreme egotist, it's hardly remarkable that Djemal and Talaat soon fell into subordinate roles.

As with Enver, there is some uncertainty about the exact details of Ahmed Djemal's birth. Some sources say he was born in 1872, others cite 1875 as the year; Baghdad, Constantinople, and the island of Midilli are variously recorded as his birthplace. His father, Mehmed Nesip Bey, was a pharmacist in the Ottoman Army, a relatively privileged position. This allowed Djemal the opportunity to be educated by a series of French tutors, followed by admission to the Kuleli Military School. In 1890 he became a cadet at the Military Academy in Constantinople and graduated in 1893.

Djemal's first posting was with the Ministry of War in Constantinople. After two years in Constantinople, he was assigned to the Kirkkilise Fortification Construction Department, part of the Second Army, posted in what is now northern Iraq. Two years later, he became the chief of staff of the Novice Division, stationed in Salonika. It was here that he was first exposed to the ideas and ideals of the Committee of Union and Progress, although he was far slower to embrace these ideals than was Enver. It wasn't until 1905, when Djemal was promoted to major and designated as the inspector of railways in the province of Rumelia, that he became sympathetic to the goals of the Turkish reformers. By 1906, however, his commitment to the revolutionary cause was strong enough that he began to exert an influence on the CUP's military policies. It was in 1907, after being transferred to the staff of the Third Army, that he first met Ismail Enver and formed the beginning bonds of a relationship, if not an actual friendship, which would in just a few years carry them to near-absolute power within the Ottoman Empire.

When Major Niyazi marched on Constantinople and triggered the revolution, Djemal was quick to decamp for the Ottoman capital. There, as a reward for his role in organizing and supporting the Young Turk movement in Macedonia, he was given the post of commandant of Constantinople, in charge of the security forces in the Ottoman capital. If Enver was a born conspirator, then Djemal was a natural counterrevolutionary: this was the first opportunity he had to exhibit his "talent" for both administration and repression. The liberal goals of the revolution notwithstanding, the CUP soon began to feel the need for a secret police organization that could be alert to any attempts to depose the new regime and return Abdul-Hamid to his autocratic ways. So successful was Djemal that when the Arab population in Mesopotamia (modern central Iraq), angered by the blatantly discriminatory, pro-Turkish policies of the new government, began to grow turbulent in early 1911, he was sent to Baghdad as the provincial governor, specifically charged with quelling the unrest. He was notably successful, although his methods did little to earn the Young Turks loyalty from the Arabs.

When the First Balkan War exploded, Djemal felt compelled to resign his governor's post so that he could return to the army and fight in the Balkans. What remains unclear to this day was exactly how his relationship with Enver developed or when Djemal became committed to the idea of a coup against the government of Grand Vizier Kiamil. Enver provided no clues: no one can say for certain precisely when he actually became determined to carry out the coup he executed on January 23. Given his mercurial temper, he himself may not have decided until that very morning. It can be reasonably assumed that Djemal's talent for counterrevolutionary repression made him attractive to Enver, in a "gamekeeper-turned-poacher" sort of way. Whatever the specifics of the bond between Djemal and Enver, it would prove to be unbreakable for nearly five years.

Just as Enver and Djemal, Talaat was an ambitious man. In his case, however, his ambition was tempered with a certain prudence, and his character lacked the darkest facets of Enver's love of intrigue or Djemal's love of repression. Still, of the "Three Pashas," Mehmed Talaat is the most difficult to clearly comprehend after the passage of so many years. In some ways, he seems to have been the most talented member of the triumvirate while possessing the most integrity, yet almost every mention of the man makes immediate reference to him with some variation on the phrase "one of the chief architects of the Armenian Genocide." Given the shrill, sometimes hysterical rhetoric that surrounds that horror, the lens of history thus becomes focused on that chapter of his life, blurring the view of the rest of his career.

Mehmed Talaat (sometimes spelled Talat) was the son of a senior officer in the Ottoman Army. He was born in Kircaali, outside of Adrianople, in 1874; his early life was marked by the comfortable, privileged existence of the empire's minor nobility. His family's social station ensured that he was given an education at Adrianople's finest private schools. Like many young men in developing nations during the last quarter of the nineteenth century, Talaat became fascinated with Western technology. In his case the object of this attention was the telegraph. In 1890 he joined the staff of the government telegraph office in Adrianople; it was a choice that would have unexpected consequences.

Like many young men making the transition from late adolescence to adulthood, Talaat found himself drawn to radical politics. It was an attraction that caused him to run afoul of Ottoman authorities, who arrested him in 1893 on a charge of subversive political activity. On his release two years later, in classically Byzantine fashion, he was appointed to a government post. As with most European nations, in the Ottoman Empire the telegraph service was not a private business but rather a branch of the post office. A skilled telegraphist, Talaat was named secretary of the postal service in Salonika, supervising both the post offices and the telegraph service there. Rising through the bureaucracy, by 1908 he was running the whole of the postal services in the province. So fond was he of his career as a telegraphist that until the end of his life, he kept a practice telegraph key on his office desk and worked it almost daily to maintain his sending skills.

But 1908 saw his career with the post office come to an end, as Talaat was dismissed when it was discovered that he had become a member of the Committee of Union and Progress. It proved to be only a temporary setback, as in July he was elected a deputy to the new Turkish parliament for his home province of Edirne. His colleagues quickly recognized his administrative talents, and he was named minister of interior affairs the following spring. He was subsequently given the office of minister of posts (that is, the post office) and in 1912 was named to be the Secretary General of the Committee of Union and Progress.

It was in this posting that he formed his political alliance with Enver and Djemal, although, like the alliance of Enver and Djemal, precisely why he chose to cast his lot with an adventurer such as Enver remains a mystery. What is not in dispute is that of the Three Pashas, he would prove to be the one indispensable to the cohesion of the Ottoman government in the five years it had remaining. In the end, Talaat was unquestionably the most determined patriot of the three.

While Enver was driven by his love of danger and intrigue—in 1913 he would organize the *Teşkilat-i Mahsusa*, the "Special Organization," as the Three Pashas' secret police force, a shadowy group of questionable characters who became Enver's personal instrument of terror and repression—Djemal was compelled by his ambition, and Talaat was the genuine patriot. The Three Pashas did share one distinct ultranationalistic sentiment, expressed in the vision of a revived Ottoman Empire, one that abandoned its quasi-Oriental trappings and medieval pretensions and was instead sophisticated and thoroughly modern: they dreamed of uniting all of the Turkic peoples in the Middle East and Central Asia into their dream of a "great and eternal land" called "Turan," with one language, Turkish, and one religion, Islam. Yet despite its veneer of sophistication, it was a dangerous vision, for it was built on a foundation of xenophobia that would lead all three men to turn their backs on the empire's subject peoples just at the moment when it would desperately need their loyalty.

Together, Enver and Talaat were responsible for an unprecedented expansion of German influence throughout the empire, which would be accompanied by consequences. Enver's passion for all things German was the by-product of his service as a military attaché in Berlin, whereas Talaat had come under the Teutonic spell in his service with the telegraph department of the post office: the department was organized and equipped by the German telegraph office, and the Turkish operators were trained by German instructors. Although German investment in the empire was already heavy, both Talaat and Enver encouraged more, while the Kaiser's military advisers were given even broader powers in their mission to reform and reorganize the Turkish Army. Rumors abounded of bribes being paid to the triumvirate—which was unlikely in the case of Djemal, who, because of his family background and education, was a convinced Francophile. It was somewhat more likely in Talaat's case, though, and was almost certainly true of Enver. At the same time, it would be incorrect to make too much of the question of bribes, if the rumors were true. Bribery had been a way of business in the empire for centuries and was not always a guarantee of cooperation: the Sublime Porte was notorious for officials who had been bought refusing to stay bought. The extent of the influence exerted on Ottoman affairs by the German military mission to Constantinople deeply worried some Turks, including Djemal, who feared Teutonic encroachment on Ottoman sovereignty, yet the need for the mission was undisputed. As its performance in Macedonia had just shown, the Turkish Army was desperately in need of an overhaul, and given the Germans' performance in their three wars of unification, no one questioned the idea of the Turks emulating a winner.

In the meantime, no one was completely surprised when, with the ink on the Treaty of London barely dry, the victors of the First Balkan War began bickering among themselves about the division of spoils. The alliance of convenience against the Turks foundered on conflicting claims by Serbia, Bulgaria, and Greece over the newly conquered territories. The smoke from the First Balkan War barely had time to dissipate before the second had begun.

Naturally, the Three Pashas saw this new Balkan debacle as an opportunity to regain some of the territory lost just a few months earlier, particularly the province of Edirne and with it the city of Adrianople. It was a task that, while successful, exhausted the Ottoman Army, although it did much to bolster the prestige of the Three Pashas among the Turkish people, as well as within the army itself. The Three Pashas wisely chose to recognize reality for what it was, deciding not to press any farther into the Balkans. When the twin treaties of Bucharest and Constantinople were signed in July 1913, the Turks officially recognized that all but the smallest remnant of the empire's European marches, which had once reached the gates of Vienna, were lost forever. What the Ottoman Empire and the Young Turks needed more than ever was peace and quiet and time to reorganize, repair, and rebuild, while redirecting the empire's limited resources toward providing a measure of economic and social stability.

CHAPTER THREE
OPENING MOVES

When August 1914 found the Great Powers of Europe plunging headlong into the abyss that would become known as the Great War, there seemed to be little, if any, reason for the Ottoman Empire to take part in the looming catastrophe. Certainly, there were no compelling causes for the Turks to join either belligerent camp (the Allies or the Central Powers), while there were numerous particularly good reasons for staying well out of the conflict. Not the least of these was the plain truth that the Ottoman economy and bureaucracy were simply too fragile to support a major war effort, while the army was exhausted, poorly trained, and demoralized: the just-ended Balkan Wars had seen to that. Equally true was that a war that preoccupied the Great Powers of Europe would present an unprecedented opportunity for the government of the Three Pashas to gain a measure of stability and legitimacy, along with time to restore imperial finances. A continent at war with itself would have little time or energy to devote to interfering in the affairs and policies of the Ottoman Empire, while there were no vital Turkish interests involved in the conflict: the blunt truth was that Turks stood to gain nothing by joining with any of the belligerents. They had the luxury of standing thoughtfully to one side while the Allies and the Central Powers mauled each other in Belgium, France, and Poland.

And yet, barely ten weeks after Austria-Hungary, France, Germany, Great Britain, and Russia had all rushed into one another's lethal embrace, the Ottoman Empire joined them. It was a disastrous decision for the Ottoman Turks, brought about by a strange combination of an overabundance of zeal on the part of the

Three Pashas, a political blunder by one of the most brilliant members of the British Cabinet, and a perfidious charade played by the German Kaiser and one of his admirals. Four years later, when the guns finally fell silent and the blood and the dust settled, the empire, which for so long had appeared to be dying but somehow managed to survive, had at last suffered truly mortal wounds.

Had the Turks taken advantage of the breathing space that the eruption of the Great War had offered, when the attention of the world would have focused away from Constantinople, they might have saved the Ottoman Empire. The Turks' situation in the summer of 1914 was such that by any realistic measure, even if they had wanted to go to war again, the Ottoman Army was in no condition to fight, no matter what the conflict's size or scope. Despite massive materiel and technical assistance from imperial Germany, the two Balkan Wars had left the army physically, morally, and materially exhausted. Prior to 1912, the Ottoman Army had been making real, if incremental, qualitative improvement, helped by a remarkable degree of stability that it enjoyed largely by providing the network of garrisons that stretched the length and breadth of the empire. In many ways, the army, rather than the creaking imperial bureaucracy, had become the framework that held together the various pieces of the empire. It is no stretch to say that Abdul-Hamid, in the one meaningful accomplishment of his reign, saved the Turkish Army from complete collapse by his willingness to allow the imperial German Army to reorganize, reequip, and retrain it in the last decade of the nineteenth century.

The German military mission to Constantinople charged with essentially reviving the Ottoman Army had quickly followed on the heels of Berlin's investment in the Berlin-to-Baghdad Railway project. The senior German adviser was Baron Colmar von der Goltz, a major in the German Army who became an Ottoman field marshal. Responsible for organizing, equipping, and training the Ottoman troops along German lines, he began by creating an organization of four field armies. He grouped the twelve infantry divisions posted around Constantinople and Adrianople into the four corps of the First Army. The Second Army, also of twelve divisions but organized into three corps, provided the garrisons for the remainder of the Ottoman Balkans. The smaller Third and Fourth Armies were stationed in the Caucasus and Mesopotamia, respectively, while independent corps garrisoned the Levant and the Arabian Peninsula. An extensive reserve system in theory provided reinforcements, while also furnishing the garrisons for strategically or politically important cities. It was a fundamentally sound organization, and had the Ottoman Turks not been compelled to disperse their forces in order to fight five foes in two widely separated wars (Libya and the Balkans), it might have allowed them to more effectively defend their provinces.

As it was, all four armies were successively thrown into the Balkan Wars, and all four were essentially shattered—some corps had been broken up to reinforce others, the fighting strengths of infantry divisions varied wildly, reservists had been hastily organized into ad hoc units, training for replacements had all but stopped, and there were shortages of weapons and ammunition everywhere as the supply services all but collapsed. The total casualties were equivalent to fifteen divisions out of forty-three committed to combat; unit cohesion had been destroyed and morale plummeted throughout the army. Only six of the pre-war regular divisions were kept completely out of the Balkans debacle. By the end of the Second Balkan War, the pre-war Turkish Army had ceased to exist as an effective fighting force.

The recovery of the army became the first priority of the Three Pashas. Berlin sent a new senior military adviser to Constantinople, Lt. Gen. Otto Liman von Sanders. Enver, as minister of war, striking a balance between necessity and his own ambition, grudgingly gave him near-plenipotentiary powers to rebuild the Ottoman Army, all the while openly jealous of Liman's authority. Seizing this opportunity, the German Army flooded the ranks of its Ottoman counterpart with nearly twenty-five thousand officers and troops brought in as advisers. Between July 1913 and August 1914, a complete reorganization took place in an effort to make good the losses and deficiencies of the Balkan Wars. At the same time, Enver, who, whatever his faults, truly loved the army, made clear his commitment to restoring the army's morale and prestige, ruthlessly purging more than a thousand officers who were deemed too old or too timid to be of value in the reconstituted army.

At first glance, it seemed that the resources available to Liman von Sanders were more than adequate for the task at hand, but a year after he began his work, his progress was limited at best. In the summer of 1914 the Turkish General Staff estimated that when the reorganization was complete, the empire would be able to mobilize a total of about 2 million men. In practice, though, this figure would prove to be wildly ambitious, for the Turks never came close to achieving it. Still, that summer the conscript classes of 1893 and 1894 (that is, young men who had been born in those two years) were called to the colors, each class numbering roughly 90,000 men. The peacetime establishment of the Turkish Army had been set at slightly more than 8,000 officers and 200,000 other ranks, so the numbers conscripted were more than sufficient to fill out the standing units. The problem was that in a departure from European practice, the Turks did not keep their first-line units at full strength in peacetime. Instead, they preferred to field formations with greatly reduced numbers: the average strength of a Turkish infantry division, in the summer of 1914, was four thousand men, which in wartime would theoretically expand to ten thousand, as reserves were called up. Called a "reduced establishment" or "cadre" structure, this doctrine was adopted after the Balkan Wars, in an effort to produce an army that could once again serve as a garrison force, be rapidly deployed to any threatened sector in a crisis, and then nearly double in strength within weeks of full mobilization, eliminating the time needed to completely assemble the units before transporting them to the front. The problem with this concept was that it required an established, robust, and efficient reserve system, something the Balkan Wars had left in a shambles, as well as a reliable transportation network.

The Germans were unquestionably the best choice for advice in organizing the Turkish reserves, for the reserve system of the Germans was (as August 1914 would prove) the most efficient such system in the world. But events would deny Liman von Sanders the time needed to rebuild the reserve organization; in any case, the overall poverty of the Ottoman rail and road network would have made it unworkable even if he had been given more time. Given the poor quality of communications within the empire, many reservists would be too long in receiving their recall and would take equally long to report for duty. As events fell out, in the more remote reaches of the empire many would choose to simply ignore the summons, confident that they would never be found by the authorities. The result was that once war was declared, although the paper strength of the Turkish Army was supposed to total some 12,500 officers and 480,000 other ranks, in practice most of its regiments, divisions, and corps would go into battle with barely half their authorized numbers.

To make matters worse, in terms of materiel, the support branches were in very poor shape. The six batteries of field artillery assigned to each infantry division were rarely, if ever, up to strength, and the guns themselves were a mixed bag of howitzers and field guns acquired over the years from Schneider in France, Krupp in Germany, and Skoda in Austria-Hungary. Corps-level artillery establishments were little better off—over all, the Turkish Army possessed barely two-thirds of the number of field guns and heavy artillery its organization tables specified. In many ways, this deficiency was an even graver problem than the potential manpower shortage: unlike infantry units, which could be raised and trained in two to three months, the manufacture of an artillery piece required a year or more. Ammunition was another problem, as shells were not interchangeable between various makes of guns of the same caliber, creating logistical nightmares for an already inadequate quartermaster service. What ammunition reserves there were averaged fewer than six hundred shells per gun.

The small arms situation was nearly as bad. Each infantry regiment was authorized four machine guns; most had only half that number. Rifles at least were plentiful—German-made 7.92mm bolt-action Mauser rifles, excellent, reliable weapons—but ammunition was not. Each infantryman was issued only 150 rounds; corps depots in theory had another 190 rounds per man available, but actual stocks for the entire army ran to only 200 million cartridges, perilously inadequate for more than a few weeks of campaigning.

Nor were the other support services in any better condition. Not surprisingly, given the shortages of weapons, which were always an army's first priority, the medical corps was inadequate: the lack of doctors, medical support personnel, medicine, and supplies was chronic. Two-fifths of all of the hospital beds in the entire empire were located in Constantinople, a fact that did not bode well for the treatment of wounded soldiers on distant fronts. Efforts to get the wounded to these hospitals faced major obstacles as well, as the numbers of wagons and draft animals were woefully deficient. Motorization barely existed outside of Constantinople and the other major cities, while there were fewer than two thousand miles of railway in the whole of the empire.

The pool of manpower was in theory very deep. All males over the age of twenty were liable to be called up—conscripts who were actually called up were obligated to serve two years on active duty with the infantry or three with the artillery and the technical services. Draft animals requisitioned for national service were retained for four years; the reserve obligation for both man and beast was for life. The result was that at any given moment, more than 2 million men could be called to the colors. Curiously, for it deprived the empire of a sizable fraction of its manpower pool, only Moslems were permitted to serve in the Ottoman Army: Christians, Jews, and other non-Moslems were compelled to pay a special "military tax" as compensation for their "exemption."

The most glaring weakness of the Turkish system, though, was its lack of a workable large-unit reserve system that could deploy full-strength reserve corps composed of reserve divisions to reinforce the regular units. It was an innovation the German Army had only recently introduced; in the event of a war, it allowed them to effectively double the mobilized strength of their army in a matter of days. It is possible that von Sanders intended to establish a similar system for the Turks—his papers make no indication one way or the other—but the Great War overtook whatever plans he had hoped to put into action. The result was that when the Turks went to war, they would be forced to fight with whatever units were already on hand. Lacking the organizational structure to create new divisions and corps while at the same time providing reinforcements for those units already committed to battle, they possessed the resources to do only one or the other but not both simultaneously. When war came, the Turkish Army would be spread precariously thin. In the end, the war would stretch both the army and the empire beyond the breaking point.

The ever more intrusive role played by the German Reich in Ottoman military affairs was a reflection of a widespread—and alarming, to some Turks—German influence throughout the empire. The process began in 1883, when a then obscure officer in the German Army, Maj. Wilhelm Leopold Colmar, Baron von der Goltz, was assigned to the post of senior adviser to the Turkish Army. He made slow but effective progress, such that he attracted the attention of the Sultan, who, as a result, began paying ever closer attention to the blandishments of the German Empire. The process accelerated later that decade when the new German Kaiser, Wilhelm II, paid the first of two formal state visits to Constantinople in October 1889. Nine years later, in October 1898, he paid a second visit, by which time Abdul-Hamid had begun to regard the Reich as the Ottoman Empire's best friend in Europe. Setting aside his general dislike of foreigners, the Sultan made it known that German advisers of every stamp and breed were welcome within the empire, where they would be put to work modernizing the creaking imperial infrastructure. That work began when German bankers and financial experts were brought in to reorganize the Ottoman government's finances. Technical advisers soon followed, and in 1899 the Sultan announced that Germany would be given the concession to build a Berlin-to-Baghdad Railway.

Meanwhile, Abdul-Hamid's German guests, always conscious of the role they were playing in advancing the power and prestige of *der Vaterland*, were careful to trowel flattery onto their hosts in thick layers. Friedrich Krupp, for example, the German munitions maker, on a corporate visit to Constantinople once referred to the homicidal Abdul-Hamid as *Wohltäter des Türkenvolkes*—"the benefactor of the Turkish peoples." The Kaiser himself got into the act, wearing a red fez at his public appearances during his state visits to Constantinople, allowing rumors to circulate that he had converted to Islam while on pilgrimage to Mecca, and declaring that "The 300 million Moslems scattered across the globe can be assured that the German emperor is, and will at all times remain, their friend." A triumphal "pilgrimage" to Jerusalem followed. By 1909 the Augusta-Victoria Sanatorium had been constructed on the Mount of Olives, nestled between an Orthodox church and a Jewish university. It had been named after Wilhelm's wife, the Kaiserin, and built with his sponsorship. Before long, the Turks were calling him Haji Wilhelm behind his back.

It is debatable whether the Sultan knew he was being taken for a ride or, if he did, that he really cared, as long as German support was directed at keeping him on his throne. At the same time, the underlying motives for Germany's friendship were neither altruistic nor disinterested. Wilhelm and the German government were determined to reduce the Sultan to little more than the Kaiser's vassal, for binding the Ottoman Empire to the German one held forth the promise of glittering rewards, military, economic, and political. Control of the Bosporus and the Dardanelles effectively neutralized Russia's Black Sea fleet by denying it access to the Mediterranean; possession of the oil fields of Mesopotamia grew in strategic, as well as economic, value as the twentieth century dawned and the industrialized world's dependence on petroleum products increased almost daily. The empire's border with Egypt stood barely seventy miles from the Suez Canal, a potential strategic threat that Great Britain could never afford to ignore. Most important, in the calculations of Wilhelm and his ministers, the Sultan's status as supreme caliph could be exploited to incite rebellion among the Moslem populations of southern Russia, Afghanistan, or western India.

The Reich's grip on the empire—always exerted with a velvet glove drawn over the iron fist—tightened dramatically with the rise of the Three Pashas, especially as the dominant figure in the new government, Enver Bey, was a passionate Germanophile. His years in Berlin had led him to embrace the whole of the spike-helmeted, goose-stepping, heel-clicking mystique of the Prussian Offizierkorps and with it a conviction that for the future of the Ottoman Empire there were but two choices: the German way and the wrong way. At one point, in the middle of a Cabinet meeting and in response to a suggestion that Germany was gaining alto-gether too much influence within the empire, Enver exclaimed, "The reason I love Germany is not sentimentality but the fact that they are not a danger to my beloved country; on the contrary, our two countries' interests go hand-in-hand."

Enver's reputation for shooting political opponents ensured that there were few individuals willing to openly disagree with him; the best that most of them could do was moderate his more severe excesses. In the name of achieving instant modernization and international power, Enver and his cronies came perilously close to reducing the Ottoman Empire to a state of vassalage to the German Reich. This was a situation the Kaiser and his ministers found eminently satisfactory: by the summer of 1914, Germans owned or operated the Turkish railway system, the telegraph system, the telephone exchange, and the power plant in Constantino-ple. Wilhelm was overheard boasting at his palace in Potsdam that "the German flag will soon fly over the fortifications of the Bosporus." A joke began to circu-late in diplomatic circles that the new Ottoman imperial anthem would be called "Deutschland über Allah."

It should never be thought, however, that the Turks were blind to German ambitions. In early 1914, when a colleague of Talaat's informed him that the Ger-man plan was to make Turkey a German colony, he admitted that he knew this to be the case. Yet he said, "We cannot put this country on its feet with our resources. We shall therefore take advantage of such technical and material assistance as the Germans can place at our disposal. We shall use Germany to help reconstruct and defend the country until we are able to govern the country with our own strength. When that day comes, we can say good-bye to the Germans within twenty-four hours." There was admittedly more than a whiff of wishful thinking in Talaat's words, but they make clear that the Turks understood the true reasons behind the German largesse.

To be his representative in Constantinople and oversee Berlin's policy of gradually subjugating the Ottoman Empire to the Germans, Kaiser Wilhelm II had personally selected Baron Hans von Wangenheim as Germany's ambassador to the Sublime Porte. It was a shrewd choice, for the Baron was particularly suited, physically and temperamentally, to the role. He was a big man, standing six feet two inches tall—broad-shouldered and muscular, he had a dominating presence that seemed to embody the physical power of the German Reich. He was also a handsome man, with a square jaw, a straight nose, and sharp blue eyes; he wore a large, somewhat drooping moustache that softened and gentled what would have otherwise been an almost frightening visage.

A native of Thüringen born in 1859, von Wangenheim was very thoroughly an aristocrat and an autocrat, believing that *Ordnung* (order), as practiced and codified by German society, and law-embodied civilization (the German word is *Kultur*) represented the best possible future for mankind. In this, his opinion exactly reflected the mind-set of the majority of the German middle class and aristocracy. There should be, as he saw it, two classes of people in the world: the rulers and the ruled. He despised the idea of class mobility and regarded the British aristocracy as effete and decadent; his opinion of the French was unprintable. It was, he believed, the manifest destiny of Germany to rule the world, and his duty, as he saw it, was to undertake any action in his role as ambassador that furthered that end. All of this made him the perfect representative in Constantinople for the Kaiser's government.

This does not mean that von Wangenheim was without personal ambition. He was convinced that if during his ambassadorship the Ottoman Empire should finally be reduced to quasicolonial status, a vassal state to Berlin, he would be rewarded with the ultimate political plum—appointment as the foreign minister of the German Empire; perhaps even the office of imperial chancellor would not be beyond his reach. With this as his goal, he brought all the force of his imposing personality to bear on the Turkish officials with whom he worked. He had a unique affinity for establishing friendly personal relations with the Turks, exercising a combination of persuasiveness, geniality, and forcefulness (with a hint of a potential for brutality), which the Turks respected and at the same time found fascinating. Unlike most of his colleagues in the German diplomatic service, von Wangenheim was capable of remarkable tact. (Barbara Tuchman once tellingly characterized the philosophy of German pre-war diplomacy: "Speak very loudly and brandish a big gun.") Rather than bully his Turkish counterparts into cooperation, he usually chose to be persuasive. The American ambassador to Constantinople, Henry Morgenthau, recalled that "von Wangenheim had in combination the jovial enthusiasm of a college student, the rapacity of a Prussian official, and the happy-go-lucky qualities of a man of the world." Yet however genuine his ebullient personality might have been, his motive was always to be of service to Germany; this was his *liebmotiv*. Von Wangenheim's character is perhaps best summed up by simply stating that he wholeheartedly embraced Otto von Bismarck's infamous dictum that a German must be ready to sacrifice for Kaiser and Fatherland not only his life but his honor as well.

The Turk who was most often called on to counter von Wangenheim's more aggressive blandishments and who did the most to moderate Enver's headlong plunge into Teutonism was a young financier, Mehmed Djaved Bey. Through his efforts, he essentially determined the boundaries of the financial ties between the Reich and the Ottoman Empire. He was thirty-four years old when he was appointed finance minister in 1909, the first Committee of Union and Progress member to serve at Cabinet rank. Despite his CUP affiliation, he was careful to become neither too closely identified with nor beholden to the Young Turk leadership, particularly by keeping Enver at arm's length. Djaved's assertion of his independence proved to be important, for it enabled him to ensure his continued place at the heart of the empire's financial administration, providing an unprecedented measure of stability to the administration of the Ottoman treasury, by standing apart from the factionalism by which the government was soon riven.

Djaved's particular talent lay in his ability to secure loans for the Turkish government in the years prior to the First World War. In doing so, he served as something of a counterweight to Enver, repeatedly tapping the Germans for fresh infusions of cash while shunting aside their demands for further economic concessions. (This was no small task, for Enver had mortgaged the empire's future so heavily to the Germans that from 1910 to 1914, the tolls collected by Turkish customs for passage through the Bosporus and the Dardanelles, the Ottoman government's single largest source of revenue, were pledged by law exclusively to the repayment of German loans.)

Djaved cleverly ensured the continued flow of money from Berlin by making it too expensive for the German bankers to refuse further loans. When pressured by Berlin to make further concessions of Ottoman economic independence, Djaved used a favorite tactic: employ the threat of nonpayment of existing loans to silence German bluster. The Germans had already invested so much money in Ottoman Turkey that they could not afford to call the Turkish bluff: had the Turks defaulted, the consequences would have been crippling for the German banking community. Consequently, new loans were made and payments continued, the stalemate allowing the Ottoman Empire to remain far less economically dependent on the German Empire than the Kaiser and his ministers had hoped it would be.

In the meantime, while the Ottoman government appeared to be mortgaging the empire's future to Berlin and the Ottoman Army was licking its wounds in the aftermath of the Balkan Wars, the Ottoman navy was attempting to resurrect itself. Here the foreign power exerting the strongest influence over Turkish policy was not Germany but rather Great Britain. Despite German efforts to entice the Turks by flaunting the rising power of the German High Seas Fleet, accompanied by the blandishments of Ambassador von Wangenheim and the German Military Mission to Constantinople, the Turkish navy—as well as its civil administration—was openly and enthusiastically pro-British.

There were a number of reasons for this, one of the most potent being the long tradition of Great Britain acting as a sort of protector of the Ottoman Empire in its declining years, dating back to the Crimean War, the symbol of which had always been the Royal Navy. Though never a formal diplomatic relationship, its intangible, almost sentimental, influence was considerable. Another was the Royal Navy's awesome reputation, built on a succession of victorious wars stretching back nearly two centuries. That reputation had only been further burnished when the Japanese, whose navy was British-trained and for the most part British-built, all but annihilated the Russian navy in 1905. A third, and by no means the least significant, was the ability of British industry to provide the Ottoman Empire with modern warships.

In this, the Germans were handicapped by their own ambition. Germany's desperate naval race with Great Britain was the culprit, for German shipyards were strained to their limits to build new warships for the Kaiser's navy; they had no building capacity to spare for new construction for other countries. Great Britain, on the other hand, had more shipyards than there were Royal Navy orders for new builds, so requests from foreign navies for British-designed and -built warships were welcomed with open arms. In the two decades before the Great War, British shipyards built battleships, dreadnoughts, battle cruisers, cruisers, and destroyers for the navies of the United States, Japan, Spain, Chile, Brazil, China—and the Ottoman Empire.

The Young Turks were very conscious of their empire's long history as the first-rank naval power of the eastern Mediterranean and were determined to reclaim the naval supremacy in the Aegean Sea that had been abandoned by Abdul-Hamid after the disaster of the Russo-Turkish War in 1878. Fearing that the fleet might revolt against him, the Sultan had ordered the Ottoman fleet into port; once there, the ships were abandoned and left to rust and rot. In 1903 Lord Selborne, the First Lord of the Admiralty, while visiting Constantinople and invited to inspect the remnants of the Ottoman navy, reported on his return to Whitehall that "there is no [Turkish] navy!"

No sooner had the Young Turks taken control of the Ottoman government than they began making an effort to reverse this deplorable state of affairs and rebuild the fleet. It was a prodigious task, for the empire had nearly five thousand miles of coastline and only thirty seaworthy ships with which to defend it, none larger than a light cruiser. First, a squadron of four French destroyers was purchased in 1909, followed by a quartet of ex-German torpedo boats a year later. A light cruiser, the English-built *Hamadiye* (sometimes spelled *Hamidieh*), was refurbished and restored to service. Finally, a pair of heavy units—pre-dreadnought battleships originally designed and built for the German navy in the mid-1890s—were acquired in 1910. Even as they bought the pair, the Turks understood that these battleships were already hopelessly obsolete; *Hayreddin Barbarrosa* (formerly, SMS *Kürfurst Friedrich Wilhelm*) and *Turgut Reiss* (ex–SMS *Weissenburg*) were small (10,500 tons), slow (15 knots), and indifferently armed and armored (they each carried four 11-inch, six 4-inch, and eight 3.5-inch guns).

Yet so feeble had the Turkish fleet become it was felt that anything was better than nothing, at least for the moment. The war with Italy in 1911 demonstrated that these efforts were a classic case of "too little, too late," as aside from a few sharp, successful actions by the cruiser *Hamadiye*, under the command of Capt. Raouf Bey, the Ottoman navy could make no showing at all against the Italian fleet, rarely leaving port and refusing to engage the enemy when it did. The Turkish navy's performance was not the fault of the Turkish sailors or their officers—as with Turkish soldiers, there has never been a lack of courage among Turkish seamen—but rather, in the simplest terms, they had been let down by their equipment. Outnumbered and outgunned by the Italians, who had just completed one of history's most ambitious building programs and by 1911 possessed one of the largest and most modern navies in the world, the handful of ships in the Ottoman navy had been completely and hopelessly outclassed.

The impetus for what was to have been a true renaissance of the Turkish navy came in late 1911, even before the war with Italy ended, when the decision was made to acquire two dreadnought battleships, to be built in Great Britain to Turkish specifications. When finished and deployed, the new ships would utterly transform the strategic situation in not only the Aegean but in the whole of the eastern Mediterranean, for they would be capable of overwhelming the pre-dreadnought battleships of the Greek fleet without fear of retaliation, and they would also be powerful enough to challenge any Italian squadron that might possibly be sent to try conclusions with them.

One of the Ottoman navy's dreadnoughts was to be built by Vickers, to be named *Rashidiye*; the other by Armstrong, to be named *Mahmud Resad V*. The two ships were based on the design of the Royal Navy's King George V class, the most modern and powerful dreadnoughts so far constructed, with modifications to allow for the particular requirements of service with the Turkish navy. They would mount a main armament of ten 13.5-inch guns each, and when completed they would form, by far and away, the most powerful squadron in the Aegean and the eastern Mediterranean. Nothing in the Greek, Russian, or Italian navies could stand up to them: when delivered in the summer of 1914, they would return naval supremacy in the Aegean and the eastern Mediterranean to the Turks.

There was only one problem with this plan: the imperial treasury was exhausted by the war with Italy and the two Balkan Wars, leaving the empire with no money to pay for both battleships. The contract with Armstrong was canceled, while the Turkish government scraped and scrimped to find the money to continue work on *Rashidiye*, which was launched with tremendous pomp and ceremony on September 3, 1913. Nevertheless, one dreadnought was not enough: the Turks needed both ships. In this case, prestige was not the determining factor; rather, naval tactics were the key consideration. There was always the possibility that an enemy fleet of individually inferior ships could overwhelm a single dreadnought; however, a pair of dreadnoughts working together as a squadron was a manifold more difficult opponent to take down.

The solution to Constantinople's dilemma presented itself when, appropriately enough, another third-rank power with naval pretensions found itself unable to pay for the warships it coveted. Brazil, which had been engaged in a comic-opera naval race with Argentina and Chile, had ordered what was at the time the largest battleship in the world, a monster displacing 31,600 tons, more than 800 feet long, armed with fourteen 12-inch guns. To be named *Rio de Janeiro*, she was almost 80 percent finished, with half of her fourteen guns mounted, when the bottom fell out of Brazil's rubber-export market and the Brazilian government suddenly ran out of money to pay for the ship.

At the same time, tensions were again rising between the Ottoman Empire and Greece. The Greeks, alarmed by the prospect of Constantinople acquiring modern dreadnoughts, began looking for battleships of their own. In the summer of 1913 a contract was quickly drawn up with Krupp, who was building the German High Seas Fleet, to construct a battle cruiser that would be armed with 14-inch guns supplied from the United States. (The agreement was disingenuous on the part of Krupp: all of the slipways at the Germaniawerft shipyard were already committed to building ships for the Kaiser's High Seas Fleet for the next five years.)

When news that *Rio de Janeiro* was being put up for auction reached Athens and Constantinople, both governments began scrambling to find financial backing in order to purchase the ship; ultimately, the Turks proved more successful than the Greeks. The Turks approached a private French bank, seeking a loan of £4 million, which was granted under the most stringent conditions: any default in the repayment schedule for any reason would be cause for the bank to seize the ship and sell it. Exhibiting a confidence that he likely did not truly feel, finance minister Mehmed Djaved signed the loan agreement, and on December 28, 1913, the Ottoman Empire bought *Rio de Janeiro* for £2,750,000; the remaining balance of the loan would pay for the completion of the ship. The largest battleship in the world, now proudly named *Sultan Osman I*, was the property of the Turkish navy. There seemed to be only one minor flaw in the plan: now that they had arranged to buy the dreadnought, how would the Turks pay for it?

Faced with yet another debacle, the Three Pashas turned it into an opportunity to secure their position by very cleverly linking the new warship to the Ottoman Turks' national identity. Overnight, *Sultan Osman I* became to the Turkish people what HMS *Victory* was to Britons or the USS *Constitution* represented to

Americans: a symbol of their empire and their national pride. Within weeks an empire-wide drive was organized to raise money to pay for the ship. Everywhere in Turkey and even in some non-Turkish parts of the empire, shopkeepers, tradesmen, peasants, fishermen, and farmers gave what money they could spare, often going without themselves, in order to be able to contribute money to buy this ship. Peasant women cut their hair to sell to wig makers in order to contribute money to the battleship fund; schoolchildren turned in carefully hoarded pennies to their teachers, who faithfully forwarded them to Constantinople. In every town and village, in taverns, cafés, and markets, everyone donated money for the Ottoman navy. A special medal, called the "Navy Donation Medal," was struck and awarded to those whose donations were particularly large or who had made some notable personal sacrifices in order to donate. Wearing the medal soon became a point of special pride among the common Turks, and long before the final payment was due, the money had been raised.

Meanwhile, January 1914 was a busy month in Constantinople. On January 7 the involuntary retirement of more than eleven hundred senior Ottoman Army officers was announced in a terse bulletin issued from the Sublime Porte. On January 25 a military convention was signed between Bulgaria and the Ottoman Empire, its intended purpose being a lessening of the tensions between the two nations by reducing the number of border incidents between their two armies. Liman von Sanders was given nominal command of the I Corps, with the additional responsibility of identifying "all the weak spots of the Turkish military organisation." It was understood that he would eventually be given the post of inspector general. Enver, the minister of war, named himself chief of staff of the Ottoman Army.

Predictably, there was friction between von Sanders and Enver: the German regarded the Turk as little more than a rank amateur playing at war, while Enver considered himself a military genius and, jealous of sharing power with anyone, resented Liman as an intrusive interloper in what should have been his own private preserve. Soon von Sanders was lodging frequent complaints with the German embassy over Enver's petty interference with Liman's command. In mid-summer, in an effort to bring Enver to heel, Liman threatened to resign his post and take the whole of the German military mission with him. Events in Europe would intervene before Enver could call his bluff.

As the end of the summer of 1914 approached, both *Rashidiye* and *Sultan Osman I* were nearing completion. A nucleus crew of five hundred officers and seamen was assembled, commanded by Capt. Raouf Bey, who had so distinguished himself in the First Balkan War. It would be incorrect to characterize this crew as experienced, for there was only a handful of real navy men among them; they had been mostly drafted from fishing villages and coastal towns, but at least they knew something of ships and the sea. When they arrived in England, they were taken in hand by instructors from both the Armstrong and the Vickers works; the two ships were scheduled to be formally handed over on August 2.

It was at this point that the growing diplomatic crisis following the assassination of Archduke Franz Ferdinand and his wife in Sarajevo on June 28 began to intrude on the Turks' plans. By the last week of July, the British Cabinet came to understand that what should have been a minor diplomatic confrontation in the Balkans had metastasized into a continent-wide war. With every passing hour the likelihood of hostilities between Great Britain and Germany grew closer to certainty, in which case the two dreadnought battleships being built for Turkey would assume an entirely unexpected importance in Great Britain's strategic calculations.

For fifteen years imperial Germany had been locked in a race for naval supremacy with Great Britain, a race that in the long run the Germans could not hope to win, but there were moments when the two opposing fleets approached something like numerical parity, a situation utterly unacceptable to the British, either politically or strategically. The First Lord of the Admiralty Winston Churchill and the senior British admirals rightly suspected that the strategy of the High Seas Fleet would be to whittle away at the strength of the Grand Fleet through a series of piecemeal actions, slowly eroding the Royal Navy's numerical superiority until the two fleets could meet as equals in the middle of the North Sea. There the Germans would rely on what they assumed would be the superior gunnery and construction of their ships to crush the Grand Fleet.

In the last days of July, the relative strengths of the two fleets stood at twenty-two dreadnoughts in the Grand Fleet opposed to the High Seas Fleet's thirteen. Churchill, however, was unwilling to settle for anything less than absolute supremacy over the High Seas Fleet. Great Britain could not afford to lose even a single naval engagement in her home waters. The Royal Navy could not win the war outright for the British, but a major defeat could, in Churchill's memorable phrase, "lose the war in an afternoon." He wanted to ensure that no matter in what circumstances German and British naval forces encountered each other in the North Sea, the Royal

Navy would be able to bring an overwhelming strength to bear, effectively nullifying Germany's strategy of attrition. Therefore, every dreadnought available would be required to take its place in the Grand Fleet's battle line—including the Ottoman Turks' *Rashidiye* and *Sultan Osman I*. On July 31, two days before the ships were to be handed over to the Turks, Churchill sent letters to Vickers and Armstrong, formally giving notice that the two dreadnoughts were being requisitioned by the Royal Navy, which would rename them HMS *Erin* and HMS *Agincourt*.

Two days were to pass before the news was relayed to Captain Raouf; the message arrived less than an hour before the ceremony formally handing over *Sultan Osman I* was to begin. Raouf immediately informed Constantinople. When the news broke in the Ottoman capital, not only was the government furious, but the Turkish people, who had made so many sacrifices to pay for the two warships, were also understandably outraged. What gave the Turks offense was not that the Royal Navy had taken over the ships. In this, Churchill was entirely within his legal rights: every contract drawn up for a warship being built for a foreign power in a British shipyard contained a provision allowing the Royal Navy to requisition said ship in the event of a war or other national emergency, and the two Turkish dreadnoughts were no exception. Another dreadnought being built by Armstrong, this one Chile's *Latorre*, would be commandeered a month later when the Royal Navy invoked the appropriate contractual clauses.

Yet the same contracts also required the British government to make payment in full for the requisitioned ship or ships at the time they were taken over by the Royal Navy. What so egregiously affronted the Turks was that their ships had been seized outright, with such a blithe disregard of Turkish feelings and dignity. The Foreign Office in Whitehall blandly informed Constantinople that compensation for the two warships would be made at such time as the British government found it convenient. As Capt. Raouf Bey recalled in his memoirs, "We paid the last installment (700,000 Turkish liras). We reached an agreement with the manufacturer that the ships would be handed over on 2 August 1914. Nevertheless, after we made our payment and half an hour before the ceremony, the British declared that they have requisitioned the ships. . . . Although we protested, nobody paid attention."

Here the British, and not only Churchill, stumbled badly, for most Britons (and most Europeans, for that matter) held the Turks in something approaching contempt and felt that where they were concerned, the niceties of contractual obligations could be ignored. This blunder created an unexpected opening for Germany's ambitions and led to the penultimate tragedy for the Ottoman Empire, for it strengthened immeasurably the position of those pro-German Turks within the Ottoman government, not the least among them being Enver and Talaat. Here was an opportunity to at last bind the Ottoman Empire to the German—not merely to align with it—and in Berlin, the German chancellor von Bethmann-Holweg was quick to seize upon it. Purely by chance, the instruments were at hand by which Berlin could administer a back-handed diplomatic blow to the British, while at the same time fundamentally alter the strategic positions of the Central Powers and the Allies.

The German navy's rather grandly named Mediterranean Division consisted of just two ships, the battle cruiser *Göben* and the light cruiser *Breslau*. When told of the Sarajevo assassinations, the squadron's commanding officer, Rear Adm. Wilhelm Souchon, immediately set out for the Austro-Hungarian naval base in Pola, at the northern end of the Adriatic Sea. Souchon's orders, in the event of war between Germany and France, were to interdict French troop convoys sailing from Algiers to Marseilles, and *Göben* wasn't ready to go to war.

Göben was a powerful warship, though by no means an awesome one. She was a battle cruiser, a class of ship that was an attempt to give cruiser speed to ships carrying dreadnought armament, at the expense of armor protection. In the case of *Göben*, on a displacement of 25,000 tons she carried a main armament of ten 11-inch guns, with a main armor belt of more than 10 inches; her designed top speed was 28 knots, and on trials in 1910 *Göben* had actually exceeded that speed by a fraction. But in the summer of 1914 her boilers were worn—many of them needed to have their tubes completely replaced—and the best she could hope to do was 24 knots. Even then, her boilers would be strained to the point of imminent failure. In Pola, *Göben*'s boilers could receive some much-needed attention from the Austrian ship fitters. *Breslau* was a different story altogether. A light cruiser, with a displacement of only 4,550 tons, she had been designed for two purposes: hunting enemy shipping and scouting for the battle fleet. Completed in 1912, she was armed with twelve 4.1-inch guns but carried no real armor to speak of. Being light, she was fast, with a top speed of 27.5 knots, but she was never meant to take a place on a battle line. Souchon's squadron was poorly balanced to do anything more than annoy the enemy if war actually came, but then it hadn't been created as a fighting force. It was a prestige posting, meant to "show the flag," providing a German presence in the Mediterranean that would look after Germany's very limited interests in the region. Souchon knew this and knew that in any event his command was hopelessly outnumbered. The French Mediterranean Fleet could deploy a half-dozen dreadnoughts and more than a score of cruisers against Souchon's two ships; there were twenty-one ships in the British Mediterranean Squadron.

When Souchon was posted to the Mediterranean Division in 1911, his orders in the event of a war involving France were to take his two ships to the coast of Algiers, where it was hoped—rather optimistically—that he could intercept and sink some of the French convoys carrying troops from North Africa to France. Equally unrealistically, the two German warships were then expected to flee westward through Gibraltar, leaving the Mediterranean and joining the High Seas Fleet, which it was hoped would be cruising the North Atlantic.

A message from Berlin arrived in Pola at noon on August 1, 1914, advising Souchon that Germany had declared war on Russia and would soon declare war on France. All work was stopped and *Göben* made ready to sail, although half of her boilers were still in need of repairs. Orders went out by wireless to *Breslau* to rendezvous with *Göben* off Taranto, at the heel of the Italian boot. This was the opening move of a cat-and-mouse game that Souchon would play with the Allied fleets for the next ten days, as he moved back and forth across the central Mediterranean, keeping the French and the British squadrons off balance and eventually being able to make a dash for Constantinople. The move east came on the morning of August 4, after a message was received from Adm. Alfred von Tirpitz, the imperial German naval secretary. It read, "Alliance with government of CUP concluded August 3. Proceed at once to Constantinople."

The message was, in fact, somewhat premature, for what was implied was far different than the reality. A treaty *had* been negotiated between von Wangenheim and the Grand Vizier, Said Halim, and on the surface it appeared that the German ambassador had gotten the better of his Turkish colleagues. The document was a typical exercise in the hypocrisy that passed for German diplomacy in those years, beginning with the first article, where both governments pledged to "observe strict neutrality in regard to the present conflict between Austria-Hungary and Serbia." Considering how Germany had exploited the Serbian crisis and used it to bully

Russia into a declaration of war, the wording was laughable. In the case of the second article, which obliged the Ottomans to join the Germans as active belligerents should Russia and Germany go to war, before the ink on the treaty draft was dry, the clock was already ticking on Germany's ultimatum to Russia, which had been specifically crafted to ensure its rejection, thus providing the German government with a *casus belli* for declaring war on imperial Russia.

It was the third article, however, that was truly absurd. It read, "In case of war, Germany will leave her military mission at the disposal of the Ottoman Empire. The latter, for her part, assures the said military mission an effective influence on the general conduct of the army, in accordance with the understanding arrived at directly between His Excellency the Minister of War [Enver] and His Excellency the Chief of the Military Mission [Liman von Sanders]." What made this article slightly ridiculous was that as few as two weeks earlier, Wangenheim had cabled Berlin with his considered opinion that there was nothing to be gained by actively seeking an alliance with the Turks; preventing them from closer association with the Entente was Germany's best option. "Turkey is today without any question worthless as an ally," he declared. "She would only be a burden to her associates, without being able to offer them the slightest advantage." Germany's best interests were served, he said, by remaining on friendly terms with the Three Pashas, while at the same time advising them to adopt a posture of benevolent neutrality and to avoid "every political adventure."

Not that the Germans were overanxious to expand the conflict into the Middle East. At this point they were still utterly confident that they would win the war in a matter of weeks. They could do so only at the price of an open confrontation with the British Empire, something the German government devoutly wished to avoid at any cost and that Berlin, even at this late date, still believed was possible. Still, the appearance of an alliance with the Ottoman Empire would be certain to divert at least a portion of Great Britain's attention and resources away from Europe, which would be just as strategically valuable as a military agreement.

Souchon, of course, knew nothing of any of this. Nonetheless, he saw the dash to the east as a brilliant ploy, for it would give the German Mediterranean Squadron—and himself—a strategic significance that neither would have otherwise possessed. At this point a sense of grandiose self-importance in the admiral's personality appeared. As he later explained, when he arrived in Constantinople he was determined, despite having no instructions from Berlin to do so, to "force the Ottoman Empire, even against their will, to spread the war to the Black Sea against their ancient enemy, Russia." At 5 p.m. on August 10, the German Mediterranean Squadron dropped anchor at the mouth of the Dardanelles (the western entrance to the Sea of Marmara, where the waters of the Black Sea flow into the Aegean). There the Germans anxiously awaited official permission to enter Turkish national waters.

In Constantinople the Three Pashas were taking their time in complying with the terms of the hasty alliance with Germany; in particular, they were in no hurry to declare war on Russia—or on anyone else, for that matter. In part, a fear of the consequences held them back: even Enver hesitated to take so great a plunge at this point, given the sad state of affairs in the Ottoman Army. There was another more mundane, pragmatic reason for Turkish foot-dragging as well. A financial crisis overtook the Sublime Porte in the first week of August, as the war swept across Europe. One by one, the Great Powers began to withdraw foreign credit in order to shore up their own treasuries, which left the Ottoman government insolvent. One provision of the treaty called for the Germans to pay the Turks a subsidy of £5,000,000 in gold, and the wily men in Constantinople were determined not to undertake any move to implement the treaty until the money was safely deposited in the imperial treasury.

Yet opportunism, rather than measured judgment, had always been Enver's guiding star, and these circumstances were no exception. Despite the just-concluded "treaty," the Turks were playing a double game with their new "allies." On Wednesday, August 5, Enver met with the Russian military attaché, offering him formal assurance that the Turkish mobilization, which had begun on August 3, was not directed against Russia. Despite what the Germans might be saying about the new treaty between them and Constantinople, the Ottoman Empire was not formally bound or beholden to anyone. The Turks would, Enver declared, act solely out of self-interest. He went on to present the possibility that the Sultan's troops in the Caucasus might be withdrawn, given assurances that the Russians would respect the integrity of Ottoman territory in the region. Should that happen, the Ottoman Army could be turned against Austria-Hungary, to fight alongside the armies of the Balkan states and perhaps even the Russians themselves. A Russo-Turkish military compact, Enver asserted, was a distinct possibility. The Russian attaché, Gen. Mikhail Leontiev, then asked the obvious question: what did Enver want in return? Enver replied that all that he expected of the Russian government was to mediate the return of the Aegean islands, an end to the Capitulations, and an adjustment of the border with Greece in Western Thrace. Leontiev dutifully reported this conversation to St. Petersburg, where the Russian foreign minister Sergei Sazonov made an ill-advised decision to temporize on the Ottoman offer.

Just how serious was Enver in his initiative to Leontiev? As always with Enver, it is impossible to say with absolute certainty. Some historians, mistaking his deviousness for subtlety, have asserted that Enver was playing a very deep game with the Russians. His offer to Leontiev, they say, was supposedly a disingenuous attempt to turn aside Russian ambitions toward Turkish territory in the Caucasus by indirectly reminding St. Petersburg of Constantinople's powerful friends in Berlin. This is to utterly misunderstand Enver's character, which was never subtle but always scheming. He doubtless wholeheartedly believed in whatever offer he was making at any given moment, but only at that moment. There was always something of the petty shopkeeper in his undertakings; he was the sort of individual who, no matter how good the deal currently at hand, was always convinced that there was a better one to be had. The offer he presented to Leontiev was potentially momentous: had Enver chosen to betray the Germans and actually align the Ottoman Empire with the Russians, the consequences for himself, the Turks, the Russians—indeed, for the entire world—would have been incalculable, and all arguably for the better. As it was, by the time the Russians got around to responding to Enver's astonishing offer, his attention had already been directed elsewhere. And when the time came, the Germans, unlike the Russians, were in a position to be able to enforce the agreement already in place.

In the meantime, the German foreign minister Gottlieb von Jagow was even at this early date far less sanguine about the prospects of German success in the west than were his military counterparts, and he began to fret when the Turks were taking their time about complying with the new treaty. He cabled Ambassador Wangenheim on the evening of August 4 that Britain was likely to declare war on Germany "as early as today or tomorrow" (the British ultimatum was only hours from expiration when the cable was sent). Jagow feared that the Turks might balk at the idea of going to war with the British as well as with the French and the Russians. Wangenheim was instructed to pressure the Turks into immediately declaring war on Russia. Wangenheim replied that "the military authorities at the Dardanelles have been instructed to let Austrian and German war-ships enter the Straits without hindrance. Grand Vizier fears, however, that if use is made of this privilege before the relations with Bulgaria have been settled, an acceleration of developments not desired at the present time by Germany or Turkey might be the result." Despite a declaration of neutrality from Sofia, Said Halim was worried about the Bulgars: if the Turks declared war on Russia and the Bulgars joined in on the side of their fellow Slavs, the Turks' strategic position would be difficult, if not impossible; consequently, he preferred to take a "wait and see" attitude. Fearing that the presence of the cruisers *Göben* and *Breslau* might provoke the Bulgars, Said denied the German ships access to Turkish territorial waters: the Dardanelles were, for the time being at least, closed.

Having painted the Germans into a corner, Said Halim now extracted the price for his cooperation. In a meeting with Wangenheim, he told the ambassador that although the Cabinet would consider allowing the German ships into the Sea of Marmara, Wangenheim should remember the six specific conditions to which he had agreed in order to gain Halim's assent to the treaty. First, Bulgaria and Romania were to be kept from taking advantage of the situation while the Turkish Army was engaged against the Russians. Second, the Germans would back the Turks in abolishing the despised Capitulations, which had essentially granted foreigners legal immunity within the empire. Third, there would be no separate peace on the part of Germany as long as enemy troops stood on Ottoman soil. Fourth, should Greece enter the war on the side of the Entente, Germany would guarantee the return of the Aegean islands. Fifth, Germany would be responsible for redrawing the eastern boundary of the Ottoman Empire "in a manner suitable for the establishment of a link with the Muslim peoples of Russia." Finally, the Germans would guarantee that when the war ended, Turkey would be compensated fairly, both financially and in territorial gains. Wangenheim, knowing he had been outfoxed, assented.

For the next five days, telegraph wires between Constantinople and Berlin ran hot as the Germans increased the pressure on the Turks to allow *Göben* and *Breslau* to enter Turkish waters and to close the Straits of the Bosporus and the Dardanelles. Doing so, the Three Pashas knew, might well provoke Russia into a declaration of war, something the Turks most devoutly wished to avoid for as long as possible. The route from the Black Sea to the Mediterranean was crucial to the Russian war effort, for it was Russia's only year-round sea lane to the west, vital for cargoes of Russian grain to be shipped out, which paid for the supplies of arms and munitions that were shipped in. When word reached Constantinople that the German ships had arrived in Turkish waters, Enver temporized: on the morning of August 11 *Göben* was given permission to pass through the Dardanelles into the Sea of Marmara, while *Breslau* stood outside the Straits, watching for any approach by British warships.

A small civilian steamer carried Admiral Souchon to Constantinople; once ashore, he immediately met with Ambassador Wangenheim, Lt. Gen. Liman von Sanders, and Enver, hoping to develop a strategy that would accelerate what the Germans in Constantinople regarded as a rather tardy mobilization by the Turks. The significance of this meeting was not its content, but that the only Turk present was the most vociferously pro-German member of the Ottoman government, as well as the most bellicose. It boded ill for Turks such as Talaat and Said Halim, who still hoped that if the Ottoman Empire could no longer maintain its neutrality, it might be able to cling to a precarious nonbelligerence. At some point the idea was raised of allowing the two German ships into the Black Sea, where they could strike at the Russians if necessary—but as a German squadron, acting without the endorsement of the Turks. Although Souchon openly favored such action, he quickly pointed out that repairs to the *Göben*'s boilers would have to be completed before it was possible.

In Berlin, meanwhile, there was still no particular sense of urgency to have the Turks become actively involved in hostilities. At this point the Schlieffen Plan was still proceeding according to its strict timetables; the French armies were, as expected, reeling back under the pressure of the relentless German advance; and the British Expeditionary Force had yet to meet the German Army in Belgium. Victory in the west seemed all but assured. A full mobilization by the Turkish Army at this moment would, without a shot being fired, facilitate German strategy, compelling the tsar's generals to redeploy part of their forces to guard the Caucasus, drawing troops away from the Russian armies now assembling on the Russo-German border just when Berlin would launch what it expected would be the decisive German attack in the east.

Ambassador Wangenheim, who understood the strategic subtleties involved, was working hard to restrain Liman von Sanders and Souchon, both of whom were advocating some sort of precipitate action to get the Turks "off the *pfennig*," as it were. Souchon, taking it for granted that the Turks would allow *Göben* and *Breslau* complete freedom of movement through Ottoman waters, cabled the Admiralty Staff in Berlin with a plan to bombard one or more of Russia's Black Sea ports in order to provoke a reaction that would compel the Turks to speed up their mobilization. The armchair sailors in Berlin quickly approved Souchon's proposal, either "with the concurrence of Turkey or against her will." Although technically subordinate to Wangenheim, the admiral was informed that he could commence operations at his discretion. Meanwhile, German engineers would take over the responsibility for the defenses of the Bosporus and the Dardanelles, repairing fortifications and artillery batteries sited there and laying new minefields in the Sea of Marmara. For four days Ambassador Wangenheim brought every bit of pressure to bear on the minister of war, Enver Pasha, while Souchon's ships steamed back and forth off the Gallipoli Peninsula. At the same time, the British and the French ambassadors did their best to counter Wangenheim's efforts, but to no avail.

On August 13 Enver finally consented to allow both German ships into the Bosporus, and events moved swiftly during the next few days. Instructions went out for a Turkish pilot boat to guide *Göben* and *Breslau* up through the Sea of Marmara to Constantinople itself, where the ships tied up within sight of the Sublime Porte. At the same time, orders went out to the Turkish defenses: any British ships pursuing *Göben* and *Breslau* into the Dardanelles were to be fired upon. Although the Turks had not yet wholeheartedly thrown their lot in with the Central Powers, one of the German military advisers in Constantinople, Col. Hans Kannergiesser, later memorably wrote, "We heard the clanking of the portcullis descending before the Dardanelles."

At first glance, it is difficult to reconcile the arrival of *Göben* off Constantinople, which seemed to symbolize the Turks' commitment to the German alliance, with Enver's overtures made just a few days earlier for a Russo-Turkish alliance, which were still on the table. It was a case of Enver being Enver, the ultimate opportunist. He knew as well as anyone that this war was not the Turks' war: he was looking for the best possible deal for the Ottoman Empire and himself, not necessarily in that order. The Russian ambassador to the Sublime Porte, the confusingly named Mikhail de Giers, saw clearly what was happening and reminded the Russian foreign minister, Sergei Sazonov, that the Germans were pressing the Turks hard, and the arrival of the two warships "may inspire [the Turks] with temerity for the most extreme steps." De Giers was specifically concerned, despite assurances from the Grand Vizier to the contrary, that *Göben* and *Breslau* would be let loose in the Black Sea, to strike at Russian shipping and ports.

This warning had the effect of finally galvanizing Sazonov into action. In his memoirs the British foreign minister Sir Edward Grey recalled how at that point he had cautioned the French and Russian governments "not to fasten any quarrel upon Turkey during the present war. . . . It would become very embarrassing for us, both in India and in Egypt, if Turkey came out against us. If she did decide to side with Germany, of course there was no help for it; but we ought not to precipitate this. If the first great battle, which was approaching in Belgium, did not go well for the Germans, it ought not to be difficult to keep Turkey neutral." It was sound advice, but instead Sazonov, who was rather high-strung and emotional, not the best traits for a foreign minister, chose to try to buy Ottoman neutrality. In exchange, he proposed that the Tsar's government would promise a guarantee of the empire's territorial integrity, give the Turks control of all of the German concessions in Asia Minor, and abolish the punitive terms of the Treaty of San Stefano, which had concluded the Russo-Turkish War of 1877–78, to end the hated "Capitulations."

It was a mistake: to the Turks, Sazonov appeared to be dealing from a position of weakness. On receiving the Russian offer, Enver called a Cabinet meeting, at which he announced that he wanted to declare war on Russia. Resorting to an old tactic, he produced a revolver and laid it on the table before him, the threat of violence explicit to those who might disagree with him. To his chagrin, all of his fellow Cabinet members then produced firearms of their own, returning Enver's threat in kind. There was no declaration of war. Nevertheless, a turning point of sorts had been reached, as Sazonov's offer was rejected, and there would be no further meaningful dialogue between the Russians and the Turks.

Reaching Constantinople on the morning of August 14, *Göben* and *Breslau* were the subjects of a particularly transparent charade in which the two ships were formally "transferred" to the Turkish navy the next day. Ambassador Wangenheim made a great show among the diplomatic community of Germany's willingness to replace the two warships seized by Great Britain with two of her own. *Göben* was renamed *Yavuz Sultan Selim*; *Breslau* became *Midilli*; the new names were mere formalities, for the ships' German officers and crews remained aboard, simply exchanging the blue hats of the imperial German navy for the red fezzes worn in the Ottoman fleet. Small numbers of Turkish sailors were brought aboard, ostensibly to begin the process of handing over the ships.

The British were furious, of course. The most immediate consequence of the "transfer" was that Admiral Sir Thomas Limpus, the chief of the British Naval Mission to Constantinople, was summarily dismissed from his task of modernizing the Turkish fleet; his responsibilities had included not only training but also operational command of all Turkish warships. Obviously, he could not remain in command of ships and crews that for all practical purposes were still German, regardless of whatever legal legerdemain had taken place. Souchon immediately replaced Limpus as the senior naval adviser to the Turks.

There was little the British could do at this point, except follow Sir Edward Grey's policy of avoiding "any quarrel with Turkey." Strong support for this position came from the Secretary of State for War, Lord Henry Kitchener. Apprehensive about the safety of the Suez Canal, which was vital to the transport of several divisions of the Indian Army to France, he was "insistent" that Turkey be kept neutral as long as possible. Grey was blunt in his memoirs: "The objective before us was therefore twofold: (1) to delay the entry of Turkey into the war as long as we could, and at all costs till the Indian troops were safely through the Canal on their way to France; and (2) to make it clear, if the worst had to come, that it come by the unprovoked aggression of Turkey."

On the morning of August 16, the Ottoman colors were hoisted aboard *Göben* and *Breslau* for the first time; it was noted by more than one observer that Souchon's personal ensign remained flying over *Göben* the entire time. Souchon soon discovered that being de facto in command of the Ottoman navy, much as Liman von Sanders commanded the Turkish Army, was a responsibility that made him as much of a desk-bound sailor as a seagoing one. Long letters to his wife were filled with his frustration at being unable to carry the war to the Russians, fettered as he was with administrative responsibilities. He also began to realize that his position was in some ways as tenuous as had been that of his predecessor, Admiral Limpus. The quite competent Captain Raouf, who had been promised command of *Göben* once she had been transferred to Turkish control and who now seethed in anger at being superceded by Souchon, was ready to replace the German admiral at a moment's notice. Souchon understood that he was being kept on a short leash, and should he try to slip it and attack the Russians, the Turks could readily disown him and his crew as "insubordinate troublemakers" and dismiss them all out of hand. Straining at the bit, eager to attack the Russians, who had just begun an unexpected and dangerous offensive into East Prussia, Souchon was forced for the time being to restrain himself. Still, although it would be far from accurate to say that the Turks were plunging headlong into the Great War, at the same time events were acquiring a momentum of their own that would carry the Ottoman Empire, willing or not, along with them.

August passed into September, and in France the "Miracle of the Marne" threw the German Army back from the gates of Paris, putting paid once and for all to the strategic ambitions of the Schlieffen Plan. There would be no swift victory for the Second Reich in the west, and now, in addition to Russia and France, Germany had to number Great Britain among her foes. At the same time, Russian offensives on the Eastern Front, which pre-war German intelligence had flatly declared to be an impossibility at such an early date, were making unexpectedly deep advances against the Austrians. The threat to East Prussia had been turned aside at the Battle of Tannenburg, but even where they were standing on the defensive, the Russians were fighting with a skill and a tenacity that startled the Germans.

Suddenly, Berlin was no longer content for the Turks to remain neutral and merely pose a looming threat to southern Russia or to Britain's Middle East possessions. The Ottoman Empire's geographic position offered attractive opportunities for the Central Powers to dissipate the strength of their enemies, by opening new fronts and posing strategic threats that the British in particular could not ignore. Closing the Bosporus and the Dardanelles had struck a severe blow to the Russians, who were heavily dependent on Britain and France for supplies of ammunition and small arms. The empire's border with British-occupied Egypt was fewer than seventy miles from the Suez Canal, Britain's priceless lifeline to India and the eastern marches of her empire. The eastern boundary of Mesopotamia was perilously close to the Red Sea ports where the black crude pumped from Persian oil fields was refined into fuel for the Royal Navy before being shipped to Britain. The strategic advantages of having Ottoman Turkey as an ally were great, the risks to the Reich minimal.

The result was that the Germans chose to follow what they termed the "jihad (holy war) strategy," inciting open uprising across the whole of the Moslem world, much of which was subject to the "infidel" European powers. Such an uprising would be a mortal threat to the British Raj in India, as well as to her presence in Egypt and parts of Africa, and could potentially paralyze the British Empire. Long before the war began, German intelligence experts had advocated such a strategy. Baron Max von Oppenheim, an eminent archaeologist and sometime spy who directed the "Oriental" Department of the German Foreign Office, was its leading advocate within Germany, waxing especially articulate in promoting this idea: "When the Turks invade Egypt, and India is set ablaze with the flames of revolt, only then will England crumble. For England is at her most vulnerable in her colonies."

In late October 1914 he submitted to the German General Staff a master plan "fomenting rebellion in the Islamic territories of our enemies," the faithful to be called to jihad by the Ottoman Sultan-caliph. Holy war was to be proclaimed against the British, the French, and the Russians, while Berlin would provide advisers, equipment, and money. Expeditions were to be sent to Afghanistan to foment a rebellion there, while a Moslem uprising in India was seen as the key to victory. In von Oppenheim's considered opinion, Islam would be one of Germany's sharpest weapons against the British. The challenge to pursuing such a strategy was how to drag the Ottoman Turks out of their comfortable nonbelligerence and bring them into the war, giving the Sultan-caliph a pretext for declaring the jihad.

What happened next is still debated—not the events, but rather who was responsible for them. The documentary record is not completely reliable, something that is to be expected whenever Enver was involved. Some authorities flatly state that Souchon acted on his own, without orders from either Constantinople or Berlin; this would be in keeping with Souchon's repeated statements that he wanted to attack the Russians in order to provoke the Turks into action. Others are adamant that the attack on Russia's Black Sea Fleet had been planned in Berlin, in order to present the Turks with a fait accompli and compel them to join the Central Powers in open hostilities against the Allies; in this case, Souchon was merely following orders, which, happily for him, coincided with his own desires. Enver, it is said, simply approved of the raid after the fact. As the tale is told, when Enver inquired as to what Rear-Admiral Souchon's intentions were for his two ships, the German replied, "I shall crush the Russian Black Sea fleet." Still other sources firmly maintain that the attack was Enver's brainchild, concocted without reference to Berlin, with Souchon simply being his willing accomplice and the German government acquiescing after the fact. Whatever the truth, and to a dispassionate observer all three scenarios appear to be equally plausible and equally likely, there can be no denying the consequences of Souchon's raid.

On October 29, 1914, Admiral Souchon took *Göben*, *Breslau*, and a squadron of smaller Turkish warships into the Black Sea; it was the point of no return for the Ottoman Empire. His confidence soaring after having eluded the Royal Navy in the Mediterranean, Souchon believed that *Göben*, now the most powerful warship in the Black Sea, was more than a match for any Russian opponent. According to reports from German naval intelligence, which cited the "poor discipline of its crews and its obsolete ships," the threat of the Russian Black Sea Fleet and port defenses was negligible. The Russians had, in fact, been expecting something like this—a few days earlier a pair of Turkish torpedo boats, *Mouavenet* and *Gairet*, had attacked the Russian port of Odessa, sinking an elderly gunboat and damaging a number of merchant ships tied up there.

Souchon was supremely confident, however, and as dawn broke on October 29, *Göben* (or *Yavuz Sultan Selim*—her crew, of course, used her German name while aboard) stood off the Russian naval base at Sebastopol, preparing to bombard the harbor, the shipyards, and any ships docked there. No declaration of war had been made, and there was still substantial opposition within the Turkish Cabinet to any active involvement in what was, by any accounting, Europe's war. To Souchon, for whatever reason, none of this mattered: he had come to raise havoc and provoke the Russians and the Turks into war.

In a bombardment lasting fewer than twenty minutes, *Göben*'s guns flung forty-seven 11-inch shells into Sebastopol; tragically, among the handful of buildings hit and actually damaged was a naval hospital. The Russian shore batteries promptly replied with startlingly accurate fire, scoring three direct hits on *Göben* before Souchon, now rudely aware of the true state of the Russian defenses, abruptly withdrew under cover of a smokescreen hastily laid by the Turkish torpedo boats escorting her. Chastened, *Göben* returned to the Bosporus, attempting to salve her wounded pride by sinking an elderly Russian minelayer and her trio of escorting torpedo boats. *Breslau*, meanwhile, had laid mines off the Kerch Strait, at the mouth of the Crimean Sea, before shelling the harbor and an oil tank farm at Novorossiysk. By October 30, both ships were back in Constantinople. Perhaps sensing that because what had been done could not be undone, the Turks refused to repudiate Souchon. Certainly, he had Enver's unquestioning support: Enver envisaged the coming war with the Allies as an opportunity for personal glory, something his outsized ego could never resist.

Materially, the raid accomplished little: the damage done to the Russian ports was comparatively minor, while *Göben* would be repaired in a matter of weeks. Strategically, however, its effects were decisive: Souchon wrote triumphantly to his wife after his return to Constantinople, "I have well and truly thrown the Turks onto the powder keg." Regardless of who planned and authorized the Black Sea raid, because Souchon's ships were at least nominally owned by the Turks and had flown the Ottoman flag, the Turks were responsible. It came as no surprise, then, that on November 2, 1914, Russia declared war on the Ottoman Empire. France and Great Britain followed suit on November 5.

On November 14 the German "holy war" strategy paid off. In Constantinople, Mehmed V, acting in his personas of both sultan and the caliph of all Islam, who was responsible for the administration of religious affairs throughout the Ottoman Empire, issued a fatwa calling on all Moslems worldwide to rise up against the British, French, and Russian infidels and wage a holy war against them. In this declaration it was absolutely forbidden for Moslems of nations that were declared to be the enemies of Islam to take up arms against fellow Moslems; the Sultan-caliph also said it would be a great sin for Moslems under British, French, or Russian rule to fight against Germany and Austria, the allies of Islam. The war was to be a war "of the mouth and the heart," that is, one of hatred of the infidel. There were three ways in which jihad could be brought to the infidel: acts of individual violence done with knives and swords; collective bands of irregular brigands who would slay infidels—soldiers and civilians alike—wherever they could be found (this included Greeks, Armenians, and Jews living within the Ottoman Empire); and by military campaigns. The question that suddenly haunted everyone's mind, from Delhi to London, was whether the faithful would answer the Sultan-caliph's call.

It had been a strange journey to war for the Ottoman Empire, one propelled by a peculiar mixture of greed, arrogance, apathy, deceit, and personal ambition, with all of these factors being present in varying measure on the part of the Allies, the Central Powers, and the Ottoman Turks themselves. The strategic situation, with Russia isolated from the west by the closure of the Straits of the Dardanelles, left the Allies with little choice but to respond. Had there been another route available to bring supplies to the Russians, the Allies could well have ignored the Turks; the material demands of the Russian war effort made this an impossibility. A new theater of war had been forced on the Allies, one potentially as vast as that of the Russian Front, bringing with it the threat of infinitely more danger. Should the Moslem peoples of the British Empire rise up in answer to the Sheikh-ul-Islam's call to jihad, the very fabric of the realm could be torn apart, with incalculable consequences for the Allies. Ancient empires would fall, the centuries-old dynasties that ruled them would be toppled, and humanity's social, political, and economic paradigm radically shifted, the unforeseen consequences of the Ottoman Turks' misguided decision to become Germany's cat's paw. The Great War in the Middle East would be fought in the shadow of the great bloodlettings of the Western Front, but its consequences would be felt all over the world into the next century.

CHAPTER FOUR

ALARUMS AND EXCURSIONS

The Russians were the first of the Allies to react to the Ottoman declarations of war. After the disastrous battles against the Germans at Tannenburg and the Masurian Lakes in August and September 1914, Stavka, the Russian high command, had drawn heavily on the Caucasus Army for replacements and reinforcements, reducing it to an effective strength of barely more than sixty thousand troops. Yet this didn't discourage Gen. Nikolai Yudenich, who commanded the Caucasus Army, from taking the offensive against the Turks. On November 2, Russian soldiers marched into Turkish Armenia, advancing seventeen miles in two days and capturing the city of Bayazid. By the beginning of December, Russian forces had taken Sarai and Bashkal, nearly fifty miles inside Ottoman territory.

As the Russians moved farther into Armenia, local militia units began to form. Supplied with Russian arms and equipment, they started to raid neighboring Turkish farms and villages. That same month, four battalions of Armenian volunteers were assembled to serve with the Russian forces advancing into Turkey, and in a particularly ill-advised move the Russian tsar, Nicholas II, during an inspection of the Caucasus front, remarked that "a brilliant future awaits the Armenians." Unknown to anyone at the time, the first steps were being taken toward what would ultimately become the great tragedy of the Armenian people, the massacres of 1915.

In the meantime, Enver responded to the Russian attack with a typical display of ego and energy. Dazzled by his own success in leading Arab irregulars against

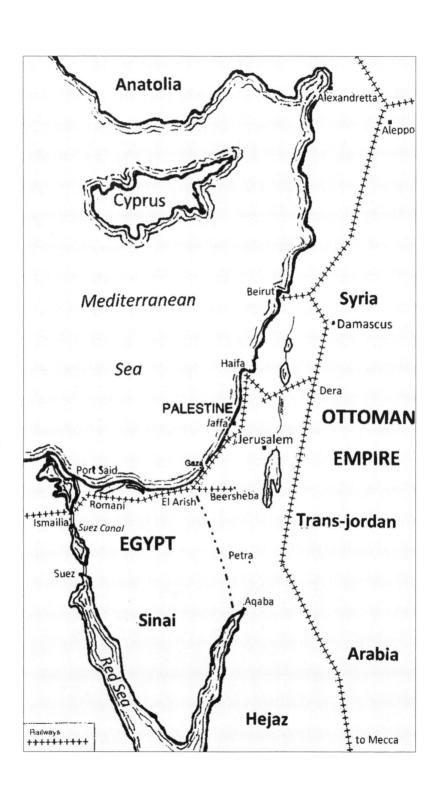

the Italians in Libya three years earlier, he indulged in his fantasy of being a military genius and set out for the Caucasus as soon as word of the Russian offensive reached Constantinople. He was convinced that his presence and leadership would inspire the Turkish troops to drive out the invaders and carry the war into the Russian Caucasus. He arrived at the front on December 14, and at his direction the Turkish Third Army launched a counteroffensive a week later.

At first, it seemed that Enver's belief in his own generalship was justified: in a little more than two weeks the Third Army had taken back much of the territory lost to the Russians, even crossing into Russia on Christmas Day. Enamored of the tactics of Frederick the Great and Napoleon, Enver then tried to emulate Bonaparte's great 1805 victory at Ulm and conceived of a complex series of converging maneuvers for Third Army's three corps to envelop the city of Sarikamish and there trap the Russian Caucasus Army. But General Yudenich quickly made it clear that Enver was very much the military amateur: making skillful use of the mountainous terrain, he directed delaying actions that fatally disrupted Enver's timetable and allowed the three Turkish corps to be defeated in detail; one, the IX Corps, was forced to surrender once it was surrounded, as were two isolated Turkish infantry divisions. It was a bloody contest, for by the time the campaign ended in mid-January 1915, the Russian force had suffered almost 30,000 killed and wounded, nearly half of its effective strength, in six weeks of fighting. Yet the Turks' Third Army, initially 112,000 strong, had for all practical purposes ceased to exist.

Having barely escaped the Russian trap—naval transports sent to Erzerum to evacuate the remnants of the Third Army were intercepted and sunk by a raiding squadron of the Russian Black Sea Fleet—Enver, once he was safely back in Constantinople, savagely blamed everyone but himself for the Third Army's destruction. He was particularly enraged by the Armenian battalions of light infantry that had fought alongside the Russians. To Enver, this bespoke of treachery, and although there was little supporting evidence, he concluded that the empire's Armenian population had actively aided the Russian forces as they advanced into Turkish Armenia.

As a military force, Enver was a spent round, but he retained his office as minister of war and would continue to exercise tremendous political influence in the Ottoman government. He would also remain an irritating influence, playing favorites with the officers of the Turkish Army and interfering with the German officers advising the Turkish commanders on various fronts as well, but the Sari-kamish disaster assured that he would never again actually command troops in action. Given the challenges that would soon be facing the Turkish Army, this could only be considered a blessing.

On January 3, 1915, in a communiqué sent to London and Paris, Tsar Nicholas of Russia rather pointedly urged Britain and France to launch attacks of their own on the Turks. In essence, Nicholas was demanding a quid pro quo for the succor Russia had provided France in August 1914, when vital reserves were withdrawn from the German armies in the west and sent east to stem the Russian offensive into East Prussia. The absence of those reserves—fully six corps—had proved pivotal in the Battle of the Marne, which had saved the French Army from defeat, and at Tannenburg especially the Russians had paid a dreadful price for the selfless support of their western ally. Now Nicholas was calling in the debt.

What had compelled Nicholas to do so was that the most serious strategic consequences of the Ottoman Empire's declaration of war on the Allies were beginning to make themselves known, with particularly unpleasant implications for Russia. Naturally, once the shooting began in earnest, the Turks had closed the Straits of the Bosporus and the Dardanelles to all shipping into and out of the Black Sea. When both sides had believed that the war would be over in a matter of a few weeks, a few months at the most, the closure of the Straits was seen as little more than an inconvenience. Yet as it became clear that the war would stretch well into the summer of 1915 or longer—in London, Lord Kitchener was predicting a war lasting three years or more—the interruption was becoming more problematic with each passing week. If it went on long enough, the closing of the Straits might have decisive—even disastrous—consequences for Russia.

The problem was geography: Russia lacked a warm-water port that had unrestricted access to the world's oceans. Sebastopol, Rostov, Odessa, all of them on the Black Sea, were major seaports, but shipping could reach them only through the Turkish-controlled Dardanelles. In the north, Russia's ports on the Baltic Sea were cut off by the German High Seas Fleet's command of that body of water, as well as of the Strait of the Skaggerak leading into it: the Allies had long understood that Russia would lose the use of the Baltic ports. The few ports that Russia possessed in the far north, such as Arkhangelsk and Murmansk, were closed as much as six months out of every year by Arctic ice. This left the Black Sea as Russia's only maritime access to the rest of the world—and none of the Allies had ever seriously considered the possibility that the Turks would become involved in a general European war and would do so allied to Germany, no less.

In peacetime, most of the wheat that Russia exported to western Europe, Africa, and South America was carried in the hulls of merchantmen that sailed from the Black Sea ports. This wheat then paid for the forges, the machine tools, the heavy equipment, the rails, the locomotives, and the railcars that were used to build Russia's industry and infrastructure, carried on those same ships sailing back to the Black Sea ports. With Russia at war, those ports ceased to be merely important and instead became vital, as whatever success the Russian armies would have at the front would depend heavily on material support from the western Allies, and that support would have to arrive via the Black Sea.

The tale is often told that in the Great War, Russia's industrial base was too tiny to be able to produce the arms, the munitions, and the supplies her armies needed. It's a story that has its roots as much in post-Revolution Soviet propaganda as it does in the truth. The Russian Army *did* run dangerously short of guns and ammunition during the first months of the war, a situation exacerbated by the crushing defeats of Tannenburg and the Masurian Lakes in the fall of 1914. Yet the deeper truth is that *all* of the Great Powers had grievously underestimated how rapidly their pre-war stocks of weapons and munitions would be exhausted once actual combat began, creating shortages for each of them at one point or another in the first nine months of the war. Although it was dwarfed in actual size by the industrial capacity of Germany, Britain, or France, when it finally geared up to full wartime capacity Russian industry would perform astonishing feats of production for the tsar's armies. Russia's *critical* weakness was in the ability to get the finished weapons and munitions to the front: specifically, in the inability of Russian industry to produce the rolling stock—the locomotives, the boxcars, and the flatcars needed to move guns, ammunition, and supplies—in the numbers needed. Stavka knew and accepted before the war began that supplying the Russian armies would depend on the western Allies' ability to provide rolling stock in sufficient numbers, but Stavka had never anticipated that Russia would be completely cut off from the west. At the same time, it seemed to Tsar Nicholas that while his army was doing battle with the bulk of the Central Powers—although the French and the British faced only the German Army, the Russians were fighting not only the Germans but the Austro-Hungarian Army as well—the least that France and Great Britain could do was find a way to break the Turkish stranglehold on the Dardanelles and reopen the supply route to the Black Sea.

The tsar's point was well taken: while the Russians were fighting the Turks in the Caucasus, the situation in the Levant and the eastern Mediterranean was much like Sherlock Holmes's "curious incident of the dog in the night-time," where said dog did nothing—"That was the curious incident." The strategic situation for France and Britain was dictated by the need to make certain that their priorities were in order. For the French, those were fairly straightforward: with *Göben* and *Breslau* out of the Mediterranean, the security of convoys moving the garrisons from North Africa was assured, allowing the French Army to concentrate on amassing the greatest number of troops possible to defend the soil of France itself and eventually—hopefully—throw back the hated Teutonic invader.

For the British, the situation was more complicated. After the German juggernaut had been repelled from the gates of Paris in the aptly named Miracle of the Marne in early September 1914, the opposing armies spent the next two months executing a series of sidesteps northward and westward that became known as the "Race to the Sea," as the Allies and the Germans sought to outflank each other, ultimately running out of real estate when they reached the English Channel. Soon two thin snakelike lines of opposing trenches, growing more and more elaborate with each passing week, had been dug from the channel to the Swiss border, depriving each side of the opportunity to maneuver and achieve any sort of decisive action. A strategic stalemate that would endure for more than three years had imposed itself on the Western Front, although neither side had yet grasped this fact.

The British and the French—and the Germans, for that matter—believed that the stalemate was only temporary. While the Germans were content for the time being to go over to the strategic defensive in the west in order to concentrate on defeating the Russians in the east, the Allies took it as an article of faith almost from the start that breaking the stalemate could be accomplished simply by massing sufficient numbers of troops at selected points in the line and driving forward into the German defenses, which would crumble under the sheer weight of their numbers.

The problem was that together the French and British armies didn't possess sufficient soldiers to properly man the trenches and at the same time assemble the number of divisions believed necessary for a major offensive. Specifically, the deficiency lay with the British Army: the original British Expeditionary Force (BEF) that was sent to France in August 1914 had numbered only 160,000 troops, a number that could be effectively trebled by sending the remaining regular divisions across the Channel to France, along with the reserve force of the Territorial Army. This was not a long-term solution to the problem, however, for even these forces represented only a fraction of the manpower needed for the offensives that were being planned. Nearly a half-million young men had answered the appeal of Lord Kitchener, the Secretary of State for War, for volunteers to make up a New Army that would go to France, tip the Huns out of their trenches, and hustle them back to Germany. Yet it would be many months before the first of those volunteer units was properly trained and equipped, so in the meantime the line had to be held, as always, by the likes of Tommy Atkins and his brethren—the regulars of the British Army.

Thus August, September, and October 1914 saw the greatest mass movement of troops in history as garrisons were recalled from every corner of the British Empire and sent to France. Thirty-nine battalions of regulars stationed in India were brought back to Great Britain, where they would become the 27th, 28th, and 29th Divisions; along with them came two divisions and a cavalry brigade of the Indian Army. In November thirty thousand Australian and New Zealand volunteers were brought up from "down under" to the Suez, where in Cairo they were formed into the Australian and New Zealand Army Corps, soon to become justly famous around the world as the ANZACs.

It was an impressive piece of work, but it took time to gather together all of the units and their equipment in the right place at the right time. While the Admiralty and the War Office were shuffling their pieces about the board and beginning to organize operations that would satisfy the tsar's politely worded demand, the Turkish Minister of Marine, Djemal Pasha, together with his German chief of staff, Friedrich Kress von Kressenstein, saw an opportunity in early 1915 to take the war to Palestine and Egypt and disrupt the British troop movements by attacking the Suez Canal, Great Britain's lifeline to India since 1869. They assembled a "Suez Expeditionary Force" of twenty-five thousand men at Beersheba, in central Palestine, and prepared to lead it across the Sinai Peninsula to the Canal.

The British had feared—and anticipated—just such an attack since the Turks declared war at the end of October 1914. The concentration of forces on the West-

ern Front remained London's first priority, but the need to honor the threat to
the Canal made it necessary to divert to Egypt an additional three divisions of the
Indian Army originally destined for Flanders. These divisions, thirty thousand
troops, would be the core of the Suez Canal defense; they would be supported by
light cruisers and destroyers stationed at Alexandria, as well as by a small aerial
reconnaissance detachment. Additionally, the ANZACs, instead of being sent on to
Flanders, were held in Cairo to be used as needed either in the defense of the Suez
or in offensive operations against the Turks when the opportunity presented itself.

These altered deployments were later regarded by some observers as part of a
larger German strategy of using the Ottoman Empire to dilute British strength and
divert reinforcements away from the Western Front. This may be true (there is no
reliable documentary evidence one way or the other), but in launching an offensive
into Egypt there were other, deeper considerations at work on the part of the Turks
themselves. Most significant among them was their hope for an Arab uprising in
Egypt that would coincide with the Ottoman drive to the Suez Canal. These hopes
rested on the peculiar political position of Egypt in 1914: nominally part of Ottoman Empire, Egypt had effectively conducted her affairs independently of the
empire since the mid-nineteenth century. It had fallen under British suzerainty in
1878, when the Ottoman viceroy, Khedive Ismail, drove the nation into bankrupt-
cy, thus leading Great Britain to take over his debts and with them effective control
of the country; a formal British protectorate was announced in December 1914.

The Turkish Army advancing across the Sinai represented a very real threat
to Britain's establishment in Cairo: there was widespread anger toward the British,
bordering on open hostility, among Egypt's Arabs. Not the least hostile of them
was the current khedive, Abbas el-Helmi, who was a passionate Egyptian nationalist. No sooner had the grand mufti proclaimed jihad in Constantinople than el-
Helmi began plotting a revolt against the British, who in turn quickly deposed him,
putting in his place his uncle Prince Hussein Kamil, whose pro-British sentiments
were widely recognized. There is evidence that Enver, at least, clung to his dreams
of a powerful Middle Eastern Moslem state dominated by the Turks and had high
hopes for an Arab uprising. Yet however effective the Three Pashas believed that
the call to jihad would be in rousing the Ottoman Empire's Arab subjects and up-
setting British plans and deployments, the threat of revolt in Egypt would cause
the War Office to keep the thirty thousand British troops originally posted there in
defense of the Canal as a permanent garrison for the remainder of the war.

The Turks' advance on the Suez Canal was constrained by a combination of topography and climate. The distance to be covered was roughly 190 miles (300 km), and there were only three practicable routes across the Sinai Peninsula. The first was along the coast, which offered the advantages of having water readily available, as well as fairly well-established tracks for the infantry to follow (there were no roads, as the term was understood by Europeans, in the Sinai), but this route was well within range of the guns of Royal Navy warships. The second possibility was a southern track, which was almost immediately rejected by both Djemal and von Kressenstein because of its near-total lack of water. The third route, which ran across the center of the peninsula, was the one the Turks chose, leading from Beersheba to Ismailia on the Canal itself.

The total absence of any rail transport meant that for this route to be used, a series of supply dumps had to be leapfrogged along the line of march. The entire distance had to be covered during the peninsula's relatively short rainy season, lasting fewer than eight weeks, before the Sinai's oppressive heat made any movement at all impossible. Djemal's plan was for the Suez Expeditionary Force to advance at least twenty miles (thirty kilometers) every day, hardly an extravagant distance until it is remembered that the Turks were moving entirely on foot, burdened with pontoon boats and collapsible rafts, without the benefit of any roads, across extremely rugged and inhospitable terrain, in a region for which there were no accurate and up-to-date maps or charts. Given the logistical situation, once the Turkish forces reached the Suez Canal they would have just four days to seize it before lack of supply, especially water, would compel them to withdraw. When von Kressenstein proposed launching diversionary attacks to the north and the south, Djemal, acutely aware of the limited number of troops he had available and the narrow window of opportunity, refused to authorize them. He was determined to achieve a decisive concentration of strength at what he hoped would be the critical point, the port of Ismailia, and set up forward positions at El Arish and Nekhl on the Canal's east bank. His plan was to capture Ismailia, then use the tracks and the roads that led to Cairo to exploit his victory, assisted, he hoped, by the expected Arab uprising against the British.

The Suez Canal is 101 miles (160 km) long, connecting the Red Sea with the Mediterranean, and the British were determined to defend its entire length, if need be. Yet Ismailia was the natural focal point of any attempt to seize the Canal: along the western bank ran a system of channels known as the Sweet Water Canal, the only large-scale source of fresh water in the region, and the pumping facilities for it were located at Ismailia. Recognizing this, the British had set up defenses on the west bank of the Suez, while pickets were posted out to the east.

Djemal had believed that he could achieve strategic surprise with his movement across the Sinai and with it tactical surprise at Ismailia. It was a vain hope, however, as the handful of British reconnaissance aircraft were able to follow the Turkish columns as they moved westward almost as soon as they left Beersheba on January 18. The few German aircraft available did their best to support the Turkish advance, but their effect was minimal. As the Ottoman troops closed in on the east bank of the Canal on January 28, a mixed squadron of French and British destroyers and gunboats took up positions in mid-channel and began intermittently shelling the Turkish columns. Turk patrols bickered with the British and Indian pickets on the east bank for the next three days, and just after midnight on February 2 the Turks made their move against Ismailia.

Inflating their pontoons and assembling their rafts, the Turkish soldiers threw themselves into the water and began paddling furiously for the western bank. The British and Indian defenders held their fire until the boats were in the middle of the channel, then opened up with machine guns that first raked the slowly moving boats, ripping them to pieces, then moved to the opposite bank, cutting wide swaths in the ranks of the assembled Turks waiting to cross. Djemal's soldiers had nothing but small arms with which to reply—it had been impossible to bring artillery across the central Sinai—and their rifles and the few machine guns they could bring to bear had little effect on the defenders. A handful of boats made it across the Canal, but their occupants surrendered almost as soon as they reached the shore. In less than an hour the attack petered out, and the Turks withdrew behind the safety of the berm that lined the eastern bank. At 6:00 a.m. another crossing was attempted, this time supported by a diversionary attack to the north of Ismailia, but when the patrolling Allied destroyers began shelling the boats in the water, as well as the troops assembled on the east bank, this assault lost its momentum as quickly as did the first. Turkish losses totaled fifteen hundred dead and almost twice as many wounded, while British casualties were barely a tenth of that number. The following day the Turks began marching back to Beersheba; the British were content to let them go, being unprepared for an advance across the desert in the rapidly approaching spring heat.

Like Enver, Djemal had botched his first—and only—opportunity at field command, although his losses were just a fraction of those that Enver's bungling had inflicted on his own army. Djemal was recalled to Constantinople, where he continued to carry out the duties of the Minister of Marine. Kress von Kressenstein would remain behind in Palestine to lead the Ottoman defense, a decision that would prove to be an inspired choice for the Turks. The failure of Enver's Caucasus offensive and the repulse of the Suez Expeditionary Force focused the attention of the government in Constantinople on the apparent shortcomings of the Ottoman forces, rather than on the fact that the Three Pashas' entire strategy was fatally flawed from the outset. The strategic importance of the Suez Canal to Great Britain's war effort meant that the British would have been prepared to defend the Canal at all costs, no matter how much manpower the Turks threw into the effort to capture it: the mission of the Suez had been doomed even before the first Turkish soldier had left Beersheba.

At the same time, the Three Pashas were blissfully unaware that when word reached Cairo of the Suez Expeditionary Force's arrival on the east bank of the Suez Canal, the reaction of the Arab populace in Egypt was one of indifference: there was never even a ghost of the sort of popular uprising against the British on which the Turks had so heavily counted. What Enver, Djemal, and Talaat failed to recognize was that the Egyptians were not prepared to simply trade one set of overlords for another. If they were going to revolt, it would be for themselves and no one else. It was an oversight for which the Turks would pay dearly less than two years later.

A more prolonged campaign than the Turkish thrust to the Suez Canal was taking shape to the northeast, at the terminus of the Persian Gulf. It had actually begun almost two months before Djemal and von Kressenstein led their soldiers out of Beersheba, but while the assault on Suez had run its course in a matter of a few weeks and had been utterly indecisive, this campaign was far slower to develop, and it had the potential to cripple the Ottoman Empire.

The British military establishment, and in particular the Royal Navy, had long understood that the Ottoman Empire was poised to threaten Great Britain's oil fields and refineries in pro-British but neutral Persia (modern Iran). The Royal Navy had begun changing over from coal-fired to oil-fired boilers for its warships, and most of its fuel oil came from Persian wells, where it was then refined. Given how Great Britain's war effort—indeed, her very survival—was utterly dependent on the navy, no threat to the fleet's fuel supply could be minimized or disregarded. Yet there was a strong divergence of opinion on what shape the strategy for that defense should take. In London the War Office, rapidly becoming obsessed with the Western Front, was prepared to carry out a static defense of the Persian oil fields, using forces drawn from the Indian Army. The government in India, however, favored a more active, "forward" defense, designed to carry the war to the Turks and away from the vulnerable oil fields and pipelines.

One of the many administrative quirks of the British Empire was that the Indian Army, whose regiments were manned by native Indian regulars led by British officers, was an entirely separate establishment from the British Army and, despite its name, not a "national" army at all. The military arm of the Raj, it took its orders from General Headquarters, India, in New Delhi, not from Whitehall. It closely cooperated with, but was in no way subordinate to, the British Army; unless an Indian unit was directly placed under the authority of the British Army, the regiments of the Indian Army always answered to their own chain of command. These particular circumstances created a peculiar situation in October 1914, as the first seven thousand Indian soldiers of what was designated Force D left Bombay on the sixteenth of that month.

Under the command of Gen. Sir Arthur Barrett, Force D was supposed to take up a defensive position along the Persian side of the Shatt al-Arab, the river formed by the confluence of the Tigris and Euphrates rivers, which then, as now, marked the border between Persia (Iran) and Mesopotamia (Iraq). This position was a precaution in case the deteriorating diplomatic situation between Great Britain and the Ottoman Empire decayed into open hostilities. By the time Force D actually arrived in the Persian Gulf, the Allies and the Turks were at war, and Barrett immediately put into motion a part of his orders from New Delhi of which London was completely unaware.

An advance force of six hundred Indian infantry captured the Ottoman forts guarding the mouth of the Shatt al-Arab on November 5, and within a week the initial five-thousand-strong contingent of Force D had been reinforced by an additional seven thousand infantry and cavalry. On November 14, in accordance with his orders from GHQ India, Barrett began moving Force D upriver: unknown to London, he had been instructed to capture the city of Basra in the event of formal hostilities breaking out between Britain and Turkey.

Even though Basra was 120 miles (192 km) upriver from the Persian Gulf, it was the region's main seaport, which naturally gave it considerable strategic value. With a population of approximately sixty thousand people, mostly Moslems but with a large Christian minority, it was garrisoned by a brigade of the Turkish 38th Division, some forty-five hundred strong, under the command of Col. Subhai Bey, who was responsible for all of the Ottoman forces in lower Mesopotamia. Given its position at the confluence of the two great rivers, which considerably simplified moving large numbers of troops or great masses of materiel, Basra could function as the staging area for any Turkish incursion into Persia: it was particularly well-suited to serve as the jump-off point for attacks on Abadan and the adjacent oil fields.

Determined to take Basra as quickly as possible, Barrett was prepared to attack the city less than a week after Force D had reached its full strength. On November 19 the Indian infantry went in on the assault, in a torrential rain that turned the approaches to the city into a sea of mud. When it wasn't raining, the daytime heat caused clouds of steam to rise up from the soaking-wet earth. Despite the rain, the mud, and the heat, the Indian attack was fierce, and on the night of November 20, the Turks broke contact and slipped away. The Indian cavalry was unable to pursue them because of the mud, so the Turks escaped intact, and Force D took possession of the city the next day. Still, despite the Turks' successful withdrawal, nearly a thousand casualties had been inflicted on them in exchange for fewer than five hundred Indians killed and wounded.

The Turkish brigade that had fled Basra had taken up position in the town of Qurna, which was fifty miles (eighty km) upriver, where the Tigris and Euphrates rivers met to form the Shatt al-Arab. Barrett decided to follow up the capture of Basra and make his position there more secure by taking the town, and he dispatched two infantry battalions supported by a small flotilla of gunboats to capture Qurna on December 4, 1914. This first attack was met with fire from both sides of the river and was compelled to withdraw; a second attack two days later was equally unsuccessful. A third attack was planned, this one combining a river assault with a strike by Indian infantry that would be landed downstream and would march overland to take Qurna from the rear. As events sorted themselves out, however, this entire operation became unnecessary as the Turks surrendered the town before the attack began. More than a thousand Turkish soldiers were taken prisoner, while British losses totaled just twenty-nine killed and wounded.

This relative ease with which the Indian troops took Basra and Qurna led Barrett—along with the rest of the British high command in Mesopotamia—into believing that the Turks' morale was rather fragile and that they lacked staying power. It quickly became the conventional wisdom that the average Turkish soldier wasn't a very skillful fighter and that the Turkish officers weren't particularly adept tactically. These assumptions came to be shared by the War Office in London, as well as by the War Cabinet, and would play heavily in the strategic assumptions on which the Allies based the planning for upcoming operations.

It was a blunder that would prove deadly for far too many Allied soldiers in the months ahead and one against which the generals of both the British and the Indian armies should have been on guard. Bonaparte had frequently warned his generals about the pitfalls of what he called "painting pictures," that is, basing one's own plans on preconceived notions of what an enemy *would* do, as opposed to what that enemy *could* do. The proof was in the pudding, as it were, for Bonaparte himself fell victim to just that weakness at Waterloo, making fatal assumptions about his British and Prussian opponents. Now the British were about to do the same by assuming that the Turks lacked both the will and the ability to fight.

It was an understandable error, though not a forgivable one, for the Indian Army HQ played heavily on the apparent Turkish ineptitude when arguing with the War Cabinet and the War Office in support of its "forward defense" strategy. Given Whitehall's rapidly growing obsession with the Western Front (and its growing casualty lists), coupled with its ever-increasing demands for manpower and equipment, the idea that the Ottoman Empire would effectively roll over and play dead with little more than the figurative prodding of a British bayonet was seductive. Politicians have always been enamored of operations that could allegedly be conducted on a shoestring, and in Britain's war against the Ottoman Turks, the politicians sitting in the British Cabinet were no different. Manpower already deemed by some to have been critical to the Allied effort in Flanders was being diverted to Egypt and Mesopotamia, but supplies were a different matter. The Western Front was given first priority on every question of munitions and equipment, and little if any thought was being given to meeting the requirements that conditions in the Middle East might dictate. It was a flawed strategy: while it could not be argued that Flanders wouldn't be the decisive theater of the war, relegating the Middle Eastern Front to the status of a bastard stepchild in the logistical train was a perilous policy, for it would lead to confrontations with the Turks where the men "at the sharp end of the stick" would be fighting with no assurance of sufficient manpower or material resources to achieve their objectives. They would be charged with carrying out operations without being given the tools to finish the job, and too many would pay for their superiors' strategic parsimony with their lives.

In Constantinople the situation was considerably different: it wasn't a question of lacking the tools to finish the job, although the Turks were in truth woefully underequipped. Rather, it was a lack of understanding precisely what was the job in the first place. As Alan Moorehead so aptly described it, the situation was one where "the Young Turks had got their country into a war which was much too big for them. They were small gamblers in a game of very high stakes, and, as it usually happens in such cases, their presence was hardly noticed by the other players for a while. They watched, they waited, they made their anxious little bids, they tried desperately to know which way the luck was going, and they put on an air of being at quite at ease which was far from being the case."

When the Three Pashas signed the alliance with Germany in August 1914, they did not have a coherent strategy in hand, although given that the Turks weren't yet actually at war it seemed that there would be no real need for one. Now that they had themselves a real shooting war, apart from Djemal's drive on the Suez Canal and Enver's abortive Caucasus offensive, they still had no idea what to do with it. It was blindingly obvious to all and sundry that there was no place within the Turks' strategic reach where they could strike decisively at the Allies. The British possessed the resources to defend the Persian oil fields and the Suez no matter what the Turks threw at them; even the closure of the Dardanelles would not begin to seriously affect the Russians for at least another year.

More fundamentally, Enver, like most of his contemporaries across Europe, accepted the basic validity of Karl von Clausewitz's dictum that "war is a means of advancing national policy through non-political methods." Inherent in this axiom, though, are two corollaries: first, that war is merely "*a* means," not "*the* means," of advancing national policy, and second is the presumption that such policy exists. In the case of the Three Pashas, neither was true: there was no national policy as such, no overarching scheme or plan to further revitalize the empire, and even had there been, there were no political objectives for the Turks that could be gained through military action. For all of his pretensions as a martial genius, Enver the shopkeeper had bargained the Ottoman Empire into a war for its own sake, without any clear conception of what he hoped to accomplish by it. What remained to be seen was whether the empire could survive the consequences of Enver's hubris.

In Mesopotamia, the lack of coherent strategy by both the Allies and the Turks led to a curious situation where the war was being fought almost by accident. While the British were determined to protect their Persian oil fields, they had no designs on Mesopotamia itself, as there was nothing of strategic value there. The Turks, in their turn, evidenced little more interest in the region: somewhat isolated from the rest of the Ottoman Empire, Mesopotamia was populated mainly by Arabs, although there were large numbers of Kurds in the north of the province, along with a handful of other tribes who held only the most tenuous loyalty to the Sultan's regime. Away from the few navigable rivers that traversed the region, transportation was all but nonexistent. Although work had begun on the fabled Berlin-to-Baghdad Railway as early as 1888, when the war began there were still huge gaps in it, and travel from Constantinople to Baghdad routinely took up to three weeks. In the war-making calculus of the Three Pashas, Mesopotamia ranked below the Caucasus, the Sinai, and the Palestinian theaters in priority.

Yet if Enver and his colleagues had no idea of what to do with Mesopotamia, this did not mean that Col. Subhai Bey was so handicapped. (The Ottoman Army was nowhere near as rank-heavy as its European counterparts, so that Turkish colonels often filled command roles that would have been assigned to brigadiers or even major-generals in the British, French, or German armies.) Before the war, the Turkish Sixth Army garrisoned Mesopotamia, its order of battle consisting of two corps: XII Corps (35th and 36th Divisions), headquartered at Mosul, and XIII Corps (37th and 38th Divisions), which had its headquarters in Baghdad. Not anticipating any significant Allied operations in the region, Enver had transferred the whole of XII Corps to Syria, while the XIII Corps headquarters and the 37th Division were moved north to the Caucasus. This left the 38th Division responsible for the defense of the entire region, which was now designated the Mesopotamia Area Command and encompassed almost 170,000 square miles (440,000 km²). In late December 1914, on his own initiative, Subhai began assembling Turkish forces in defensive positions near the village of Ruta, upstream on the Euphrates from Qurna. The relative positions of the Turks and the Anglo-Indian forces remained essentially unchanged for the best part of four months until Subhai launched an offensive of his own in April. His objective: to retake Basra.

General Barrett had begun to fortify Basra almost as soon as he had taken the city, and by early April he had close to thirty thousand British and Indian troops at his disposal, five thousand more than Subhai had available in his command. Nonetheless, the Turks went in on the attack on April 13, after their artillery had bombarded the Allied positions for two days. Subhai's plan was to attract and hold the attention of the British forces with a frontal attack by cavalry, while his own infantry outflanked Basra itself and took the city from the rear. It was a realistic plan with a fair chance of success, even allowing for the Turks' numerical inferiority, but a British counterattack preempted the Turkish cavalry and drove it off before it could properly form up for its own strike; the flanking force was then contained with relative ease. Turkish casualties numbered some twenty-four hundred killed and wounded, while British losses were roughly half that number.

A few days before Colonel Subhai's attack on Basra, another British general appeared on the scene, Sir John Nixon, who was designated the regional commander. As such, he superseded General Barrett as commander of all Anglo-Indian forces in Mesopotamia, although Barrett retained command of Force D. Nixon wisely refrained from interfering with Barrett's defensive arrangements around Basra, and when the Turkish attack there was driven off, he quickly came to share Barrett's rather low opinion of the Turks as soldiers. This in turn led him to conceive of attempting even more ambitious, sweeping operations up the Tigris-Euphrates Valley, culminating in, hopefully, the capture of Baghdad itself.

The first stage of this projected advance would be to take the city of Amara, an important commercial center on the Tigris 100 miles (160 km) north of Qurna. Spring rains, coupled with the runoff from snow melting in the mountains far to the north, had created flood conditions reaching several miles inland along the length of the Tigris and Euphrates Rivers. The average depth of the water was three feet, which made an approach to Amara possible only by shallow-draft riverboats and barges. The flooding also effectively eliminated any possibility of maneuver by the British and restricted the axis of their advance to the Tigris itself. This gave the Turks the advantage of knowing exactly where the British would strike; they could also guess with reasonable accuracy when and in what strength. At the same time, caught up in the euphoria of their successes at Basra and Qurna, the British missed the straws in the wind that might have warned of potential disaster ahead.

In Djemal and von Kressenstein's attack on the Suez Canal, the Turks were attempting an all-but-impossible operation: an assault across a river (which, tactically, was what the Canal was) against an entrenched enemy who possessed superior numbers and firepower. Everything was against Djemal's soldiers at Ismailia; outnumbered, outgunned, with no artillery support, and attempting to cross a channel 300 yards (290 m) wide, the Turks had no chance of success, something that was readily apparent to them all too quickly once the shooting began. For most of the Turkish soldiers caught in open boats on the Canal itself and under a vicious crossfire from Indian machine guns, surrender was the only option available, other than dying—for no purpose. Consequently, the attack on Ismailia was in no way a real measure of the Turkish soldier. More telling was the grueling 190-mile march across the Sinai, where the Turks had to construct their own supply network as they advanced. That they accomplished it in the space of ten days was a remarkable demonstration of the tenacity and endurance of the Turkish soldier, a display that the British ignored or else misunderstood completely.

In Mesopotamia the situation was muddled, although there were signs for perceptive observers to read. Colonel Subhai's willingness to withdraw from Basra and Qurna was mistakenly regarded as a sign of weakness by the officers commanding the Anglo-Indian forces. While there is no evidence to suggest that Colonel Subhai had been pursuing some deeper long-range strategy for the defense of Mesopotamia, he could readily appreciate that holding Basra and Qurna were not vital to the Turks' defense of the region. Whatever his limitations as a strategist may have been, Subhai knew full well the waste of throwing away the lives of his soldiers in attempting to hold either city, efforts that the Anglo-Indian numerical superiority would have rendered futile in any case. By moving upriver to Amara, he shortened his own supply lines, while forcing the Anglo-Indian units to lengthen theirs, and at the same time further concentrated his troop strength. None of this was particularly brilliant generalship; it was, however, fundamentally sound strategy.

There were lessons for the Anglo-Indian commanders to learn in the Turkish attack on Basra as well, if they had been willing to take note of these. The high casualties suffered by the Turks in the infantry assault—nearly 10 percent of the attacking force—were a clear demonstration that the Turkish soldier *could* fight with tenacity and determination. The withdrawals from Basra and Qurna, while unquestionably aided by an inexcusable laxity on the part of the British in pressing any pursuit, evidenced a surprising degree of discipline among the Turks.

None of this appears to have registered with General Nixon, who tasked Maj. Gen. Sir Charles Townshend and his newly arrived 6th (Poona) Division of the Indian Army with taking Amara. A ragtag fleet of some five hundred river boats of all descriptions, quickly christened "Townshend's regatta," was assembled to move the division's artillery and heavy weapons up the river. Aerial reconnaissance showed that the Turks had abandoned their forward posts at the town of Ruta and took up defensive positions north of Amara, leaving a garrison of approximately two battalions to hold the town itself. On May 31 Townshend sent his "regatta" up the Tigris, supported by gunboats of the Royal Navy.

Arriving at Amara on the afternoon of June 3, Townshend staged a colossal bluff. With his forces numbering perhaps a hundred British sailors and a few hundred soldiers manning the regatta's artillery and machine guns, he persuaded the city's garrison of two thousand Turkish infantry that the whole of the 6th Division was coming up hard behind him (when it was, in fact, still more than fifty miles [eighty km] downriver). Panicked, the Turks surrendered en masse, and Townshend was able to sustain the bluff through the next day, until the 6th Division was able to join him. The garrison's capitulation pushed Nixon's disdain for the Turks' apparent lack of fighting spirit into something approaching contempt, a sentiment Townshend shared, and which encouraged his plans to push farther up the Tigris.

Despite long supply lines and critical equipment shortages—particularly medical supplies and transport for fresh water—Nixon was determined to occupy the whole of southern Mesopotamia. In order to accomplish this, he conceived of a two-pronged offensive, using the two rivers, Tigris and Euphrates, to define his lines of advance. In order to bring the left wing of his army up even with the position of the 6th Division at Amara, Nixon determined that the Turkish Army garrisoning the city of Nasiriyeh had to be turned out from its positions, with an Anglo-Indian force taking its place. If successful, the impact of this action on Nixon's drive toward Baghdad would be twofold: first, it would secure the Anglo-Indian left flank against a possible Turkish counterattack, and because Nasiriyeh was the main Turkish supply depot for southern Mesopotamia, it would impose a serious, possibly decisive, disruption on Turkish operations in the entire region.

Brig. George Gorringe was ordered to push his 30th Brigade up the flooded banks of the Euphrates, and on June 27, 1915, his troops opened their attack on the Turkish garrison at Nasiriyeh. The conditions were deplorable: mid-day temperatures reached 115°F (46°C), and the troops were plagued by swarms of mosquitoes; the plains surrounding the city were still flooded, some to a depth of more than three feet (one meter), while the countryside was home to some twenty thousand aggressive Budhoos tribesmen who were equally hostile to British and Turks. Gorringe emulated Townshend's example in carrying his artillery and machine guns up the river on shallow-draft barges, while moving his troops overland.

The British and Indian infantry first encountered the Turks while still ten miles (sixteen kilometers) downriver from Nasiriyeh. A solid earthwork built across the Hakika Channel blocked any further advance, forcing Gorringe's troops to spend thirty-six hours breaking it down, all the while under heavy and accurate artillery fire from Turkish batteries dug in farther up the river. Once the earthwork was down, the 30th Brigade spent the next four days clearing out those field guns. When the brigade began to advance again, the Turks were waiting for it six miles (ten kilometers) south of Nasiriyeh: an assault by part of Gorringe's brigade was driven off when it attempted a surprise attack, forcing the troops to dig in and wait for further reinforcements from General Nixon. Repeated, unexpected attacks on their outposts by Budhoos tribesmen complicated the Anglo-Indian situation, while nearly half of Gorringe's men fell ill from a combination of the searing heat and contaminated water.

The reinforcements duly arrived, and after a two-day bombardment by the British artillery, on July 24 two brigades of Indian infantry, with the usual support by Royal Navy gunboats from the Euphrates River, attacked the main Turkish position at Nasiriyeh. Unexpectedly, the Turks fought back hard, but the gunboats proved decisive, allowing the Indian troops to turn the Turks' position on the riverbank. Both sides lost more than 500 dead each in the battle alone; the Turks lost a further 1,000 wounded, along with 1,000 men taken prisoner. The capture of Nasiriyeh gave Sir John Nixon the secure flank he had sought and cemented his intention to drive on to Baghdad, despite his perilous supply situation, and he ordered General Townshend to take the 6th Division up the Tigris and capture the city of Kut, the last major obstacle before Baghdad.

Yet before the 6th Division could begin its advance, before the fall of Nasiriyeh, even before Townshend had bluffed his way into Amara, the focus of the Allied command in the Middle East—indeed, the attention of the whole of the British Empire—had shifted dramatically, to center on a narrow peninsula on the Turkish shore of the Aegean Sea. There, on April 15, the ANZACs had launched an amphibious assault against a poorly prepared Turkish defense. The original objective of the ANZACs had been to advance up the peninsula and eventually take the city of Constantinople. Instead, the Australians and the New Zealanders had found themselves fighting for their lives: the Turks were preparing to pitch them back into the sea. Suddenly, a name that few people had ever heard before was on the lips of the whole world: Gallipoli.

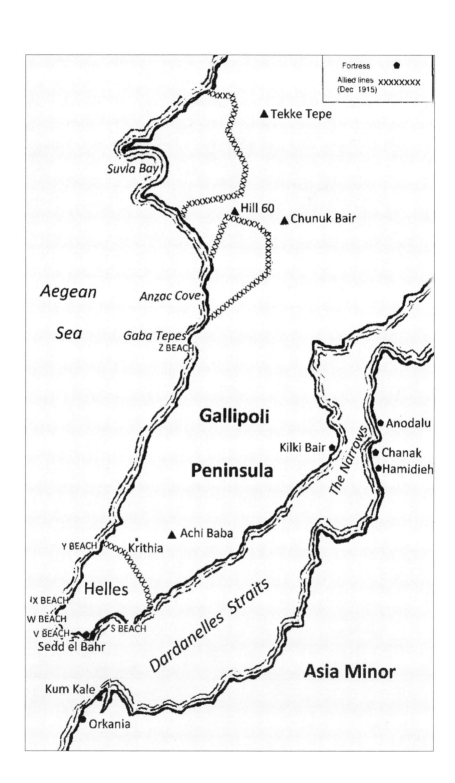

CHAPTER FIVE
GALLIPOLI

"Gallipoli"—just the mention of the name stirs pride, sadness, anger, shame, compassion, patriotism, and a curious sense of shared humanity, singly, in combination, or all simultaneously, in places separated by thousands of miles and by decades, even centuries, of culture on three separate continents. To millions of Turks, Britons, Australians, and New Zealanders, it represents more than a collection of battles for an otherwise obscure peninsula on the Turkish shore of the Aegean Sea, more than a military campaign to change the course of a war. Gallipoli was not the ultimate campaign of the Great War in the Middle East. It was not even particularly decisive or significant in terms of the war's outcome. Yet it was one of history's most perfectly defined turning points, its aftermath altering the destinies of hundreds of millions of lives for the next four generations. Entire nations had their identities forged, shaped, altered, defined, or refined in the events on the scrub-covered hills and ridges of the Gallipoli peninsula or as a consequence of them.

No one ever intended for the Gallipoli campaign to change the world; no one ever really intended for there to be a Gallipoli campaign at all. The entire operation was an afterthought, really, grafted onto a naval operation that was drawn up to knock the Turks out of the war by a coup de main at the heart of the Ottoman Empire, Constantinople.

The idea of an Allied attack directed at the Ottoman capital was given its first serious impetus when the Russian tsar, Nicholas II, in his diplomatic communication to London and Paris on January 3, 1915, pointedly urged the French and the

British to take action against the Turks. The idea of attacking Turkey had first been put forward in November 1914, when it was suggested by French minister of justice Aristide Briand in November 1914. Briand's ideas were heavy with generalities but light on specifics and were given short shrift by both the French the British high command. That same month First Lord of the Admiralty Winston Churchill, using (grossly erroneous, as it turned out) information supplied by a young intelligence officer named T. E. Lawrence, advanced a rather more detailed plan for a naval attack through the Straits of the Dardanelles, up the Sea of Marmara, and ending at the Bosporus, abreast of Constantinople. Again the idea was ignored, in no small part because it was still believed on both sides that the war would be over in a matter of weeks.

As November faded into December and then 1914 passed into 1915, growing casualty lists on both the Western and the Eastern Fronts, coupled with the accumulating evidence of a strategic stalemate, particularly in France and Belgium, made it increasingly clear to all of the belligerents that the war was going to last much longer than anyone had anticipated, and the idea of some sort of direct action against the Turks began to gain limited favor within the British War Cabinet and the whole of the Cabinet itself. Prodded by the Tsar's note, Churchill once more took up his idea of a naval assault on the Dardanelles and began to argue in its favor, with the dual purpose of opening up access to the Black Sea and restoring the supply lines to Russia, while at the same time bringing about the collapse of the Three Pashas' regime and removing Turkey from the war. Pointing to the large number of "pre-dreadnought" battleships that the Royal Navy had mobilized at the war's outbreak but that were relegated to secondary duties because of their obsolescence versus modern dreadnoughts, he conceived of an operation that could be carried out by the Royal Navy alone, using these elderly ships, which could no longer take their place in the line of battle but whose guns (many of the ships mounted 12-inch main batteries) were far more powerful than anything that the Turkish defenses possessed. As envisaged by Churchill, there would be no requirement for committing any major land forces, only a relative handful of troops being needed for occupation duties once the Turks had capitulated.

At Churchill's direction, Adm. Sir Sackville Carden, the commander of British naval forces in the Mediterranean, drew up a detailed plan for a naval attack on the Straits. Though he personally doubted the likelihood of such an attack being successful, Carden did a professional job in carrying out the First Lord's directive, such that when Churchill placed his plans before the War Cabinet on January 13, 1915, its members, including Prime Minister Herbert Asquith, Field Marshal Lord Kitchener, the Secretary of State for War, and Adm. Sir John Fisher, the First Sea Lord, agreed to give action in the Dardanelles active consideration.

The Cabinet's approval was somewhat ambiguously worded, however, and Churchill, given his naturally aggressive personality, came away believing that he had been given the authority to put Carden's plans into action. A date of February 19 was set for the first attack to go in; when the plans were presented to the War Cabinet on January 28, Churchill made his case so forcefully and with such conviction that his colleagues, swept up by his enthusiasm, formally approved them. Later Churchill's political and personal enemies would make much ado about how he had "railroaded" the War Cabinet into giving its consent to a reckless and risky operation that offered a very small chance of success in return for the potential for catastrophic losses. Yet these critics, who would spring up long after the fact, usually lumped the naval attack on the Straits, which was Churchill's brainchild, together with the landings on the Gallipoli Peninsula, which were never part of the First Lord's planning.

As conceived by Churchill, developed by Carden, and approved by the War Cabinet, the naval attack would be a swift, sudden strike at the Turks' defenses along the Dardanelles, ultimately carrying the attacking fleet to Constantinople, leaving the Ottoman capital at the mercy of the Royal Navy's guns. Should something go wrong during the operation or the Turkish resistance prove unexpectedly fierce, the fleet could be withdrawn altogether. The ships to be deployed could be risked without compromising the Royal Navy's strategic superiority over the German High Seas Fleet, and compared to the daily carnage of the Western Front, even the potential loss of life had to be regarded as encouragingly small. The only possible genuine criticism of the plan—and it was a valid point—was that it remained unclear as to exactly what would be the Allied strategy in the event of an immediate decisive breakthrough.

Yet even this criticism was anticipated by Churchill: he was certain that the appearance of a fleet of Allied warships in the waters off Constantinople would lead to the immediate collapse of the government of the Three Pashas and a swift capitulation by the Young Turks. This element of political consideration was more the product of Churchill's instincts than of any firm diplomatic or military intelligence in the plan that could not be quantified and committed to paper, but it was a premise on which depended the entire calculus of the proposed operation. In conceiving of the Dardanelles operation, the First Lord presumed the fragility of the Turks' morale; the plan's strategic keystone was to strike a crippling blow at not just the ability of both the government and the people to keep fighting, but also at the Turks' willingness to do so. It's unclear from just what information Churchill drew this conclusion—it may have been private communications from the American ambassador in Constantinople, Henry Morgenthau, who had assumed the role of caretaker for British and French interests there after the war began—but it was an even more accurate assessment of conditions in the Ottoman capital than he may have realized.

Ever since war had been declared, there had been an undercurrent of apprehension running through Constantinople, as both government and populace alike realized that the Three Pashas had most certainly bitten off more than they could chew: the Allies were expected to appear in the Bosporus any day. The city was extraordinarily vulnerable: there were no modern defenses, and what few heavy guns the Turks possessed were desperately short of ammunition. (At one point a coded cablegram to Berlin from the German embassy in Constantinople almost hysterically requesting an immediate resupply had been intercepted by Admiralty intelligence code breakers and passed on to Churchill.)

In the immediate aftermath of their revolution in 1908, the Young Turks had enjoyed a level of confidence among the Turkish people that the Sultanate had not possessed for decades, but as members of the new government began to squabble among themselves, that confidence soon began to devolve into much the same sullen indifference that had marked the Turks' attitude toward the Sultan's regime. After the twin disasters of the Suez and Caucasus campaigns, what little remaining confidence the Turkish people reposed in the Young Turks and especially in Enver, Djemal, and Talaat was rapidly evaporating. Placards began to appear in the capital denouncing the government, which was increasingly feared by the minorities living inside the city: Greeks, Armenians, Arabs, Balkan Christians, and even Jews were prepared to see the government off. Well-to-do Turkish families were fleeing Constantinople for the interior of Anatolia, while banks were quietly making arrangements to transfer their gold reserves out of the city, and the government made their own preparations to evacuate Constantinople.

By February the tension had evolved into an almost incipient panic, as the disaster in the Caucasus, the repulse of the Suez Expedition, and the rapid Anglo-Indian thrust up the Tigris-Euphrates Valley bespoke of impending defeat. The Treasury was empty, and confiscation of private property—especially food and farm animals—was increasing daily. The government did little to inspire confidence among the populace. After their respective defeats in the Caucasus and the Suez, Enver swung between moods of transparently false bravado and hand-wringing despair, while Djemal brooded in his Ministry office. In early February Talaat met in secret with Liman von Sanders; General von Bronsart, a German serving as the Turks' chief of staff; and Admiral Usedom, who commanded the Dardanelles defenses. Rumors of a pending Allied attack on the Straits had been swirling about Constantinople for weeks, and all four men agreed that if the Allies struck and pressed their attack, they would get through. Once past the Straits and into the Sea of Marmara, the guns of the Royal Navy's battleships would be able to range on any spot in the city. Most critically, the only two ammunition factories the Turks possessed were located in Constantinople: with their loss, there could be no further resupply of Turkish forces in the field.

Meanwhile, the planned naval attack on the Straits was gaining strength among the Allies. Three days before the first bombardment was to begin, Lord Kitchener detailed the 29th Division, the British Army's single remaining division not already committed to the Western Front, to stand by for deployment to the Dardanelles if need be. Likewise, the planned transfer of the ANZACs to France was postponed and the troops held in Egypt. Finally, the French Minister of Marine, Churchill's counterpart, agreed to add a squadron of French pre-dreadnoughts to the order of battle for the February 19 operation.

The Sea of Marmara, which connects the Aegean Sea and the Black Sea, is shaped like a giant crouching eastward-facing rat, some 175 miles (280 km) long and 50 miles (80 km) wide. Geographically, it separates Europe, on the northern side, from Asia, on the south. The city of Constantinople sits on the northern shore, just where the rat's ears would be. Trailing out and down to the southwest and ending in the Aegean Sea is the rat's tail, the 31-mile (65 km) long Straits of the Dardanelles; the Straits are 5 miles (7 km) from shore to shore at their widest point. Once an invading fleet of warships is past the upper mouth of the Straits and into the Marmara itself, there are no obstacles between it and the city of Constantinople. Whoever controls the Dardanelles then essentially controls the entire waterway from the Black Sea to the Aegean.

Silencing the Turkish coast defense batteries protecting the Straits was the objective of the first attempt to force the Dardanelles, made on February 19, 1915. The Allied fleet included the new dreadnought *Queen Elizabeth*, sent out to calibrate her massive 15-inch guns, three battle cruisers, sixteen pre-dreadnoughts (including four French vessels), four cruisers, eighteen destroyers, six submarines, and twenty-one trawlers, plus the seaplane carrier *Ark Royal*. Admiral Carden was in overall command; he intended for his plan of attack to unfold in three distinct stages. First, the "outer forts," those sited below the Narrows, that section of the Straits where the northern and southern shores most closely approached each other, would be neutralized by long-range gunfire, keeping the battleships out of effective range of the Turkish guns. Once this was accomplished, the Allied fleet would move up to engage any remaining shore batteries while minesweepers cleared the minefields, which were located in the Narrows itself, roughly halfway up the Straits. The final phase envisaged the destruction of the "inner forts," which were positioned above the Narrows.

The bombardment began at 8:00 a.m. By the end of the day the Turkish positions had suffered tremendous punishment, although fewer guns were actually destroyed than the British had anticipated. A series of storms moving across the Straits prevented the bombardment from being continued until February 25, when again the Turkish positions in the "outer forts," those positioned along the shoreline, were subjected to heavy bombardment, then occupied by the Royal Marines. Still, the Allied ships couldn't silence the Turkish mobile batteries positioned farther inland, sited to protect the elaborate minefield located roughly midway along the Straits.

Here Carden's plan ran into its first serious obstacle, although it wasn't insurmountable. The mobile batteries weren't heavy enough to pose even a middling threat to the Allied battleships, but they were a genuine threat to the Allies' lightly constructed minesweepers. As long as the minefields were in place, the fleet could not move forward; as long as the mobile batteries remained in action, the minesweepers could not remove the mines without facing the risk of destruction.

Nevertheless, Churchill urged Admiral Carden to resume the bombardment at the earliest opportunity and press home the attack so that the minesweepers could clear the Narrows. After Carden read an Admiralty intercept of a Turkish signal that indicated that the Dardanelles forts had all but exhausted their ammunition, he found a new confidence in his own planning and on March 4 he informed Churchill that he expected the Allied fleet to arrive off Constantinople within two weeks. On his instructions the bombardment would be resumed on March 18.

Yet when the sun rose over the Dardanelles on March 18, Carden wasn't there to see it. High-strung and anxious, the admiral had almost collapsed from nervous exhaustion. He was evacuated to the fleet shore headquarters on the island of Lemnos, and command of the Allied fleet passed to Adm. Sir John de Robeck. This would prove to be a significant development: Carden was not a dynamic commander, but he had drawn up the Allied fleet's plan of attack and so naturally had a considerable personal interest in its success. De Robeck, while not actually a timid officer, was far less enthusiastic about the basic premise that a naval attack alone could carry the day against the Turks without being supported by a large-scale amphibious assault on the north side of the Straits, the Gallipoli Peninsula.

For the Turks, or at least the Turkish government, that first naval attack on February 19 seemed to be their worst nightmare come true; Churchill's reading of the Ottoman political situation was even better than he knew. The panic that had been lurking just under the surface in Constantinople since the war began was ready to break through. Two trains were readied in the capital, prepared to depart for the Anatolian interior on an hour's notice, one for the Sultan and his harem, the other for foreign diplomats and their staffs. Fearing riots, the government posted troops to keep order. On instructions from Talaat and Enver, demolition charges were rigged at all of the city's most prominent structures and all public buildings: the government offices, the two arsenals, the telegraph office, the train station, the power plant—even in mosques and churches. When American ambassador Henry Morgenthau protested and asked Talaat to at least spare the Hagia Sophia, the foreign minister scoffed, replying, "There are not six men in the Committee of Union and Progress who care for anything that is old. We like new things." The German ambassador, von Wangenheim, sent a secret cable to Berlin expressing his fears that if the naval attack on the Straits continued, the Three Pashas would conclude a separate peace with the Allies. Whether or not this was true remains unclear. There are no contemporary Turkish documents indicating that such a drastic step was being contemplated, but it was not impossible, and that a normally unflappable character like von Wangenheim should communicate such a possibility to his superiors is a powerful indicator of just how high tensions in Constantinople had been ratcheted by the Allied attack.

The Allied fleet that opened fire on the Turkish positions on March 18 now consisted of eighteen battleships along with the array of battle cruisers, cruisers, and destroyers. With them went a flotilla of minesweepers tasked with removing the eleven lines of mines that had been laid in the Narrows and that posed the greatest threat to any Allied warships attempting to move out of the Straits and into the Sea of Marmara itself. For several hours the scene was essentially a replay of February 19, with the fixed fortifications receiving most of the attention of the British and French battleships. The elderly—in some cases, ancient—Turkish fortifications were no match for modern heavy guns and suffered accordingly. The records of the Turkish General Staff note that by 2:00 p.m., "All telephone wires were cut, all communications with the forts were interrupted, some of the guns had been knocked out. . . . In consequence the artillery fire of the defense had slackened considerably." It was a masterful understatement: most of the Turks' heavy guns had been disabled or their emplacements rendered unworkable—one entire fort was obliterated when a magazine blew up—and what few pieces remained in action were almost out of ammunition. In fact, a lack of shells began plaguing all of the Turkish guns, including the mobile batteries scattered up and down the heights of the Straits.

Within this shortage of ammunition lurked the potential for disaster for the Turks, for it was the mobile batteries of medium guns that actually posed the greatest threat to the success of the Allied operation. Churchill had, in fact, been quite correct in the basic premises of the naval attack when he maintained that the guns of the Turkish forts were too old and weak to present any real threat to even predreadnought battleships. Turkish gunners, fighting with a heroism and a determination that aroused open admiration from their British and French opponents, were able to score hits on several of Allied battleships but failed to do more than superficial damage to any of them. The medium guns of the mobile batteries were another story, however: while they were utterly powerless against the armor of even obsolete battleships, they were able to bring a heavy and accurate fire down on the small, flimsy minesweepers attempting to clear the Narrows. As long as the minesweepers could be prevented from sweeping the channel, the Allied battleships,

Ismail Enver. Charming, dynamic, ambitious, and egotistical, he was the acknowledged leader among the Three Pashas who ruled the Ottoman Empire in its final years. Not intellectually gifted, Enver possessed a style of leadership that was better suited to a shopkeeper than to a statesman.

Mehmed Talaat. The most intelligent and pragmatic of the Three Pashas, he was also the most closely identified with the Armenian Massacres of 1915.

Ahmed Djemal. The third of the Three Pashas, he was given the responsibility of formulating the Ottoman Empire's domestic and foreign policies, most of which eventually proved to be failures.

Sultan Mehmed V. With the Sultanate politically emasculated by the time he came to the throne in 1909, the only significant act of his reign was his declaration of jihad against the Allies on November 14, 1914.

Kaiser Wilhelm II of Germany. So greatly did Wilhelm and his government covet the Ottoman Empire that the Kaiser went to considerable lengths to endear himself to the Turks, including being photographed in a Turkish uniform and allowing the rumor to spread that he had secretly converted to Islam.

Colmar Freiherr von der Goltz. The German general (later field marshal) responsible for reorganizing and modernizing the Ottoman Army, he would die at the front in Mesopotamia in 1916.

Hans Freiherr von Wangenheim. German Ambassador to the Sublime Porte (the Sultan's Palace), von Wangenheim played a pivotal role in bringing about the Turkish-German alliance.

The Grand Mufti of Constantinople, the senior cleric of Islam, publicly proclaims the Sultan's declaration of Holy War (jihad) on the Allies, on November 14, 1914. It was hoped that the proclamation would lead to rebellion among the British Empire's Moslem subjects, which proved to be a vain effort.

A graphic example of the violence of the Royal Navy's initial bombardment of the Turkish forts guarding the Gallipoli Peninsula, this 10" heavy gun has been blown completely off its mountings. Had the British followed up with an immediate landing on the peninsula, there would have been almost no resistance.

Otto Liman von Sanders. A German *generalleutnant* who was part of the German Military Mission to the Ottoman Empire, he was the senior officer on the Gallipoli Peninsula when the British landed.

Mustafa Kemal. A colonel in the Turkish Army in command of the 19th Infantry Division, his tactics stopped the Allies in their tracks wherever they attacked on the Gallipoli Peninsula, and his leadership made him a national hero to the Turks.

W Beach at Gallipoli. An eloquent image repeated at all of the Allied landing sites, showing the tight confines of the beachheads.

Armenian irregulars who banded together to support the Russian invasion of eastern Anatolia in late 1914. Their actions provided the Three Pashas with the pretext used to justify the Armenian Massacres in 1915 and 1916.

Sayyid Hussein ibn Ali, Sherrif of Mecca, proclaiming the Sultan's declaration of jihad to be invalid; in effect, this was a declaration of open rebellion against the Turks by the Arabs of the Hejaz.

A division of Turkish infantry prepares to march from the outskirts of Jerusalem into defensive positions in the Sinai Peninsula, made necessary when the Turkish offensive to capture the Suez Canal was routed in early 1915 and the British moved eastward across the Canal into Turkish territory.

A column of Turkish reinforcements marching eastward to the province of Mesopotamia, where the British Indian Army was methodically advancing up the Tigris and Euphrates Rivers. Though often let down by incompetent leaders, Turkish soldiers were admired by their Allied counterparts for their skill and courage.

A troop of Turkish cavalry. Excellent horsemen riding sturdy Arab mounts, the cavalry was the eyes and ears of the Turkish Army in Mesopotamia and on the Palestine-Sinai front. The availability of aerial reconnaissance was extremely limited for the Turks, making the work of the cavalry especially vital.

A Turkish artillery position in Palestine. Turkish guns were for the most part obsolete, and available in far fewer numbers than the Allies could deploy, but they were well served and when available used effectively.

Turkish Aid Station near the Suez Canal, early 1915. The Ottoman Army's support services were woefully inadequate by Allied standards, but Turkish medical personnel, despite shortages of equipment and supplies, were admired by Allied soldiers for their willingness to treat wounded of any nationality.

A column of Australian Light Horse on the march to Beersheba, where, on October 31, 1917, they carried the town in what became known as "the last cavalry charge of the British Empire."

The town of Beersheba, with its six wells, was the strategic key to General Allenby's plan to outflank the Turks' defensive positions that blocked his advance to Jerusalem.

Indian infantry in Mesopotamia. The British Indian Army was responsible for the Mesopotamian Campaign in what is modern Iraq, and the majority of the troops deployed there were Indian, both Hindu and Moslem. The hoped-for rebellion by Indian Moslems in response to the Sultan's call to Holy War never materialized in any substantial or effective form.

General Maude (at the head of the column) leading his troops into Baghdad. The fall of the city, the de facto eastern capital of the Ottoman Empire, was a severe blow to the Turks' morale.

Lt. Col. T. E. Lawrence, "Lawrence of Arabia." Although the exploits of his Arab irregulars were romanticized and exaggerated, his understanding of the Arabs and their aspirations were far more realistic than those of anyone in Cairo or London— and were essentially ignored.

Lt. Gen. Sir Edmund Allenby. A fighting soldier who had not particularly distinguished himself on the Western Front, in the Sinai and Palestine he proved to be a brilliant tactician and a first-class leader.

Maj. Gen. Friedrich Freiherr Kress von Kressenstein. Part of General von der Goltz's military mission to the Ottoman Empire, von Kressenstein masterminded the disastrous first offensive against the Suez Canal, but later redeemed himself with his skilled defense of the Sinai and southern Palestine.

Turkish machine gun sections in a defensive position. The Ottoman Army wholeheartedly embraced the German Army's tactical use of the machine gun, and used them to good effect in their defense of Gallipoli, Mesopotamia, and Palestine, often forcing the Allies into prolonged and expensive diversions and flanking maneuvers.

Lieutenant General Allenby proclaiming martial law in Jerusalem, after having entered the city on foot, representative of a pilgrim, rather than as a conqueror on horseback, on December 9, 1917.

The last Ottoman Sultan, Mehmed VI, who had succeeded his brother in July 1918, leaving the Sublime Porte for the last time, on November 1, 1922, having been formally stripped of his title and power by the new Republic of Turkey, led by Mustafa Kemal.

for all their superiority of firepower, could not risk sailing through the minefield for fear—a very real one—of a fatal encounter with one of the underwater devices. That the medium batteries were mobile meant that they could shift their positions from time to time, denying the battleships the opportunity of ranging in on them, all the while dropping a lethal fire among the minesweepers, preventing them from clearing the minefields. But should the medium guns exhaust their ammunition, the minesweepers would be able to move forward unhindered, and soon the way would be clear for the Allied fleet to steam into Constantinople.

Here, as it so often does in warfare, chance played an unexpected and, as events would have it, decisive hand. On the night of March 9, a Turkish cruiser had laid a single line of mines in the Straits, south of and at right angles to the eleven minefields about which the Allies already knew. Intelligence updates to Admiralty charts showed the area to be swept where these new mines lay lurking, so the Allied battleships and battle cruisers steamed through it with blithe confidence, unaware of the danger below. The inevitable soon happened, and right before 2:00 p.m., just as the situation was approaching the worst for the Turks, the French battleship *Bouvet* exploded, capsized, and sank in two minutes, taking her entire crew with her. Not realizing that *Bouvet* had struck a mine, believing that she had suffered some freak hit from the Turkish guns, the remaining battleships continued to fire at the Turkish positions while the minesweepers went forward. Then, two hours later, HMS *Irresistible* and HMS *Inflexible* were both shaken by heavy underwater explosions not far from where *Bouvet* had disappeared, and it began to dawn on Admiral de Robeck that there might be another undetected minefield in the waters where his battleships were cruising. A few minutes later, HMS *Ocean*, sent to take *Irresistible* under tow, struck another mine and within minutes she was on her way to the bottom, where *Irresistible* soon joined her.

After watching his minesweepers driven off by the Turkish field batteries and having three of his battleships sunk and a fourth heavily damaged in little more than two hours, de Robeck decided he'd had enough. The fleet was recalled to the safety of the Aegean, and the admiral sent a signal to the Admiralty in London stating his considered opinion that naval power alone could not clear the Straits. Ground forces were necessary to eliminate the Turkish mobile artillery. Only once this was done would the minesweepers be able to clear the way to Constantinople for the battleships.

De Robeck's signal caused tremendous consternation in London. A fundamental part of the planning of the attack on the Dardanelles was the premise that its success was not dependent on the use of ground forces. At the same time, the use of old and obsolete battleships for the naval attack had been predicated on the knowledge that some of them would certainly be sunk by enemy action. While the loss of life among the crews of the three sunken battleships was regrettable, the casualties had been incurred in what promised to be one of the war's decisive operations and numbered fewer than those being suffered each day by the British Army on the Western Front for transparently indecisive results. Now, according to de Robeck, the entire concept was hopelessly flawed, and the only prospect of salvaging anything of the operation was to resort to exactly the sort of action its planners had sought to avoid in the first place. One of the great attractions of Churchill's original idea was that the naval attack was a self-limiting operation. If it were not a success, then there would be no need to attempt to sustain or redeem it with further actions or reinforcements—the Allied squadron could simply steam away.

De Robeck's signal broke open a deep fissure that had formed in the War Cabinet and the Admiralty over the wisdom and viability of the Dardanelles operation, one that would eventually fragment both bodies. For the time being, however, its immediate consequence, once the dust had settled from the acrimonious debates in Whitehall over who was ultimately responsible for this setback, was the decision by Lord Kitchener to appoint Gen. Sir Ian Hamilton as commander of the newly designated "Mediterranean Expeditionary Force," with the mission of seizing the Gallipoli Peninsula and in so doing permanently silence all of the Turkish artillery covering the Straits. To accomplish this, Hamilton would be given the Australian and New Zealand Army Corps (ANZAC), formed by the Australian 1st Division and the New Zealand and Australian Division; the British 29th Division, a unit of pre-war regulars; the Royal Naval Division, composed of Royal Marines and hastily drafted naval recruits; and the French Oriental Expeditionary Corps, a hodgepodge body of various units of native troops recruited from French colonies.

Six weeks would pass before all of Hamilton's units were assembled in Alexandria and Cairo—the 29th Division had to be transported from England—and in that time a number of Royal Navy officers, including de Robeck's chief of staff, Com. Roger Keyes, were insistent that another effort be made to force the Narrows with just naval units alone. The Turks, they believed, were well and truly on the ropes, and another effort on the scale of March 18 would, they argued, be the knock-out blow for the Ottoman Army. Within the Royal Navy itself, the outcome of March 18 wasn't regarded so much as a defeat as merely a temporary setback. While Admiral de Robeck might have been unduly pessimistic about the fleet's chances of success against the remaining Ottoman defenses, the majority of ships' officers and ratings were confident of their ability to overwhelm the Turkish guns and force their way past the minefields and on to Constantinople.

Yet if the British saw the action of March 18 and its immediate consequences as nothing more than a check to their plans, the Turks saw it as something completely different, and it is here that the Gallipoli campaign begins to gain momentum toward becoming something of far greater historical significance than merely a military operation. For the Turks, March 18, 1915, was nothing less than a miraculous victory. The defenders of the Dardanelles forts had watched almost helplessly as their fortifications were pulverized under a rain of 11- and 12-inch shells; they knew how close they had come to exhausting their own ammunition; they also knew that when what shells were to hand ran out, there was no hope of resupply. The gunners and the garrisons had watched three Allied battleships sink on March 18 and watched as three others limped away, seriously damaged, but the Turks knew they were facing the might and determination of the Royal Navy and fully expected when the sun rose on March 19 to see the Allied fleet again steaming up the Straits, determined once more to try conclusions with the Turkish batteries. And the Turks knew full well this time that after an hour or two, there would be no more resistance to the Allied fleet. Constantinople and with it the Ottoman Empire were doomed.

Yet when March 19 dawned and no Allied warships appeared, the only conclusion the Turkish defenders could draw, once it became clear that the Allies really weren't going to renew their attack, was that the British and the French had indeed been turned back. How or why didn't matter; they had turned back. As the news, unbelievable as it might have seemed, percolated back to Constantinople, a sea change began to overtake the Turks, both within the government and among the common people, first in the capital and then flowing out into the countryside as news of the victory at the Narrows began to spread. For decades, victories of any kind had been rare for Ottoman armies: now the Turks could boast of a triumph over not some minor Balkan principality or an Italian rabble-in-arms in Libya, but over the most powerful fleet in the world, almost at the gates of Constantinople.

The most immediate consequence of this apparent victory was to give the Turks a sense of pride in their army and, by extension, their government that they never had during the seven years of the Young Turks' rule. This was no small thing, for it legitimized the government in the eyes of the common Turk in a way that nothing the regime had done previously ever could. Moreover, it gave the Turks a sense that they did have a measure of control over their own destiny: for months now the Greeks, the Bulgars, the Romanians, and the Armenians had been hovering like vultures, ready to rend and devour the corpse of Ottoman Turkey, and for much of the populace it had seemed only a question of when, not if, they would descend. After March 18, the Turks not only discovered that they had the strength, but rediscovered that they had the will to resist the powers arrayed against them. If the Ottoman Empire were to fall, at least the Ottoman Turks would make a fight of it. Any hopes to which the Allies may have clung of easy victories or a Turkish collapse, whether in the Dardanelles, Mesopotamia, or Palestine, evaporated.

No matter that from the British and French perspective, breaking off the action on March 18 was not a defeat at all: the Allied fleet could renew the bombardment at any time of its choosing. What mattered for the Turks was the perception of victory: they had no idea why the Allied battleships had suddenly turned back from the Straits, and they could draw their conclusions only from the evidence of their own eyes. They had witnessed three Allied battleships sink in a little more than two hours and two others suffer serious damage at the same time. Shortly thereafter the Allied warships steamed away: ergo, they had been defeated. And as events would prove, sometimes perception can exert a more powerful influence than reality.

Inevitably and understandably, Enver, Talaat, and Djemal immediately sought to take credit for the Allied repulse. Enver in particular, conveniently forgetting his days of near panic in February, when any minute he expected to see the battleships of the Allied fleet steam into the Constantinople waterfront, was loud in proclaiming that he had always had complete confidence that the defenses of the Straits would never fall. The Turkish people, having no recourse to any other source of information but the government, naturally believed the Three Pashas' claims of being instrumental in repelling the Royal Navy: that belief, coupled with the rekindled pride the Turks felt in their victory at the Straits, translated into a linkage between the government and the people that the Turks had never known under the Ottoman sultans. What eventually emerged from the aftermath of March 18, 1915, was an unusual sense of unity between government and governed: it was perceived as having been a *Turkish* victory, not an Ottoman triumph, and for the first time, the Turks began to identify themselves as not merely subjects of the Ottoman Empire, but as the people of the Turkish nation.

Meanwhile, as the Turks celebrated, the British and the French began preparations for the amphibious assault on Gallipoli. It would take six weeks for the British 29th Division to reach Egypt, where it, along with the ANZACs and the Naval Division, would embark on transports bound for the Aegean Sea and the Gallipoli Peninsula. The date of the attack was set for April 25, 1915, and General Hamilton's staff worked around the clock to prepare the plans that would put seventy thousand Allied soldiers ashore the first day. Given the situation that developed almost from the moment the first troops landed, it should be remembered that Hamilton and his staff were expected to produce an operational plan in less than two months that was as complicated in nature and almost as large in scope as the "Overlord" landings on D-Day nineteen years later, to which more than two years of planning and preparation were devoted. The handicaps he faced were enormous: he had no specialized landing craft, the troops he had been given had no training in amphibious landings, nor had they ever fought or even trained together; the supply situation was hopelessly muddled, as munitions and equipment were loaded aboard transports in whatever manner suited the quartermaster, rather than on the basis of priority needs. Hamilton also believed that the Royal Navy would continue with its attacks on the Straits while the landings were taking place, creating vital diversions among the Turkish defenders. Admiral de Robeck, however, who had never been in favor of the naval action, feared losing more ships and refused to continue the bombardment.

Hamilton's plan was for the 29th Division to land at Cape Helles on the tip of the Gallipoli Peninsula and then advance on the Turkish forts at Kilitbahir. The ANZACs were to land simultaneously with the 29th at a small cove, to be known forever as ANZAC Cove, north of Gaba Tepe, their objective being to advance across the peninsula and prevent the Turks from withdrawing from Kilitbahir or reinforcing the positions there. The 29th's operational sector became known as simply Helles, while the ANZAC position was called, inevitably, ANZAC. The French Oriental Corps was given the task of a diversionary landing at Kum Kale on the far side of the Straits, while the Royal Naval Division would first make a diversion of its own at Bulair, then withdraw and serve as a general reserve.

Hardly had the Allied fleet withdrawn from the Straits than rumors began to circulate among the Turks about a planned Allied landing on Gallipoli. They wasted no time in preparing for such an assault, although the Ottoman commanders argued hotly among themselves as to the best means of defending the peninsula. None disagreed that the best defense would be to hold the ridge: the point of contention was over exactly where the British and the French would land. A mistake in divining the Allied intentions would put the Turkish divisions holding the wrong places, almost certainly with disastrous results. Otto Liman von Sanders, the German general in overall command of the Turkish Fifth Army, which was responsible for the defense of the Dardanelles, believed that Besika Bay, on the south, or Asiatic, side of the Straits, posed the greatest danger. British forces landing there would find the terrain easier than on the north side of the Straits, and from there Allied artillery would be able to target most of the Ottoman medium batteries guarding the Narrows and the minefields. Sanders placed two divisions, a third of the Fifth Army's strength, around Besika. Another two divisions were deployed at the isthmus of Bulair, far up the Aegean coast from where the Allied naval attacks had taken place. Liman was convinced that the opportunity to cut off this narrow neck of land and so sever the Turks' supply lines and communications to the rest of the peninsula would be one the British could not pass up. Finally, from Cape Helles, on the tip of the peninsula, northeast along the Aegean shore, the two remaining divisions, the 9th and the 19th, were deployed in a thin screen. The 19th was placed under the command of a thirty-four-year-old lieutenant colonel, Mustafa Kemal.

Gallipoli would introduce the name Mustafa Kemal to the Ottoman Turks and the world alike; before the battle he was just another unknown Turkish officer. Born in 1881, in the then Ottoman province of Thessaloniki, Mustafa (the name *Kemal*, meaning "mature" or "complete," would be given to him by a teacher) demonstrated very early in his life a remarkable intelligence, coupled with a capacity for deep thinking that impressed all who met him but did not make him particularly approachable. He scorned the religious education his mother tried to force on him, preferring a private, secular school. The first step toward a military career, rather than one in trade as his parents would have preferred, came when Mustafa entered a military junior high school in Thessaloniki, then went on to the military high school in Monastir. In 1899 he enrolled at the War College in Constantinople and graduated in 1902; in 1905 he finished the course of the Ottoman War Academy.

Two years later, while posted in Damascus, he was promoted to captain. In the meantime, he had become politically active, joining a small secret revolutionary society called Vatan ve Hürriyet (Motherland and Liberty) made up of Ottoman officers dedicated to reforming the Sultan's regime. While serving back in Monastir, he joined the Committee of Union and Progress and took an active part in the 1908 revolution. Despite his political activities, he was still first and foremost a dedicated professional soldier: in 1910 he was in France as the empire's official observer at the French Army's annual autumn maneuvers; he then went to the Ministry of War, working under Enver, who came to dislike and mistrust the intelligent, dedicated, and honest young officer. When the war with Italy erupted in 1911, Mustafa fought in Libya, and during the First Balkan War he fought the Bulgars at Gallipoli and Bulair. With peace restored in 1913, he was appointed military attaché to Sofia and promoted to lieutenant colonel the following spring.

Despite Enver's suspicions of, and hostility toward, Mustafa Kemal (Enver was suspicious of and hostile toward anyone cleverer or more intelligent than himself, which meant he suspected and disliked almost everyone), the minister of war could not deny the young lieutenant colonel's ability. When the Turkish Fifth Army was formed on March 24, 1915, and charged with the defense of the Gallipoli Peninsula, Mustafa was an inevitable choice for a senior posting and so was given the task of organizing and commanding the 19th Division. Quiet, thoughtful, given over to periods of deep thought that others mistook for moodiness, Mustafa Kemal was about to show the world that he was a born soldier, a brilliant tactician, and a clever strategist.

Kemal was convinced that Liman's deployments left the Turkish forces too widely dispersed to be able to respond to an Allied landing in strength. He was certain, as Field Marshal Erwin Rommel would understand twenty-nine years later while attempting to defend the Normandy beaches, that an amphibious landing was at its most vulnerable when the troops were coming ashore. An enemy landing had to be met immediately and driven into the sea before it had time to consolidate and organize. Kemal also believed that Cape Helles and Gaba Tepe, not Besika Bay and Bulair, would be the two most likely targets for a British landing. By attacking Cape Helles, the British would be able to use the guns of the Royal Navy to dominate the entire position, while at Gaba Tepe the short distance across the peninsula to the shore of the Straits meant that a swiftly moving attacker could simultaneously cut off any retreating Turk units, while at the same time blocking the advance of any fresh reinforcements.

In shape, the Gallipoli Peninsula (its name in Turkish is rendered "Gelibolu") is 63 miles (101 km) in length and 13 miles (21 km) at its widest point. It resembles a human foot seen in profile: Cape Helles is at the toe, the Straits run along the arch of the sole, the Narrows are located at the heel; Gaba Tepe, the site of what would become known to the world as ANZAC Cove, sits where the instep meets the ankle. There is nothing podiatary about the terrain of the peninsula, however. To call it "hilly" is an understatement, for in most places the land rises out from the narrowest of beaches in steep slopes—in some places at angles of nearly 70 degrees—to heights of more than a thousand feet (340 m). The hills form into criss-cross patterns of high ridges that alternate with deep ravines, some running parallel to the peninsula's long axis, others at almost right angles to it, offering countless positions of natural concealment and defilade. The soil is rocky, the vegetation is mostly scrub pine. It is, in short, a defender's dream and an attacker's nightmare.

The Turks didn't waste the time given them between the end of the Allied naval bombardment and the British landings: it was well spent on preparing their defenses. Liman von Sanders recalled in his memoirs that "the British allowed us four good weeks of respite for all this work before their great disembarkation. . . . This respite just sufficed for the most indispensable measures to be taken." Barbed wire was strung on beaches considered likely landing sites; mines improvised from old navy torpedo warheads were cobbled together; machine guns were carefully sited and zeroed; trenches were dug and reinforced; communication lines were laid; defensive positions were connected by hastily constructed roads; small boats were collected to quickly move troops and equipment to critical areas; and the regimen of constant drills and training kept the men fit.

The British landings took place on April 25, 1915: the 29th Division came ashore at Cape Helles, its mission to advance northeast up the peninsula to the forts at Kilitbahir. As Kemal had predicted, the ANZACs landed north of Gaba Tepe, the plan being for them to move southeast across the peninsula and cut off the Turks at Kilitbahir from either retreat or reinforcement. To divert Turkish strength and attention from the ANZAC landing, the Royal Naval Division made a feint at Bulair, while the French made a diversionary landing on the Asian side of the Straits, at Kum Kale, before later reembarking to then hold the Helles beaches.

The ANZACs landed first, at about 3:30 a.m. on April 25. The landing force was split into two waves, and a navigational error caused the first wave to come ashore roughly 1.5 miles (2.4 km) north of its designated beaches. There was almost no resistance, but the Australian troops could find no recognizable landmarks to guide them toward their objectives, so most of them waited on the beach for fresh orders. Two battalions that did try to move inland found themselves in dead-end gullies. Troops in the second wave landed closer to their assigned beaches but still well north of where they were supposed to be.

The handful of Turkish defenders at Gaba Tepe, once they became aware of the magnitude of the ANZAC operation, brought every weapon available to bear. Liman von Sanders was convinced that this landing was a diversion and that the Royal Naval Division's demonstration at Bulair was the real threat, the exact opposite of the actual situation, but Mustafa Kemal immediately saw the situation with perfect clarity and quickly directed reinforcements to the Gaba Tepe sector. It was at this point that he famously ordered the Turkish 57th regiment to execute an immediate counterattack with the words "I do not expect you to attack, I order you to die! In the time which passes until we die, other troops and commanders can take your place!"

The fighting during the whole of April 25 was confused and bitter, as the ANZACs were determined to recover from the botched landings and take their assigned objectives, and the Turks were equally determined to hold them off. By the end of the day, it was clear that a state of equilibrium had been reached—the Australians could not advance, and the Turks could not drive them back. As April 26 dawned, it seemed impossible that the ANZACs could hold off the Turkish counterattack that the combatants believed would come within the next twenty-four hours. It was suggested to General Hamilton that the ANZACs be withdrawn and the beachhead north of Gaba Tepe, already known as ANZAC Cove, be abandoned: the Australian and New Zealand units would be used to reinforce the Helles positions. Hamilton refused to consider any withdrawal, instead telling the ANZACs, "You have got through the difficult business, now you have only to dig, dig, dig, until you are safe." Almost immediately on hearing this, the Australian troops began to call themselves "Diggers," and a legend was in the process of being born.

There were five separate landing sites at Cape Helles, in an arc around the tip of the peninsula, designated, from east to west, as S, V, W, X, and Y Beaches; however, they would become known collectively as Helles. The strength of the Turkish defenses varied wildly from beach to beach: the commander of the Y Beach landing was able to walk unopposed to within fifteen hundred feet (five hundred meters) of Krithia, from which any force holding the village could dominate the central ridge of the peninsula. Inexplicably, the village was deserted, but word of this never got back to General Hamilton, who had set up his headquarters aboard the dreadnought *Queen Elizabeth*, and a golden opportunity was missed for the Allies. The Turks quickly moved troops into Krithia, and the British never came near to taking the village again, as Y Beach was evacuated the following day to reinforce the other Helles beaches.

The main landings were made at W Beach and at V Beach, on more or less opposite sides of the Cape Helles headland, the site of V Beach sitting just below the ancient, crumbling fortress of Seddulbahir. On both beaches the Turks fought ferociously, inflicting appalling casualties on the landing infantry. At W Beach, a small beach overlooked by dunes and obstructed with barbed wire, the First Lancashire Fusiliers landed in open boats and were met by murderous machine-gun and rifle fire. The Lancashires were able to eventually overwhelm the Turkish defenders but at a horrendous cost: out of a strength of eleven hundred officers and other ranks, six hundred were killed or wounded in that first morning. Six Victoria Crosses were awarded for heroism during the storming of the beach that would always be called "Lancashire Landing."

V Beach would never receive such a moniker, the words "V Beach" being enough to speak volumes. The initial force storming the shore was drawn from the Royal Munster Fusiliers and the Royal Hampshires and was brought to the beach aboard a converted collier, the SS *River Clyde*, which was run aground beneath the ramparts of the Seddulbahir in the hope that it would provide cover for them until the last possible moment. Instead, the Turkish machine gunners in the ruined fortress were able to aim directly at the sally ports in the steamer's side, so that the troops attempting to disembark walked directly into their line of fire. The Royal Dublin Fusiliers would land at V Beach from open boats. Out of the first two hundred soldiers to disembark, only twenty-one men made it onto the beach. Other battalions landing on V Beach in open boats also took terrible casualties: almost

70 percent of the officers and other ranks committed to V Beach were killed or wounded, and like W Beach, six Victoria Crosses were awarded among the infantry and the sailors at V Beach.

Just as Kemal had predicted, however, once the British troops were ashore, Liman's deployment had stretched the Turkish defenses too thin, leaving them too weak to be able to drive the British off the beaches, despite the fearsome casualties they had inflicted during the landings. Yet once the British and the ANZACs got ashore, they seemed to have no idea of what to do next: so much emphasis had been placed on getting ashore that Hamilton had failed to impress on his divisional commanders the urgency of striking inland as quickly and deeply as possible once the troops had carved out their beachheads. Nor had Hamilton expected anything like the ferocity of the Turkish resistance: he had been in Egypt during Djemal's Suez fiasco and knew from reports received from Mesopotamia of the Turkish Army's poor performance there. The landings, then, were expected to be little more than walkovers, but the Turks refused to be so cooperative.

Kemal launched his first organized counterattack on the afternoon of April 27, determined to drive the ANZACs back into the sea. The Australians, with superior numbers and the fire support of destroyers offshore, held the Turks off during the night and into the next day before Kemal gave up and called a halt to the attack. The next day the British made their first effort to break out of the Helles position but gained little ground. The Turks counterattacked at Helles three days later and were quickly repulsed. These actions set the tone for the next four months, in which the British and the ANZACs tried to break out of their beachheads, and the Turks in turn attempted to tip them into the sea. Casualties were always high for whichever side was attacking at any given moment, while those suffered by the defenders were usually absurdly low by comparison. In one Ottoman attack at ANZAC Cove, on May 19, 42,000 Turks struck at 17,000 Australians and New Zealanders: when the assault finally petered out, the Turks had suffered about 10,000 casualties, while the ANZAC losses were 160 killed and 468 wounded. On June 4, when 25,000 British soldiers struck out toward the village of Krithia (it was their third attempt at taking it), more than 4,500 became casualties by day's end.

The front lines on the Gallipoli Peninsula had evolved into a small-scale replica of the Western Front. Opposing networks of trenches, dugouts, listening posts, and communications laterals sprang into being on each side of the rocky, scrub-strewn no-man's-land, where an injudicious movement during the day or a poorly concealed match at night could bring a fusillade of bullets or a quick burst of shells. Firepower asserted its superiority over movement on Gallipoli as surely as it had done in Flanders, and the British generals pacing the decks of the Royal Navy warships in the Aegean Sea were as frustrated in their attempts to find a method of breaking the stalemate as any of their chateau-dwelling counterparts in France and Belgium. Hamilton, in particular, never intended for the Gallipoli operation to descend into such pointless and expensive exertions. Yet in his own way, Hamilton had made such a debacle inevitable, for while he was an excellent administrator and a competent strategist, he simply did not possess the sort of ruthless aggressiveness that was needed to drive—not simply direct—an operation such as the Gallipoli campaign. He lacked the capacity to embrace the sort of cold-hearted calculus that causes successful generals to understand that in losing thousands of lives today, it may be possible to save tens or even hundreds of thousands of lives in the morrow. At the same time, he lacked the moral strength to be able to admit that his original planning had failed. Instead, he felt the necessity to try to redeem the landings at Helles and ANZAC Cove, choosing to reinforce failure, and so during the summer of 1915 he continued in his attempts to force a way out of the Helles bridgehead and up the peninsula.

Back in London, the lack of any swift, decisive result from the landings at Gallipoli, coupled with the failure of the British Army's attack on Aubers Ridge in Belgium, its largest offensive action so far in the war, produced political upheavals that resulted in a Cabinet crisis for Prime Minister Herbert Asquith. The ramshackle political alliance he had cobbled together in the spring of 1914 to enable his Liberal government to remain in power now began to fall apart, as it became clear that his managerial style of handling the responsibilities of his office were not equal to the task of effectively running a wartime government. In the House of Commons, the Conservatives made it clear that the only way Asquith could retain his office was to accept a coalition government, with Conservatives appointed to several key Cabinet posts. One additional price of their participation was Churchill, who was anathema to them for reasons both political and personal and who, though he had never proposed the landings at Helles and ANZAC Cove, would become the scapegoat for the failure of the Dardanelles operation. More critical for Asquith, although perhaps he did not realize it at the time, was that his authority as prime minister had been fatally undermined, as the more ambitious members of his Cabinet, and in particular David Lloyd George, the Chancellor of the Exchequer and in effect the deputy prime minister, began scheming to replace him.

The repeated failure of the Allies to break out of the Helles beaches eventually forced General Hamilton to acknowledge the strategic and tactical realities and draw up a new plan to revitalize the entire campaign by landing in a completely new sector of the peninsula. On the night of August 6, two fresh divisions of British infantry were put ashore at a small bay called Suvla, five miles (eight kilometers) north of ANZAC Cove. In order to divert the Turks' attention from this new landing, the ANZACs were ordered to attack up the spine of the Sari Bair Range, a mountain ridge that ran northeast from the heights above ANZAC Cove and that dominated the narrow neck of the peninsula. Hamilton's plan called for the British troops to drive eastward from Suvla and eventually hook up with the ANZACs, and together the two corps would achieve the original objective of cutting off the Turkish forces on the southern end of the peninsula and, in doing so, opening up the passage of the Straits, which had been the goal of the entire campaign from the beginning.

The British landing at Suvla Bay was virtually unopposed, but the British commander, Lt. Gen. Sir Frederick Stopford, an officer of little imagination and even less drive, halted his troops in place as soon as the initial objectives were taken, which meant in practice that the British had seized little more than the landing beaches themselves. Mustafa Kemal reacted with his usual furious energy and was able to get his troops positioned on the high ground above the Suvla beaches before the British could take them. (One of history's greatest "what ifs" is the question of what might have happened at Gallipoli had even one of the British commanders possessed even a fraction of the energy and determination Kemal displayed throughout the entire campaign.) The result was that within a matter of days, the same sort of trench warfare that characterized Helles and ANZAC Cove supervened at Suvla.

While the Suvla position stagnated with relatively light casualties, the Australian and New Zealander assault on August 7 against the Sari Bair Range was an altogether different situation. The plan of attack was unnecessarily complicated and too dependent on each element achieving success on schedule. The terrain once more worked entirely in the defenders' favor, with ravines and gullies channeling the ANZAC attacks, sometimes leaving units in open ground without cover in the face of withering enemy fire. The steep ridges threw timetables hopelessly out of kilter, with heartbreaking consequences. In one action the Australian Third Light Horse Brigade, who were fighting as dismounted infantry, attempted to take a narrow section of ridge called the Nek. In seven minutes, 372 troopers and officers, more than two-thirds of the brigade's strength, were killed or wounded. The ANZACs would continue to press their attacks for another ten days, but for all of their courage and determination, the operation was a failure and the Turkish defenses held.

Yet something unexpected came out of the Sari Bair attacks. If the naval bombardment of March 18 was a defining day for the Turkish Army, the Turkish people, and the Turkish nation, then Sari Bair was equally defining for the AN-ZACs, particularly the Australians. Just as the men who were even now filling out the ranks of Lord Kitchener's "New Army" in England were the finest examples, physically, intellectually, and morally, of Britain's pre-war generation, so, too, were the ANZACs the avatars of their own homelands. Young, vital, brash, confident, irreverent, perhaps a bit naive, though not so susceptible to the same sort of rose-colored idealism as their European counterparts and more self-reliant, the Australians and the New Zealanders were carving out national identities for themselves and their homelands on the slopes of ANZAC Cove and the Sari Bair Range just as surely as were the Turks they fought. Dominion status and autonomy had come to both Australia and New Zealand only as recently as 1907: in the case of Australia, it had assembled a nation out of what had been six separate colonial administrations. Gallipoli was the Australians' first shared national experience, and the courage, the sorrow, the glory, and the pain that the "Diggers" knew came to be part of their legacy to their country. They became the exemplars of what it would mean to be an "Aussie," a source of pride and a touchstone of unity for all Australians, just as the "Kiwis," their New Zealander comrades-in-arms, did for their own young nation, one that strongly endures to this day.

When the August battles petered out, and it became clear that there would be no breakout from Suvla or ANZAC Cove, Hamilton and his staff, as well as Kitchener and the War Cabinet in London, argued over what to do next. It was a debate being conducted in an increasingly tense atmosphere, for the British public, as well as that of Australia and New Zealand, was at last beginning to become aware of the scale and the human cost of the failure in the Dardanelles. Led by Australian war correspondents Keith Murdoch and Ellis Ashmead-Bartlett, reporters began to increasingly defy General Hamilton's restrictions on their coverage of the campaign, and rather than depict the rosy and ever-confident official version of events, they presented a picture of the true conditions on the peninsula. They wrote of the desertlike heat of the summer and the bitter cold of autumn, which played havoc on the soldiers' health; the bland, unimaginative diet of bully beef and biscuit, which was all too often the only food that men in the trenches had; the constant, yet unpredictable, danger from intermittent shelling and sniper fire; the muddled supply situation; and, of course, the casualties suffered as a consequence of poor strategy and tactics. By mid-October Hamilton had been completely discredited in the eyes of Whitehall, and on October 16 he was recalled to London, with command of the Dardanelles forces then given to Lt. Gen. Sir Charles Munro.

Within days of assuming command, Munro informed Whitehall that he believed the whole Gallipoli operation had become a strategic dead end and recommended evacuation of all of the Allied forces from the peninsula. Kitchener wasn't convinced that such drastic action was necessary and so made a personal visit to Gallipoli to view for himself the tactical situations at Helles, ANZAC, and Suvla and learn firsthand the truth of conditions on the peninsula. What he saw convinced him that Munro had been right, and the order to begin preparations to evacuate went out on December 7, 1915.

The task was an immense challenge: fourteen infantry divisions, all in contact with the enemy and in extremely vulnerable positions, were to be withdrawn by sea, at night, in the winter, with a minimum of casualties. In the opinion of some senior British officers, including Sir Ian Hamilton, fully 50 percent losses among the troops being withdrawn could be expected by the time the last man had left the beach. Nevertheless, the evacuation went ahead as planned, the first withdrawals being made at Suvla and ANZAC Cove beginning on December 10 and ending ten days later as the last Digger left the sand of ANZAC Cove. Clever ruses—prepositioned rifles with improvised timers set to fire off random shots, or grenades with delayed fuses that exploded unexpectedly—and careful planning had kept the Turks unaware of what was happening until after all of the Allied troops had been taken off the beaches. On December 27 it was the turn of the Cape Helles beachheads; the success of ANZAC and Suvla was repeated and the last British troops were rowed away from Lancashire Landing on January 9, 1916.

In what was perhaps the greatest irony in a campaign filled with a lifetime's worth of ironies, the evacuation was the most successful part of the entire Dardanelles operation: not a single Allied soldier lost his life during the withdrawal, despite the dire predictions of General Hamilton and others. That was no small mercy, for it had been a costly campaign for both sides. The accounting would be imperfect, for there were many soldiers on both sides who vanished without a trace, but in the final reckoning Allied casualties exceeded 265,000, of whom some 46,000 were killed in action or died of wounds or disease. The Turkish losses were around 215,000, including 86,000 dead. Gallipoli, conceived and planned as a way to get around the carnage of blood-soaked Flanders, had ultimately proved to be every bit as deadly as the Western Front.

It is no exaggeration to say that what had happened there would reverberate for generations to come: the Gallipoli battlefields had been the crucible that gave shape to three nations, Australia, New Zealand, and Turkey, and laid an unforgettable blow to the imperial power Great Britain. A library's worth of books would be written about Gallipoli—debating, deprecating, or vindicating the wisdom of the campaign or detailing it to one end or another. Yet in the end, the verdict of the battlefield stands: the Turks won, the Allies lost; Russia would remain unsuccored and because of this would collapse in revolution two years later, almost handing victory in the Great War to the Germans; and the war in the Middle East would continue. But now it was also clear to everyone who wished to understand it that the Ottoman Empire would not allow itself to be trammeled by the Allies. Gallipoli had redeemed the Turks in their own eyes and showed the rest of the world that Ottoman power, so long disparaged, was still a force with which to be reckoned.

War would not come again to the Gallipoli Peninsula, although in many ways it would never leave it, either. Almost all of the British, Australian, and New Zealand dead were buried in military cemeteries on the peninsula, after the British fashion to inter their dead where they fell. The cemeteries are meticulously maintained to this day by the Imperial War Graves Commission, with the active assistance of the Turkish government. The Ottoman dead were buried in mass unmarked graves; nevertheless, they share the soil with their onetime foes, so that in death each side retains its hold on what it struggled so tenaciously to keep in life. In one final, fitting irony, it would be Mustafa Kemal, now known as Atatürk, "the father of the Turks," who would provide the benediction for all of them. His words are carved on a monument overlooking ANZAC Cove:

Those heroes that shed their blood and lost their lives . . . you are now lying in the soil of a friendly country. Therefore rest in peace. There is no difference between the Johnnies and the Mehmets where they lie side by side here in this country of ours. . . . You the mothers who sent their sons from far away countries, wipe away your tears. Your sons are now lying in our bosom and are in peace. Having lost their lives on this land they have become our sons as well.

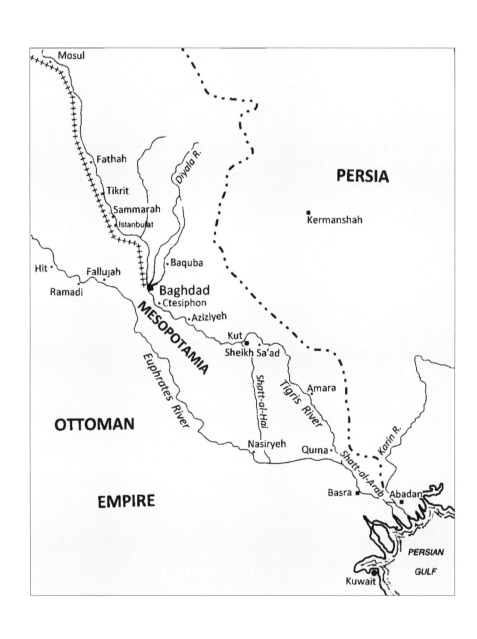

CHAPTER SIX
KUT

While the epic fight for Gallipoli held the world's attention (that is, those few parts of the world aside from Australia, New Zealand, and Turkey that paid any heed at all to the war in the Middle East), another drama was unfolding in Mesopotamia as the British continued their thrust up the Tigris-Euphrates Valley. For seven months the Anglo-Indian Army under Gen. Sir John Nixon strung together a series of victories over an outnumbered Turkish command tasked with holding the whole of Mesopotamia (which corresponds more or less to modern Iraq) with only two divisions.

The British captured Nasiriyeh at the end of June 1915, on the Euphrates River, which anchored their left flank. The right moved steadily up the Tigris, although a deteriorating supply situation slowed the advance, and the city of Kut-al-Amara, usually called simply Kut, was captured on September 28 by the Sixth (Poona) Division under Gen. Sir Charles Townshend. The town itself had little strategic significance, but its geographic position made it invaluable: it sat where the Shatt-al-Hai branched off from the Tigris to join the Euphrates at Nasiriyeh. Holding both cities and both ends of the waterway would simplify the movements of troops and equipment between the two rivers; the British position had every appearance of being extremely strong.

Hardly had Townshend begun to consolidate at Kut, however, than Nixon pressed him to continue the advance: Nixon had his sights set on capturing Baghdad.

From a purely military perspective, there was little about Baghdad to justify Nixon's eagerness to take it. The city had only minor intrinsic military value, with little to offer in the way of natural resources, inhabited by an Arab populace that was only marginally loyal to its Turkish masters. As made clear with their deployments, the Turks regarded Baghdad, along with the rest of Mesopotamia, as a strategic backwater. Nixon understood this: his determination to capture Baghdad was motivated not by military necessity, but rather by politics and questions of prestige.

Nixon's drive to take Baghdad had the firm support of the Indian government, as well as the Indian Army. Here imperial politics—British imperial politics—were driving the situation and in particular the peculiar status of the Indian Army within the British military establishment. One of the quirks of the British Empire, itself a collection of administrative eccentricities masquerading as a government, was that when the Empire of India was created in 1858, the Indian viceroy ruled as "the Raj"—the direct representative of the reigning monarch but without direct responsibility to or oversight by Parliament. In practice, this meant that Britain's Indian government could, and often did, conduct its affairs independent of Whitehall. This included the responsibility for the Indian Army, which was organized along the lines of the British Army and officered entirely by Britons. While its NCOs and other ranks were drawn from the native Indian population, it was not a "national" army in the European sense—there was no "nation" of India at this point in time—but rather the military arm of the Raj. Charged with the defense of the Indian subcontinent, as well as a limited degree of policing duties, the Indian Army followed instructions and policies set forth by the British government of India—the Raj—and answered to it only.

In his desire to take Baghdad, General Nixon enjoyed the open and wholehearted support of the Indian government, despite the official position of the British government that merely assuring the security of the Persian oil fields was all that was expected, required, or desired of the Indian infantry divisions being shipped to the head of the Persian Gulf. The enthusiasm with which the Indian government promoted the idea of a "forward defense" of the Persian oil fields by taking the offensive into Mesopotamia was inspired by several different sources, none of them particularly military.

In no small part this determination to take the war to the Turks, rather than sit passively on the defensive in Persia, was motivated by an animosity, almost a hostility, felt by officers of the Indian Army toward their brethren in its British counterpart. British officers serving with the British Army regarded a commission in the Indian Army as being somehow inferior, both professionally and socially, to their own service. The officers of the Indian Army were determined to prove to their British counterparts that they were every bit as competent and professional as the Brits, and that Indian soldiers lacked nothing in courage or fighting spirit when compared to the British "Tommies." As Nixon's successful progress up the Tigris and Euphrates rivers continued, London began to share some of the Indian government's enthusiasm, in no small part because the success was being accomplished at no cost to Britain, in either money, manpower, or material, but was being borne entirely by the Indian Empire.

Also, both London and New Delhi considered the political benefits of capturing Baghdad to more than justify the effort to take the city, for it was one of the four great cities of Islam (Mecca, Medina, and Damascus being the other three). Although it is easy in the early years of the twenty-first century, given the West's experience of the last decade, to overrate the importance of religion in the military, political, and social equation of the war in the Middle East, it cannot be marginalized or altogether dismissed either. The fatwa of November 14, 1914, which was issued in the name of the Sultan, Mehmed V, and endorsed by Essad Effendi, Sheikh-ul-Islam, commanded all Moslems around the world to rise up in arms against the Allies and assured them that "Of those who go to the Jihad for the sake of happiness and salvation of the believers in God's victory, the lot of those who remain alive is felicity, while the rank of those who depart to the next world is martyrdom. In accordance with God's beautiful promise, those who sacrifice their lives to give life to the truth will have honor in this world, and their latter end is paradise." The fatwa was at first a cause for serious alarm, particularly among the British, who feared uprisings in Egypt and India. Those fears were somewhat dispelled, at least where Egypt was concerned, following the failure of Djemal's Suez offensive, when the anticipated uprising among the Egyptians proved to be a damp squib.

In the case of the Indian Army, however, the question was whether Moslem Indians would fight against fellow Moslems. Ultimately, those fears would prove baseless, as India rallied to the Allied cause: more than 1.5 million Indians, two-fifths of whom were Moslem, volunteered to fight for the Allies during the course of the Great War. Eventually, some 800,000 Indian troops saw action, serving in every theater of the war. It was a costly effort, as, all told, 47,746 Indians were listed as killed or missing in action, with a further 65,000 wounded. The Indian soldiers were awarded 13,000 medals for gallantry, including 12 Victoria Crosses.

Yet all of this was in the future. In the days and the weeks immediately following the announcement of the fatwa calling for Holy War, the British and Indian governments had valid reasons to be chary of its effects. The modern fantasies of Western liberals notwithstanding, the Indian peoples have long traditions of warrior cultures, which played a crucial role in the way in which Indian soldiers resolved their attitudes to the war. Some Hindus held to the belief that soldiers killed in battle, in the service of the king, would end the cycle of death and reincarnation and send the soldier directly to paradise. Sikh soldiers were known to refer to fellow Sikhs who had fallen in battle as having "suffered martyrdom."

Most Moslem Indians came to accept the war against the Ottoman Turks as lawful, especially when Sheikh Hussein ibn Ali, the emir of Mecca, refused to endorse the Ottoman declaration of jihad, a vital point because the emir's approval was necessary for the Holy War to be spiritually binding on the faithful. The central point of his refusal, that "the Holy War is doctrinally incompatible with an aggressive war, and absurd with a Christian ally, namely Germany," laid bare the hypocrisy of Sheikh-ul-Islam's proclamation, for Enver, Djemal, and Talaat, who had drafted the fatwa and persuaded ul-Islam to publish it, were clearly not fighting for Islam but for their own worldly ends. For his part, Nixon believed that by taking Baghdad, any remaining credibility still clinging to the November 1914 proclamation would be stripped away, the city's fall being a clear demonstration of Allah's indifference to the Ottomans' illegitimate call to jihad. True, there were desertions by small numbers of Indian soldiers in the wake of the fatwa and at least three mutinies by Indian Moslems in other theaters of war, prompted by suspicions that they were going to be sent to fight against the Turks. But the most common reaction among the Indian soldiers, Moslem and Hindu alike, when they learned of such desertions or mutinies was unqualified disdain.

These motives, then, were propelling Nixon to press Townshend to drive on Baghdad with all due haste, while Townshend argued that further extending the British supply line—already some 360 miles (600 km) from the ports of the Persian Gulf—was reckless. Townshend also made specific requests for additional transports, extra machine guns, and trench mortars, as well as medical supplies, which were already becoming scarce, stating that his requisitions had to be filled before he could advance any farther up the Tigris. Nixon flatly overrode Townshend's objections and declined his requests, and ordered him to proceed; the advance of Nixon's Anglo-Indian command, now styled "the Tigris Corps," resumed in early October.

After Kut was taken, the Turks, now led by Col. Sakall Nureddin Pasha, fell back to the ruins of the ancient city of Ctesiphon, which sits astride the Tigris. There Nureddin began the construction of a carefully sited defensive position. Nureddin had chosen this site with skill: upstream of where the Shatt-al-Hai connects the Tigris with the Euphrates, the two rivers begin to gradually converge, until, when they are abreast of Ctesiphon, they are barely fifteen miles (twenty-four kilometers) apart. Because Nixon used the rivers as his supply routes, his troops could not operate far from them, and when the rivers were so close together, it restricted Nixon's operational radius, eliminating the possibility of sweeping flanking maneuvers that would allow the British to bypass Nureddin's defenses. Instead, in order to take Baghdad, they would have to fight the Turks on ground of Nureddin's choosing.

Sakall Nureddin was a fifty-two-year-old infantry officer born in Bursa, the son of an officer and a graduate of the Ottoman War Academy. The typical Ottoman Army officer regarded his position as a sinecure and, despite the best efforts of the German advisers, rarely considered his profession as one requiring intellectual effort. Nureddin was an exception. Intelligent—he spoke Arabic, French, Russian, and German, in addition to his native Turkish—he was one of the handful of Ottoman officers who were genuine students of military affairs. Wounded in the Greco-Turkish War of 1897, he was also decorated for bravery in the same conflict; by 1902 he was fighting insurgents in Macedonia. Assigned to headquarters, Third Army, in Salonika in 1907, he joined the march on Constantinople led by Major Niyazi in 1908. Although he doesn't appear to have been politically ambitious, his professional status rose swiftly following the 1908 revolution. That same year he was given command of an infantry battalion; an infantry regiment followed in 1910. The next year saw him in Yemen, fighting to suppress an Arab insurgency in the province. The real plum came in 1913, when he was named to the staff of Liman von Sanders's German Military Mission in Constantinople. Here he worked daily with the men who were reshaping the Ottoman Army, and he took to heart the lessons in warfare the German officers on the mission had to teach. A posting as officer commanding the Fourth Infantry Division was given to Nureddin in April 1914, and a year later he was given command of the Sixth Army. He arrived in Mesopotamia in June to take over for Colonel Subhai.

Subhai had done well in his efforts to defend Mesopotamia, given the limits placed on him by geography and the relatively few troops he had available. Nureddin realized that however unwittingly he may have done so, Subhai had drawn the Tigris Corps into a trap: by falling back along the two rivers, he had induced the Anglo-Indian Army into overextending its supply lines at the same time that its numbers were being reduced by combat and disease. It was obvious to everyone that Baghdad was the British objective. There was nothing else of military value in Mesopotamia, and the city would act as a magnet for British forces, hastening their destruction. Nureddin decided that the ground surrounding the ancient city of Ctesiphon, twenty miles (thirty-two kilometers) south of Baghdad and sitting astride the Tigris River, offered the best defensive possibilities and chose to make his stand there.

Colonel Nureddin had some eighteen thousand Turkish troops concentrated around Ctesiphon, many of them veterans of Subhai's withdrawal up the Tigris-Euphrates Valley. These experienced men were invaluable to Nureddin, as was the news coming out of Gallipoli, where the Turks were standing firm against the Allied landings, for the colonel was confident that he could stop the advance of the Tigris Corps. Plans were drawn up for creating two concentric lines of entrenchments around the southeastern perimeter of the ruins at Ctesiphon, which, given the flooding along the Tigris, was the only practical route of advance for the British. The defenders made judicious use of the terrain and carefully sited the Turkish artillery and machine guns. In order to negate the firepower advantage that the British gunboats gave Tigris Corps, mines were improvised and moored in the river.

As he advanced toward Ctesiphon, General Townshend had no idea that the eleven thousand troops of the Poona Division were outnumbered by the Turks waiting for him. He did know that reinforcement was unlikely but was confident that with the pair of Royal Navy gunboats accompanying his advance, he would have sufficient firepower to overwhelm the Turks when his forces finally encountered them. That happened on November 22, 1915, when Townshend sent his division into action against Nureddin's defenses on the east bank of the Tigris. His tactics were dictated, just as Nureddin had planned, by the impassible flood plain of the west bank and his limited numbers of troops.

Townshend was hoping to repeat the success of his attack on Kut six weeks earlier, when a night march set up a flanking maneuver supported by close-range shelling from the gunboats. But when one of his columns got lost approaching the Turkish positions at Ctesiphon, all surprise was lost, and the Indian infantry was pinned down by intense rifle and machine-gun fire from the Turkish entrenchments. The gunboats were unable to intervene, as they were repeatedly harassed by the Turks' artillery while at the same time having to dodge mines set drifting down the river.

Still, the Indian infantry fought as fiercely as always, breaking through the first line of trenches, but then bogged down before reaching the second line. The morning of November 23 brought a Turkish counterattack intended to retake the lost trench line. It was beaten back, but casualties on both sides were rising. By the end of the day, Townshend's division had lost forty-five hundred killed and wounded, while inflicting more than double that number on Nureddin's forces. Nureddin, startled by the determination with which the Indian soldiers pressed their attack, contemplated withdrawing from Ctesiphon before the Anglo-Indian reserves came up and cut off his line of retreat, but when no such reinforcements materialized, he began cautiously moving his units forward. Townshend, for his part, expecting that Turkish reserves were already making their way to Ctesiphon from Baghdad, ordered the Sixth Division to retreat back to Kut-al-Amara.

The retreat to Kut took ten days, the Indian infantry harried the entire way not only by the Turks, but by tribes of marsh Arabs who were equally hostile to British, Indian, and Turkish soldiers. Once within the perimeter at Kut, Townshend began organizing the defense of the town in the hope that support and relief were on their way. His troops were exhausted and disorganized, worn out by more than eight months of fighting and marching up the valley of the two rivers, wracked by disease, and plagued by a shortage of clean fresh water. The two gunboats that had accompanied the Poona Division to Ctesiphon had been left behind there, knocked out by Turkish artillery.

The Turks arrived on December 7, 1915, led by the man who had begun modernizing and reorganizing the Ottoman Army more than thirty years earlier, Wilhelm Leopold Colmar, Baron von der Goltz. Promoted to field marshal in 1911, von der Goltz had been sent back to the Ottoman Empire within days of the Turks' declaration of war on the Allies. Once back in Constantinople, he quickly found himself at odds with Enver: inevitably, the war minister recognized von der Goltz as being in the flesh the sort of soldier that Enver could only pretend to be. Consequently, using a professional disagreement between the field marshal and Gen. Liman von Sanders as a pretext, Enver effectively banished von der Goltz to what was anticipated to be a strategic and professional backwater—Mesopotamia.

Working as a team, von der Goltz and Nureddin quickly boxed in Townshend's forces at Kut, then made three attempts to drive through the Indian defenses, all of which were thrown back. Rather than persist in such pointless attacks, Nureddin chose to blockade the Sixth Division, keeping it bottled up at Kut while at the same time preventing any relief force from reaching it. What followed in the next 143 days would become known in history as the Siege of Kut.

While being cut off and surrounded by the enemy is not a position in which any general ever wants to find himself, Townshend didn't feel unduly alarmed. He was confident, given his supply situation, that with careful rationing his troops could hold out at Kut for at least two months. Surely, that would be enough time for General Nixon to bring up reinforcements, break through the Turkish perimeter, and relieve the Sixth Division. But then a message from Nixon got through to Townshend, informing him that it would be a minimum of two months before a relief operation could be organized and set into motion. On learning this, Townshend proposed to attempt a breakout by the Sixth Division down the Tigris, but Nixon, trying to save as much from the rapidly deteriorating situation as he could, insisted that Townshend and his troops remain at Kut.

Between the first week of January 1916 and the third week of April 1916, the British made five attempts to break through the Turkish defenses across the Tigris and rescue Townshend's trapped division. Inside the Kut perimeter, conditions went from bad to worse: food supplies began to run low, while fresh water, a problem during the entire campaign, all but ran out. The water of the Tigris and Euphrates rivers, though drinkable to the local populace, who had generations to physically adapt to the impurities and the parasites that thrived there, was undrinkable to the British and Indian soldiers. Those who tried were quickly laid low by disease. Sickness, especially typhus, began running through the ranks of Townshend's Indians, and a small but steady toll of casualties was being taken daily by sporadic Turkish rifle and artillery fire. By the fourth week of April, Townshend's men had lost on average more than 30 percent of their body weight, and half of them were incapacitated by wounds or disease. On April 26, almost five months after being cut off at Kut and with no real prospect of relief, Townshend contacted Colonel Nureddin and requested a six-day armistice, pending the surrender of his force. Nureddin, though he would later prove himself capable of extraordinarily ruthless actions, was in this case compassionate and agreed to send ten days' rations into the Indian position, along with supplies of water.

While the armistice ran its course, Townshend made certain that anything of military value inside his perimeter and within the town of Kut was destroyed. Townshend then sent a message to the military governor of Baghdad, Khalil Pasha, offering to buy a parole for his men, to the sum of £1 million, plus a guarantee that none of them would again be deployed in combat against Ottoman forces. Khalil was inclined to accept the offer, but when he forwarded it to Constantinople, Enver, now feeling far more courageous than he had a year earlier, refused, instead demanding Townshend's immediate surrender. The British general was informed of this on April 29, 1916, and Townshend, convinced, rightly as it turned out, that he had no other choice, surrendered. (As it happened, Field Marshal von der Goltz did not live to see the culmination of his final campaign: he died of typhus ten days before Townshend's capitulation.)

Approximately eight thousand Anglo-Indian troops became prisoners of war, all that was left of Townshend's division, which had begun the campaign with a strength of eleven thousand on the books. The number of remaining troops is necessarily vague, given what happened after the capitulation: Townshend was treated with great respect and courtesy, but his men suffered in Turkish captivity through harsh treatment, neglect, inadequate food, and lack of medical care. The exact numbers of those who surrendered and those who perished in captivity were never accurately totaled, Turkish record keeping being shoddy and incomplete, but it was determined that at least half of the Indian infantry who surrendered died during their time as POWs; the corresponding figure for British prisoners was seven in ten. In addition to the loss of the Sixth Division at Kut, the British also suffered twenty-three thousand additional killed, wounded, and sick during the five attempts at relieving Kut; Turkish casualties numbered some ten thousand.

The surrender of Townshend's garrison at Kut was the greatest humiliation ever suffered by an imperial army in the whole history of the British Empire. Coming as it did just three short months after the final withdrawal from Gallipoli, it sent a shock through the entire British military establishment. The War Cabinet, seeing the disaster as a direct consequence of the Indian government's aggressive "forward defense" policy, removed the entire Mesopotamian theater from Indian authority and replaced its Indian Army commanders with British Army officers. Maj. Gen. Sir Frederick Maude took command of the entire front in June 1916 and began an effective reorganization of the supply system and the medical services, but it would be more than six months before any new offensive action would be possible.

In purely military terms, Kut was neither a great victory for the Turks nor a truly serious defeat for the British. Constantinople continued to have little use for Mesopotamia, and the loss of a single under-strength division was far from critical to Britain's war effort, in the Middle East or elsewhere. Yet what Kut *represented* was something else entirely. The blunt truth of the strategic situation in the Middle East at the beginning of the summer of 1916 was that the Turkish Army, after its initial reverses and contrary to all expectations, had fought the Allies to a standstill on every front. Outmanned, outgunned, underequipped, poorly fed, and inadequately trained, *it had fought the Allies to a standstill.* Even more astonishing was that it had done so single-handedly, for aside from the scattering of advisers sent to the Ottoman Empire by the German Army, the Turks had been given no assistance, apart from munitions and supplies, and none of the sort of reinforcement that Germany was already using to prop up the sagging Austro-Hungarian armies. Even the Russians had been turned back in June 1916, having tried to advance into Mesopotamia from the northeast, through Persia.

June 1916 could have been the defining moment for the Three Pashas, the Young Turks, and the Ottoman Empire, had Enver, Talaat, and Djemal possessed the wisdom to recognize it. Had they been men as big as they pretended to be, they would have seized it; had they been the statesmen they imagined they were, they would have embraced it. The opportunity was presented to them to make the presence of the Ottoman Empire in the Great War, for which there had been no real reason or purpose, actually meaningful: it would have legitimized all of their follies and mitigated all of their errors. Instead, they let the moment pass without so much as a word of acknowledgment or recognition.

That moment was the opportunity to seek peace with the Allies on terms that would have cost Great Britain, France, and Russia but little in prestige, treasure, or territory, yet would have gained for the Ottoman Turks tremendous stature among the powers of the world. The summer of 1916 would be the psychological turning point of the Great War, when feelings on both sides, Allies and Central Powers, would begin to irrevocably harden and the opportunities for a negotiated peace rapidly diminish into nothing. Already in Great Britain, a powerful bitterness toward Germany was growing, fueled by reports of officially sanctioned atrocities committed against Belgian civilians by the German Army, the sinking of the passenger liner *Lusitania* in May 1915, and the execution of Nurse Edith Cavell in October of that same year. The French, of course, were already irredeemably hostile to the Germans, while the Russians despised their German foes equally with their Austro-Hungarian ones. For all three of the Allied powers, however, the Ottoman Empire was a minor player, regarded with disdain, even contempt, but with none of the hatred that was daily increasing toward the German Empire.

This lack of any deep-seated animosity toward the Turks would have allowed the Allies to make peace with the Ottoman Empire—*if only the Turks were to make an offer.* The realities of international politics were such that none of the Allied powers could approach the Turks with an offer to make peace. Such a gesture could never come from Whitehall in London or the Quai D'Orsay in Paris. To make such an offer would, in political terms, be perceived as an admission of weakness, with a commensurate loss of prestige, the currency of international diplomacy. But should the offer come from Constantinople, it would be seen as being made from a position of strength, in effect saying, "We have withstood your best efforts to defeat us, now let us all be reasonable and end this fighting that is gaining none of us anything." Accepting such an offer would have allowed the Allied governments to appear deliberate and rational and would have placed significant pressure on imperial Germany to begin exploring similar options, lest her own reputation be diminished among the neutral powers whose goodwill German diplomats were working so assiduously to cultivate.

Such a settlement was neither unreasonable nor impossible. The Turks could not have realistically expected any sort of territorial concessions from the Allies, but guarantees of the territorial integrity of the Ottoman Empire would have been a given. Indemnities would have been paid, by the Turks to Russia for the destruction caused by Admiral Souchon in the autumn of 1914, and by the British and the French for the havoc created at Gallipoli. The amounts might have been more symbolic than substantial but would have served their purpose. A settlement would have released tens of thousands of British and imperial troops to be transferred to France, along with scores of Royal Navy cruisers and destroyers for service with the Grand Fleet in the North Sea or in the open reaches of the North Atlantic. The sea route to Russia, through the Bosporus and the Dardanelles, would have been re-opened, averting the disasters of the two revolutions of 1917 and the seven decades of Bolshevik terror that followed them. With a decently equipped and supplied Russian Army still fighting in 1917, the Allies' numerical superiority might well have proved decisive and brought the war to a halt a year before it actually ended.

For the Ottomans, especially the Young Turks and in particular the Three Pashas, peace would have given them and their regime an unshakable legitimacy: the international prestige of the Ottoman Empire would have been revived and the legacy of the "Sick Man of Europe" laid to rest once and for all. The Turks could no longer be marginalized as they had been for the last century; if not quite perceived as one of the Great Powers, the rest of the world would understand that the Ottoman Empire was strong, and the voice of the Turks would be heard in the councils of the world.

Even more important was that with such legitimacy, the Young Turks would have bought themselves time. It was their misfortune, as well as that of the empire, that hardly had they taken power in 1908 and begun learning how to govern that they were thrown into three successive wars that drained away the time, the money, and the resources that were badly needed for the reforms they wanted to enact. A peace settlement with the Allies in 1916 would have given them that time and in the same moment would have assured them that the Greeks, the Bulgars, or the Macedonians were not about to try conclusions with a newly resurgent Turkish Army.

Yet the offer was never made. There is, in fact, no evidence to suggest that such an offer was ever even considered by the Three Pashas or anyone else in the Turkish Cabinet. This failure, more than anything else a failure of perception, of vision, of imagination, reveals just what little men Enver, Djemal, and Talaat truly were. Enver, with his shopkeeper mentality, could only imagine what bigger and better deals he could make at the negotiating table if his armies won even greater victories. Djemal, the eternal counterrevolutionary, simply lacked the intellectual breadth and depth to embrace the political calculus of such an idea: his horizons defined by the murky world of plot and counterplot, he lacked the mental machinery to think in truly international terms.

Yet although the failure of Enver and Djemal, the petty merchant and the conspirator, to imagine the possibilities inherent in making peace with the Allies in 1916 is understandable, the inability of Talaat to conceive of them is almost impossible to comprehend. Far better educated, more sophisticated, and more urbane than Enver or Djemal, Talaat, because of his aristocratic background, was also better acquainted with the nuances of international relations. There was certainly an element of loyalty to the alliance with Germany that Talaat and Enver had labored hard to cultivate and that Enver had finally sprung on the Ottoman Turks as a fait accompli, but invocations of loyalty to an alliance with foreign power do not excuse senior statesmen from their duty to do their best by their country. Yet it appears, as absurd as it may seem nearly a century later, that Enver, Talaat, and Djemal, separately and together, never saw the wisdom of ending the war in the Middle East at the moment when the Ottoman Empire could come out of the conflict on the positive side of the balance ledger. Had they truly regarded the situation thoughtfully, they would have seen that this was an opportunity that could never again come the Turks' way. Fully half of the Turkish Army had been deployed in Gallipoli trying to stop the British advance up the peninsula. For Great Britain, that was just one of many fronts the British Empire was able to sustain and even expand. The British forces in Mesopotamia were being reorganized and reinforced, while a new army was assembling in Egypt for an offensive into Palestine, with its ultimate objective being the capture of Damascus. The Ottoman Army had already run out of reserves: there would be no more reinforcements for units already in the field, and new units could be created only by scraping together the remnants of other units already broken up in battle. The Turks had indeed stopped the Allies cold in the summer of 1916, but in doing so they had drawn on every last bit of strength the Ottoman Empire could muster. Worse was to come, for instead of making peace at the moment when it would have held the moral high ground, the Ottoman Empire was about to suffer near universal condemnation that would last decades, as the world began to learn in the autumn of 1916 that the Ottoman Turks stood accused of one of the most barbaric acts of the twentieth century—the Armenian holocaust.

CHAPTER SEVEN
ARMENIAN AGONY

No one could have believed that when the Russian Caucasus Army struck across the Ottoman border in November 1914, driving toward the city of Bayazid, it was setting into motion a series of events that would culminate in one of the great human tragedies of the twentieth century. No one could have dreamed that the mere presence of four battalions of Russian-born Armenian infantry would have such dreadful consequences for the millions of Armenians who were subjects of the Ottoman Empire. Few men even considered the existence of an "Armenian question" before the events of 1915, and yet by the time the dust, the blood, and the tears had settled three years later, a chasm of bitter hatred yawned between Armenian and Turk, one that remains, gaping and ugly, to this day, with no sign yet visible of its closing.

Of course, the presence of those four battalions of infantry was itself hardly sufficient cause to trigger what would come to be called the Armenian Genocide; the origins of the tragedy went much deeper. Yet they undeniably acted as the catalyst for the events that followed, and so they serve as an appropriate, as well as convenient, point of departure for any accounting of that tragedy. Like so many of the other threats that hedged about the Sultan's realm in its last decade, however, the origins of the "Armenian question"—what was to become of the Armenian people—were to be found both within and without the Ottoman Empire long before the Great War.

One of the most pernicious problems besetting the Ottoman Turks lay in the persistence with which they maintained the exclusivity of their "Ottoman" Empire, existing and functioning solely for the benefit of the Ottoman Turks. The Sultan's non-Turkish subjects—Armenians, Kurds, Arabs, Jews, Farsi, Greeks, Bulgars, and such—were naturally consigned to second-class-citizen status, in strict accordance with the Moslem *dhimmi* law, which carefully prescribes and proscribes the legal status of non-Moslems living in a Moslem state. As such, they were assured of the right to worship as they chose, which to most of these peoples was no small matter, but, in the eyes of Ottoman law, in all other respects they were never considered the equal of the Sultan's Moslem subjects. The exclusions were numerous and petty: non-Moslems were forbidden to ride horses or carry weapons, their houses could not be sited higher than those of their Moslem neighbors, and religious practices would have to defer to Islamic customs. In the courts, Jews and Christians were not allowed to act as witnesses giving evidence against Moslems, nor were they permitted to bring criminal charges or civil actions against Moslems. Punishment for violating these laws was harsh, execution being the most common retribution. Even the Arabs, who were fellow Moslems, had many of the same limitations imposed on them in regard to Turks.

While such customs had been characteristic of empires throughout history, what set apart the relationship between the Ottoman Turks and their non-Turkish subjects was the absence of anything that resembled a social contract. The Christians and the Jews could till their farms, mind their shops, and ply their trades, the Arabs and the Kurds could tend their flocks and herds, all in relative peace and security, so long as they paid their taxes and obeyed the Sultan's laws. Yet there was no hope for any of them that they could ever better their condition: their children, grandchildren, and great-grandchildren would be born into, then live and die in the same second-class status their parents and grandparents had known. There were no opportunities for a non-Turk to serve in the bureaucracy or the imperial army or navy, to find a better station in Ottoman society. It was this consignment to eternal inferiority that had made the prospect of giving their sons to the Janissaries so attractive to the empire's Christians until the regiments were disbanded, because a Janissary's descendants were considered Ottoman Turks in the eyes of the laws of the empire.

Nor were the numbers of the minorities so stigmatized insignificant. Experts put the population of the empire in 1914 at almost 21 million people, a quarter of whom weren't Turkish. (Figures for the empire's population at the beginning of the First World War range from a low of 18 million to a high of 26 million, but the figure of 21 million is best supported by the limited documentation available. Compared to European bureaucracies, particularly those of Germany and Great Britain, Ottoman record keeping was abysmally bad.) That such a large proportion of the Sultan's subjects were thus marginalized might have been a cause for anxiety in the Sublime Porte, had any of them felt in the slightest way empowered. But they were not: in the realpolitik calculus of nineteenth-century diplomacy and international position jockeying, advocating for any of the minorities of the Ottoman Empire offered no advantage to the Great Powers. There was no one to give those minorities a voice, and so they remained marginalized.

That is, until the last quarter of the nineteenth century. In the wake of the Russo-Turkish War of 1877, Tsar Alexander II of Russia, having already made himself the champion of the Balkan Christians, decided to take a paternal interest in all of the Christians in the Ottoman Empire—including the Christians of Armenia. As a region, Armenia was geographically divided almost evenly between the Ottoman Empire and imperial Russia. It embraced what is now the northeast corner of modern Turkey, northern Iraq, northwestern Iran, southern Georgia, and Azerbaijan and was home to Kurds as well as Armenians. Under Alexander's rule, Russia's Armenians had seen their culture, particularly Armenian literature, undergo something of a renaissance at the same time that Russian rule began to have a "Westernizing" effect on Armenia, turning the focus of the region more toward Europe and away from the Middle East.

When Alexander III took the Russian throne following the assassination of his father in 1881, the attitude of the Russian government toward ethnic minorities living within the Russian Empire changed dramatically. Ultraconservative and determined to create a highly centralized, autocratic state, the new tsar feared that encouraging non-Russian cultural identities would result in separatism and rebellion. His solution was to introduce a sweeping program he called Russification, hoping to create a homogenous Russian culture throughout the whole of his empire; the key to accomplishing this was the suppression of non-Russian ethnic cultures.

Alexander III undoubtedly knew that this was a hopeless objective, but he clearly believed that Russification could create a society where all of his subjects identified themselves as Russian first and then as part of an ethnic group second.

However unrealistic his goals within his own borders, what was painfully obvious to Armenians living in the Ottoman Empire was that their brethren living under the tsar were not subject to the permanent social stratification that they knew under Turkish rule, with its corresponding consignment to inferiority. Although the ideal of a separate, independent Armenian homeland may have been the dream of the most ardent Armenian patriot, even the reality of life under the tsar was, for the vast majority of Turkish Armenians, a far more attractive alternative than the reality of their current existence.

A corner was turned in the relationship between the Turks and the Armenians in 1894, when, without any apparent provocation, the Sultan, Abdul-Hamid II, began to encourage increasingly violent persecution of the Christian minorities living in Anatolia, which resulted in a succession of massacres. Specifically targeted were the Armenians, who in turn resisted as best they could, believing that the protections assured them under the Treaty of Berlin, which had ended the Russo-Turkish War in 1878, would compel the European powers to intervene—by force if need be—should the Sultan revert to his homicidal habits. Yet the Armenians lacked any champions in the capitals of Europe to press their case, which, coupled with the Europeans' general indifference to the empire's internal affairs, meant that such protection was not forthcoming. In response, however, a number of provincial governors began inciting the local Turkish population against their non-Moslem neighbors. The violence spread to nearly every Armenian town and village in the empire, while the Sultan sent the army into Armenia proper, where, at times working with bands of Kurdish irregulars armed with Ottoman-supplied weapons, tens of thousands of Armenians were slaughtered. The most notorious incident took place in the city of Urfa, where the cathedral, with some three thousand Armenian refugees huddled inside seeking sanctuary, was burned to the ground.

Some Europeans did take note of what was happening but offered little more than rhetoric. The French ambassador, in an official report to the Quai D'Orsay in Paris, described Turkey as "literally in flames," with "massacres everywhere"; the Turks were "gradually annihilating the Christian element" by "giving the Kurdish chieftains carte blanche to do whatever they please, to enrich themselves at the Christians' expense and to satisfy their men's whims." The killing lasted for more than two years; in 1897 Abdul-Hamid, as abruptly as he had begun, declared the Armenian question "closed." Naturally, Turkish records were imprecise, but the death toll, once the smoke cleared and the blood and the dust settled, counted between 100,000 and 300,000 Armenians killed.

For the next decade, a sort of uneasy truce existed, but in 1908, when the Young Turks stripped the Sultan of all effective power, it seemed that the relationship between the Turks and the Armenians had finally taken a decisive turn for the better. The inclusion of Armenian representatives in the first Turkish parliament seemed to assure their people a secure place in the empire. While ties between Armenians living on either side of the Russo-Turkish border inevitably remained close, there was little evidence that those living in Anatolia were still anxiously coveting a separate homeland.

Even when the Turks unexpectedly declared war on the Allies at the end of October 1914, no one in Constantinople anticipated trouble from the Armenians. Yet circumstances abruptly changed that expectation. The Turks' declaration of war caught the Russian forces in the Caucasus off guard. Having been used as a reserve of trained troops to reinforce the Russian Army units embattled with the Germans and the Austro-Hungarians, the Caucasus Army was badly under strength, so it was hardly surprising that the Russians would seek to exploit the resentment that still burned bright among Armenians on both sides of the Russo-Turkish border by enlisting Armenian irregulars to fight alongside Russian units. When the Caucasus Army lunged into northeastern Anatolia, four battalions of Armenian troops marched with it; ultimately, more than 150,000 Armenians would serve with the tsar's armies.

The Russians were quick to give credit to their Armenian auxiliaries for a large measure of the Caucasus Army's success in trapping the Turkish IX Corps at the Battle of Sakiramish, encouraging open resistance to the Turks among the more fiery elements of the empire's Armenian population. Whether the tsar's government ever truly intended to incite a revolt is still unclear, but in Constantinople the prospect of collusion between the Russians and the Armenians appeared to be a very real possibility. This came as a surprise to the Three Pashas, as the Young Turks, in an effort to distance themselves from the barbarities of Abdul-Hamid, had tried to address the worst of the inequities of the old imperial social system and believed that they had succeeded. But "address" was not "redress," and fully integrating the empire's minorities with the Turkish population was incompatible with Enver and Talaat's ideas of a greater Turkish state and "Ottomanism."

Djevdet Bey, who was, ominously enough, Enver's brother-in-law, was the governor of Van province, the heart of Turkish Armenia, and seems to be the catalyst for the tragedy that would follow. He was described by a foreign contemporary as "a man of dangerously unpredictable moods, friendly one moment, ferociously hostile the next, capable of treacherous brutality"—hardly a sterling character reference but unquestionably describing an individual capable of enormous cruelty. In February 1915, determined to test the loyalty of the empire's Armenian population, he demanded that the city of Van provide a levy of four thousand conscripts, in direct contravention of Ottoman law forbidding Christians to bear arms or serve in the army. Suspecting that his intent was to hold them as hostages or execute them outright—Djevdet had ordered the execution of eight hundred men, women, and children in Salmas province in early March—the leaders of Van temporized; negotiations went back and forth for several weeks, until mid-April, when tensions finally ratcheted to the breaking point.

On February 25, 1915, Talaat's ministry of the interior, in a state of near panic over the defeat of the Suez Expedition, Enver's humiliation in the Caucasus, and the rumors of a pending British naval assault on Constantinople, issued Directive 8682, "Increased Security Precautions." Specifically directed at the Sultan's Armenian subjects, the directive was prompted by the increasingly open activities of dissidents across Turkish Armenia. There was evidence, attested to by foreign observers, that some Armenian communities had been stockpiling weapons and bombs. Djevdet seized on this as an excuse for punitive raids that burned villages and towns, and he randomly ordered the execution of their inhabitants when the mood struck him. On April 24 Talaat attempted to defuse a situation that he realized was ready to explode by depriving any pending Armenian revolt of its leadership, issuing an order for the arrest of the leaders of the Armenian community in Constantinople, along with those in the larger Armenian towns and villages. They were to be transported to two holding centers located near Ankara, in the heart of Anatolia. A crucial passage (that is, in light of what would shortly transpire) of the order read, "The measures taken shall be realized justly; and should there be any arrests after the thorough investigations of the documents the criminals shall be sent to the military courts immediately"—a clear statement of Talaat's intent to follow established legal procedures.

Yet Talaat's order, though carried out, came as too little, too late. On April 20, in response to an alleged affront to an Armenian woman by a pair of Turkish soldiers, agitators in Van attacked a Turkish patrol. The Ottoman garrison reacted

predictably, turning its artillery on the sections of the city where the suspected at-
tackers lived. Turkish units began to converge on Van, and within days the city was
effectively under siege. In advance of the Turkish troops came a flood of refugees
from the surrounding countryside, numbering approximately fifteen thousand. A
local government was formed inside the city, and the Turks living within Van began evacuating—by the middle of May the last of them had been able to escape by
sailing west across Lake Van.

A week after the revolt began, a Russian column started to move toward the
city, with the intent of raising the siege. The first Russian forces reached Van on
May 18, with a detachment under General Yudenich arriving on May 23. Yudenich
promptly recognized the provisional government, a disastrous decision for the Armenians, for it provided the justification for the actions taken by the Turks in retaliation for the revolt.

On May 29, 1915, six days after Yudenich's entry into Van, the Central Committee of the CUP passed the "Temporary Law of Deportation" (called the Tehcir
Law), granting the Turkish civil and military authorities the power to deport anyone who was deemed a threat to national security. Written in four parts, it was a
civil law, rather than a military one. It first addressed the military measures against
anyone who opposed the orders of the government or obstructed the national defense, as well as those who were responsible for organizing armed resistance, and
the treatment of rebels during wartime. Next, it dealt with the transfer of people
in villages or towns deemed to be in rebellion against the Constantinople regime,
the temporary nature of the law, and its applicability, that is, to whom it was to
be applied. Under the circumstances, there could be little doubt toward which of
the empire's subject peoples the law was directed (the law was provisionally titled
"Regulation for the settlement of Armenians relocated to other places because of
war conditions and emergency political requirements"), although it was in letter
only marginally more harsh than similar legislation passed by the warring European powers in regard to foreign nationals within their own borders.

What turned the Tehcir Law into a nightmare was the incompetence and inefficiency of the Ottoman bureaucracy. Orders went out to regional authorities and
provincial governors across Anatolia to relocate hundreds of thousands of Armenians in an effort to dislocate and defuse what Constantinople feared was a rising
Armenian rebellion, orders that had to be carried out under the threat of answering

to the *Teşkilat-i Mahsusa*, who had a particular expertise in making people who crossed or displeased the Three Pashas disappear. Yet with the orders came no instructions or guidance as to how they were to be accomplished. In essence, the provincial authorities were told, "Get the Armenians out," without being instructed how it was expected that this would be accomplished or where the displaced people were to go. If the plan was to be a deportation and a relocation, then transportation, routing, supplies of food and water, shelter—the necessities required to move so many people—were nowhere to be found. Instead, local government officials and mid-level army officers, knowing that they were expected to comply with their orders—or else—resorted to whatever means were at hand in order to carry them out. The results were predictably tragic and horrible and produced an Armenian agony that has since evolved into the tale of the Armenian Genocide.

Beginning in early June 1915, hundreds of thousands of Armenians were turned out of their homes at gun and bayonet point. For months to come, on roads across the length of Anatolia could be seen processions, some small, others large, some just a handful of individuals, men, women, and children, their only belongings what they could carry on their backs, with literally nowhere to go. Tens of thousands would die of starvation and exposure; other tens of thousands would succumb to disease, most particularly typhus. Often their bodies were left to decompose where they died. More sinister, off in distant fields or gullies would be found rows of corpses, Armenians of both genders and all ages shot out of hand by Turkish soldiers. A sort of frenzy overtook the Ottoman Army units assigned to the task of removing the Armenians from their homes, and scenes of wholesale rape and slaughter were common as Turkish troops moved through Armenian villages and towns.

In some places, detention areas (they were far too crude to call them "camps") were created, but they were little more than vast open tracts lacking water and shelter. Kurdish tribesmen hired as guards were given carte blanche to rob, pillage, rape, and plunder the refugees. One eyewitness reported seeing the bodies of nearly ten thousand Armenians dumped into several ravines near Lake Göeljuk, later referring to this region as the "slaughterhouse province." Elsewhere—and whether this was done out of convenience or sadism will never be known—schools were used as holding centers for children, who were then executed in the classrooms. Neutral governments, including that of the United States, tried to intervene on behalf of the Armenians, as did Pope Benedict XV, but their overtures were rebuffed by Enver, who claimed that the deportations were being carried out in retaliation for the pro-Russian insurrection at Van.

Exactly how and why the Turks committed such a monstrous atrocity is hotly, even violently, debated to this day. Ethnic Armenians, particularly those living abroad, argue that Constantinople's policy of deportation was a thinly disguised attempt at systematically eliminating the entire Armenian people—an Armenian holocaust, the first example of what would become a dismayingly recurrent theme in the twentieth century: genocide. Claims are made by some Armenian apologists that as many as 1.5 million Armenian men, women, and children were methodically put to death by their Turkish overlords between 1915 and 1918. It was, they claim, an effort to rid the empire of a particularly troublesome minority, a process begun in the early 1880s under Abdul-Hamid II and continued during the regime of the Three Pashas. The massacres of 1915–18 are said to be the ultimate expression of the Young Turks' philosophy of "Ottomanism," which was halted only when the Ottoman government and the imperial infrastructure collapsed in October 1918. Not surprisingly, Turkish officials to this day deny—with considerable vehemence—that there was ever any deliberate government policy promulgated to exterminate the Armenian people. That there were deaths numbering in the hundreds of thousands among the empire's Armenian population is not denied: what is contested is the scale of the slaughter, the methods by which it was carried out, and the ultimate responsibility for the atrocities.

There is no consensus on how many Armenians lost their lives during the Armenian holocaust, and the death toll will never be known with any exactitude. Estimates vary between 300,000 (the figure acknowledged by modern Turkey) to 1.5 million (according to some of the more extreme Armenian spokespersons); there is a general agreement among Western scholars that at least 500,000 Armenians died between 1914 and 1918. British historian Arnold Toynbee, who served as an intelligence officer of the British Foreign Office during the Great War, put forward an estimate that 600,000 Armenians "died or were massacred during deportation" as the Tehcir Law was carried out. Whatever the final figure, the undeniable truth is that the Armenian people had suffered dreadfully. The pre-war Armenian population of the Ottoman Empire has been reliably estimated by Professor Guenter Lewy at 1,750,000: whatever figure is cited for the final death toll of the Armenian deportations and massacres, both in absolute numbers and as a proportion of the Armenian populace, it was a catastrophe—and undeniably a crime against humanity.

But was it a genocide?

That is a loaded question, one fraught with an unbelievable weight of emotional, political, and social baggage. Hundreds of thousands of Armenians fled Ottoman Turkey between 1915 and 1918, escaping as best they could into Russia, Persia, Greece, or the islands of the Aegean Sea, many of them eventually making their way into western Europe and the United States. With them, they brought tales of the Tehcir Law deportations and the deaths that followed in their wake. The tales grew in the telling, aided by receptive Western audiences who, imbued with centuries of prejudice against the horrid Turks, were ready to believe any story, however lurid, put forward about the Ottoman Empire. The Armenians were perceived (and were careful to present themselves) as fellow Christians fearsomely persecuted by the Islamic infidels who were capable of any cruelty against true believers.

To bolster the Armenian case, an impressive array of documentation supporting their claims has been assembled in the years since 1918. During the war, tracts, pamphlets, and a few book-length works produced under the supervision of various Allied governments appeared in the West purporting to document the Armenian genocide. (The word "genocide" itself would not be created until 1943, so the events depicted were usually termed "massacres.") After the war, the testimonies of hundreds of eyewitnesses to some aspect or another of the massacres were collected, and it should be noted that not all of the statements came from the Turks' former foes. Significantly, among the documents were accounts from German and Austro-Hungarian officers and government officials, erstwhile allies of the Ottoman Turks. Numerous atrocities committed by Turkish soldiers or Kurdish irregulars in Turkish service were documented by missionaries living and working in Anatolia. Winston Churchill openly declared that the massacres were "an administrative holocaust." During the war, the American ambassador (the United States remained neutral until April 1917), Henry Morgenthau, confronted both Enver and Talaat with accounts he had gathered of the extent and the ruthlessness of the deportations and their lethal consequences, demanding a cessation of the deportations. Morgenthau's reports would become a cornerstone of the evidentiary edifice supporting the Armenians' claims that they had been the subjects of a genuine, systematic process of genocide. The body of evidence, if sheer bulk alone were sufficient, would appear to be compelling.

And yet there is something patently phony about the Armenian version of the events of 1915. Like the Player Queen, the Armenians "doth protest too much." They are too shrill, too strident, too adamant in their refusal to answer rational queries or respond to objections with reason and evidence. Objectors are shouted down or overwhelmed with scorn or derision. Anyone questioning their evidence or their conclusions is immediately accused of having a "pro-Turkish" bias or being "anti-Armenian." Nor does the Armenian persecution of those who refuse to unquestioningly embrace their version of the events of 1915–18 stop at mere verbal harassment. Armenian interest groups have persistently tried to have major American and European universities suppress the academic work of faculty who refuse to parrot the Armenian story. In 1978, Armenian activists bombed the Los Angeles, California, home of a UCLA professor who specialized in Turkish studies and who in his course work did not sufficiently demonize the Turks or present the Armenians in a properly martyrlike light.

The volume alone of the recollections and the testimony of people who claimed to have been eyewitnesses to some aspect of the death toll in Anatolia must give a degree of credence to the overall story told by the Armenian survivors. At the same time, it is impossible to ignore the propaganda value, both during the war and in its immediate aftermath, of such reports of atrocities. They were as invaluable to the Allies as the tales of German atrocities in Belgium (which were much better documented but still suffered from elements of exaggeration and fabrication) in sustaining civilian morale at home by reassuring the public of the rightness of the Allied cause and the necessity of ultimate victory over the Central Powers. After the war, such sustenance became even more vital, in order to assuage the grief of the bereaved among the populations of the "victorious" Allies, suffusing them with the knowledge that their sons, brothers, husbands, and fathers had not died in vain but had made their supreme sacrifice in order that such horrors would never again be perpetrated. Consequently, those eyewitness accounts of the Armenian massacres must be taken with a few grains of salt, not for doubts of their overall veracity, but rather for the selectivity with which they have been presented.

Moreover, in their zeal to make their case, the Armenians have been known to resort to outright fabrication. Rumors have been spread, without supporting evidence, about gas chambers, germ warfare, doctors who were recruited to aid in the extermination by extensive lethal-injection programs, special execution squads, and concentration camps that became extermination centers. As the years pass the story grows, until the Armenian massacres begin to take on the appearance of the dress rehearsal for Nazi Germany's "Final Solution" of 1942–45.

Perhaps the best example of this sort of fabrication is found in the history of one of the pieces of "evidence" that is the most damning to the Turks. Repeatedly cited as proof that the Tehcir deportations were part of a larger government-led conspiracy to exterminate the Armenian people is the text of a telegram that is said to be authored by Talaat himself. The communication first appeared in a book titled *The Memoirs of Naim Bey: Turkish Official Documents Relating to the Deportation and the Massacres of Armenians*, written by Aram Andonian and published in London by Hodder & Stoughton in 1920. The documents have become known collectively as "the Talaat telegrams"; the key passage is an alleged order from the minister of the interior that reads, "Although the extermination of the Armenians had been decided upon earlier than this, circumstances did not permit us to carry out this sacred intention. Now that all obstacles are removed, it is urgently recommended that you should not be moved for feelings of pity on seeing their miserable plight, but by putting an end to them all, try with all your might for obliterate the very name 'Armenia' from Turkey."

When subjected to critical analysis, the telegrams, which were reproduced in the book in facsimile form, proved to be of extremely dubious provenance. Signatures were shown to be obvious forgeries, dates do not correlate, there are errors in the cipher groups supposedly used to encode the telegrams, and the texts themselves are fraught with the sort of grammatical and idiomatic mistakes that someone translating into Turkish from another language would make. Perhaps most damning of all in regard to the authenticity of the telegrams is that it has been variously claimed by some sources that the originals are in the possession of an Armenian Studies Centre in Manchester, England, where repeated requests to view them and compare them with the facsimiles have been denied without explanation; other sources state that the originals were lost while in the keeping of Aram Andonian.

One of the most persuasive voices of counterpoint to the charge of genocide is that of a British scholar, Professor Bernard Lewis. A former intelligence officer with the British Army and a specialist on the Middle East, he had at one time written of "the terrible holocaust of 1915," accepting the figure of 1.5 million Armenian dead. Later, however, he came to believe that the term "genocide" was inapplicable, because the massacres, though undeniable, were not "a deliberate preconceived decision of the Turkish government." This opinion has been joined by Guenter Lewy, one of the world's preeminent genocide scholars.

The Ottoman Empire, they argue, simply did not possess the resources necessary for such a program of genocide, even had one been formulated and implemented; the atrocities and the acts of violence were the actions of low- and mid-level officials and officers taking their orders to extreme ends and exceeding their authority. Given the near legendary incompetence and inefficiency of the Ottoman bureaucracy in the empire's waning years, it is inconceivable that a conspiracy as far-flung and complex as a campaign of ethnic extermination could have been put into motion across the whole of Anatolia and with the degree of success that Armenian apologists maintain was achieved. Moreover, the manpower required for killings on such a massive scale simply was not available to the Turks. In the summer, the fall, and the winter of 1915, full half of the Ottoman Army was deployed in the Gallipoli Peninsula, holding off the British and the ANZACs, while more than two-thirds of the army's remaining eighteen divisions were stationed in Mesopotamia, Palestine, and Arabia, with three others posted along Ottoman borders shared with Bulgaria and Greece. There was even a division of Ottoman infantry fighting alongside the Austrians in Hungary, where no Turkish soldier had set foot in more than two centuries. Perhaps two divisions of infantry —twenty thousand troops—were available for deployment in the whole of Anatolia, far from sufficient numbers to be able to carry out the sort of wholesale slaughter of which they are accused. Killings on such a scale were simply beyond the manpower available to the Ottoman Turks.

The obstacle that looms largest before the Armenian claims of genocide is the absence of premeditation: to truly be called a genocide, the acts so described must be part of an overall plan of extermination, conceived as such in advance of the deed and carried out at the behest of the government in power. The existence of such premeditation and planning the Armenians have never been able to establish against the Turks without resort to distorting or falsifying the evidence.

The massacres of 1915–18 were, beyond question, a catastrophe for the Armenian people. In some ways, it could even be argued that they were worse than a genocide, for undertaking a campaign of racial or ethnic extermination implies that the people to be extinguished are in some way possessed of sufficient power to represent a clear and present danger to the society demanding their destruction. And that lack of premeditation is, in its own perverse way, a greater humiliation. In some respects, indifference is even more degrading than damnation—the victims, the Ottoman Empire's Armenians, were denied even the perverse dignity of open condemnation. Rather than being the product of deliberate policy, the massacres were the consequence of ill-conceived orders, rashly issued without explanation or elaboration to mid-level officers and officials, who in turn lacked the means to carry them out properly. Left to their own devices, in order to be able to fulfill the letter of their instructions, the men responsible simply resorted to whatever methods were at hand to do so. The simplest and most effective solution was often to simply put the Armenians literally on the road to nowhere and let nature, banditry, and the more bloodthirsty of their soldiers have their way. And it cannot be denied that some interpreted their instructions as authorization for mass executions: those thousands of corpses found in ravines near Lake Göeljuk weren't figment of some fevered imagination. Yet to characterize the Armenian massacres of 1915–18 as a genocide is to misunderstand the word, the situation, the peoples, and the deeds.

None of this should be construed as an exoneration of the Ottoman Empire, the Young Turks, or the Three Pashas, however: their hands remain covered with innocent blood. What happened in Anatolia between 1915 and 1918 may not have been a genocide in the strict definition of the word, but it was beyond any argument a crime against humanity. There is no way to ignore or explain away how between 500,000 and 600,000 Armenians died as a direct or indirect consequence of actions taken by the Ottoman Turks. In the decades since the war, the Republic of Turkey has striven to promote the idea that the Armenians who perished were somehow legitimate casualties of war. There was no genocide, it is said—correctly—but there *was* a war being waged, and the hundreds of thousands of Armenian deaths, while regrettable, are construed as being somehow justifiable as the inevitable consequence of the Turks' suppression of a violent internal rebellion.

In appropriately Byzantine fashion, then, the deaths of a half-million Armenians are presented as some form of "collateral damage," a regrettable yet inescapable fact of war. But that very idea collapses under the moral weight of what followed: on September 13, 1915, the Ottoman parliament passed the "Temporary Law of Expropriation and Confiscation," which declared all property, including homes, land, livestock, and possessions, belonging to the deported Armenians to be forfeited to the government in Constantinople. Whatever justification may have been offered for the massacres, this "law" was out-and-out brigandage. To the Three Pashas and the Young Turks, Armenian property was worth more consideration than were Armenian lives: the provision of the basic necessities of survival for the men, the women, and the children driven from their homes was less important than assuring the proper accounting and redistribution of the possessions they left behind. There can be no more sharply defined confirmation than the "Temporary Law of Expropriation and Confiscation" of the Ottoman Turks' utter indifference to the ultimate fate of the Armenian deportees. No matter what befell them on the roads and the open tracts of Anatolia, even had they lived, in the end they would have had nothing to which they could return.

It is that broad streak of indifference toward the Armenians and their fate that will not allow the Ottoman Turks to be relieved of their rightful burden of guilt for the Armenian catastrophe. Invoking the argument that the hundreds of thousands of Armenian dead were somehow legitimate casualties of war in exculpation invokes the words of United States Supreme Court Justice Robert H. Jackson, arguing the guilt of Nazi war criminals before the International Military Tribunal in Nuremburg in 1946. They stand, he declared, "as bloodstained Gloucester stood by the body of his slain king. He begged of the widow, as they beg of you, 'Say I slew them not.' If you are to say of these men that they are not guilty, it would be as true to say that there has been no war, there are no slain, there has been no crime."

The Armenian massacres were one of the final bloody pages in the blood-soaked history of the Ottoman Empire. Their legacy has been one of perpetuated anger, enmity, and bitterness. Forgiveness, let alone reconciliation, has been made impossible by the intransigence of both sides, Armenian and Turk alike. No one wants to talk about the Armenian massacres, but all want to shout about them, and in the shouting much is said but nothing is heard. The continuing tragedy of Armenia's agony in the Great War is that the hatred that caused it continues. Armenia's dead deserve a better memorial.

CHAPTER EIGHT
EL AURENS

As autumn came in 1916 and the Great War entered its third year, the Allies faced a bleak strategic picture. In France, the French Army was being systematically bled to death by its German counterpart in an apparently endless artillery duel around the fortress city of Verdun. To the north, the great British offensive, which was to smash through the German trenches and break the stalemate of the Western Front, died, along with tens of thousands of Tommies, on the German barbed wire and machine guns that stretched across the gently rolling slopes just east of the River Somme. In Russia, the Brusilov Offensive had come within a whisker of knocking the Austro-Hungarian Army to its knees in the summer, bringing the Dual Monarchy with it, but German reinforcements had saved their Austrian comrades from collapse, and now the Russian Army, beginning to suffer the effects of its faltering supply system, was being slowly forced back from all of its earlier gains. At sea, the German U-boats were beginning to once again take aim at civilian merchant shipping, threatening to sever the sea lanes that were Britain's lifelines. And finally, improbable as the idea might have been even a year earlier, through a combination of Allied mistakes, good luck, and the courage of the common Turkish soldier, the Ottoman Empire had managed to fight the Allies to a standstill.

What made the Turks' accomplishment all the more improbable was that apart from the supplies, the munitions, and a relative handful of advisers who were provided by Berlin, it had been achieved entirely through their own exertions. There were no German infantry divisions being rushed to Gallipoli or Mesopotamia or Palestine, as had been sent to prop up the faltering Austro-Hungarians both on the Eastern Front and against the Italians, who had entered the war on the side of the Allies in the spring of 1915.

Significantly, there appears to be no record of the Turks asking for such support or of the Germans offering it. Enver, despite the assiduousness with which he had pursued the alliance with Germany, was terribly suspicious of German intentions toward the Ottoman Empire. It was a justifiable suspicion: given Germany's thinly disguised pre-war ambition of reducing the Ottoman Empire into a vassal state, a handful of German divisions sent by Berlin to bolster Turkish forces at the fronts could easily turn into an army of occupation once peace was restored. The Germans, for their part, had long been disdainful of Turkish military abilities and regarded the alliance as little more than a means of expediting Germany's eventual subversion of the Sultan's realm.

Of course, the fact that Germany offered the Ottoman Empire nothing more than material and financial support—and in terms of Germany's overall expenditures, very small amounts and very minor sums—gives lie to the idea that the Germans had hoped to use the Turks to draw off significant Allied strength from the Eastern and Western Fronts. The grand strategic picture of 1916 was no different than it had been in 1914: there was still no place for the Turks to strike decisively at the British or the French with any hope of success, and in terms of both absolute and relative strength, they were still overmatched. The Turks had no choice but to stand on the defensive, and as they did so, they could only grow weaker. They were like a man standing in a corner of a room, trying to bar the door on either adjoining wall: he can concentrate his full exertions on neither door, lest the intruder at the other break in. Eventually, his strength must give out, and both doors will be forced open. The Allies could eventually bring a slow, inexorable pressure against the Turks with the resources already at hand in Egypt and Mesopotamia. The forces diverted to the Middle East had been significant, but in the sense of altering the strategic balance on the Western Front or materially affecting events there, their absence was not decisive.

Yet as the Allies, and particularly the British, licked their wounds in the autumn of 1916, such considerations were far from obvious. It would be too much to say that the British were stunned, far less reeling, from the defeats at Gallipoli and Kut. They were nonetheless amazed at the revitalized Ottoman Empire. It was clear that the sort of "have a dash at Johnny Turk and watch him run away" tactics that had characterized much of the planning for operations in Mesopotamia and Gallipoli were not going to work. Defeating the Turks would require more careful planning and preparation, as well as officers at every level of command who possessed a drive and a determination to "get forward and get on with it."

These changes would take time, though, and while they were being put in hand there seemed to be little opportunity for the British to take the war to the Turks. The sole bright spot for the British in the Middle East came toward the end of 1916, provided by a hitherto obscure British officer leading an Arab "Army" that was little more than a rabble in arms in lightning raids against Ottoman outposts and installations in the Arabian Peninsula and Palestine. His name was T. E. Lawrence; he would be remembered by history as "Lawrence of Arabia." Among his devoted Arab followers, he was known by his Arab name: El Aurens.

Lawrence is one of those romantic historical figures of the Great War who must be taken with a rather large grain of salt, for his life would become so enshrouded in myth and enmeshed in controversy that the boundary between fact and fabrication sometimes blurs into indistinction. He claimed to have performed amazing feats of bravery, intrigue, and sometimes blatant recklessness. When official records were released decades after his death, they showed that some of his claims were exaggerations or even out-and-out falsehoods, yet at the same time the same records revealed truths about exploits even more amazing of which he had never spoken. Arguably no other single individual would play such a pivotal role in the creation of the modern Middle East, even though it would ultimately bear little resemblance to what he had hoped it would become. Yet many historians devote more time and effort to debating the truth of his alleged homosexuality than they do to understanding how he helped accelerate the Allies' efforts to wrench apart the Ottoman Empire.

Thomas Edward Lawrence, known to his family as Ned, was born in Wales in 1888. He was one of five illegitimate children born to Sir Thomas Chapman, an Anglo-Irish baronet, and Sarah Junner, who had eloped together after Chapman left his wife. He took the surname "Lawrence" from his mother, who had at one time adopted it to hide her own illegitimacy. The family moved to Oxford when Ned was eight. Lawrence would remain associated with the city for the rest of his life, graduating from Oxford University in 1910 with First Class Honours in history. His dream was to become an archaeologist. Four years of field work for the British Museum followed, most significantly on the museum's dig at Carchemish, on the Euphrates River, where Lawrence was introduced to Arab culture and the Arab language. He developed a remarkable empathy with the local Arabs, as well as an ability to motivate them through sheer force of personality.

The outbreak of the war found Lawrence still at Carchemish. Based on his education and experience, he was offered a commission and a posting to the Geographical Section of the General Staff in London. A few months later he was shipped off to Cairo, where he went to work for the Military Intelligence Department. His familiarity with the Arabs led him to be slotted as an expert on Arab nationalism and independence movements in the Turkish provinces of the Levant and the Arabian Peninsula. He also provided intelligence on the Ottoman Empire as a whole, usually of excellent quality, although some of it, including the briefings he prepared for First Lord of the Admiralty Winston Churchill prior to the naval attack on the Dardanelles, proved to be less than perfect.

With a brilliant mind, a caustic wit, and a restless spirit, Lawrence chafed in the confining role of a staff officer, even in as relatively free-wheeling a posting as Cairo. It wasn't until October 1916 that he finally found his niche, or, rather, it found him. The overall quality of his intelligence work, coupled with his empathy with the Arabs and particularly their leaders, made him a natural for the posting as the British liaison officer in the Arab Revolt, serving with the Emir Faisal, the son of Sherrif Sayyid Hussein ibn Ali of Mecca.

Lawrence's affinity for the Arabs never developed to the degree where he "went native," as some colonial officials were known to do, but he did readily adopt the most practical, as well as the most physically intriguing, aspects of Arab life into his own lifestyle, which included his wardrobe (he habitually went about dressed as a Bedouin), his diet, and his personal habits. His years of working at Carchemish had convinced him that by virtue of being a more "primitive" people, Arabs were "morally superior" to Europeans but intellectually inferior. Like so many other Britons who lived and worked among native populations in the various corners of the British Empire, he found himself regarding the "locals" with a mixture of fascination and paternalistic condescension that would characterize his entire experience in the Middle East.

On his first mission as the Arab liaison, he was sent on a fact-finding mission to the Hejaz at the heart of the Arabian Peninsula, where Sherrif Hussein was in open rebellion against the Turks. Hussein's goal was nothing less than a complete separation of Arabia from the Ottoman Empire, bringing an end to the Sultan's hegemony, which dated back to the sixteenth-century authority. In addition, Hussein was fighting for the creation of an independent Arab state that would span from Aleppo in Syria to Aden in Yemen.

Arabia had been a part of the Ottoman Empire since the sixteenth century, although the Turks never managed to fully establish their authority over the peninsula. Nomadic Arab tribes refused to recognize the rule of the Sultan and frequently took to raiding Ottoman settlements. Moving swiftly, appearing from and then vanishing into the endless Arabian desert, they defied the Ottoman Army to stop them. Most Arabs gave their primary loyalty to their religion or sect, their tribe, or their own local potentates; to them, the Sultan was a far-off interloper who had not earned and thus did not deserve their allegiance. Met with a sometimes irrational but constant resistance at every turn to its efforts to bring order and stability to Arabia, eventually the best that Constantinople could hope to achieve was to bribe the more aggressive tribes to cease attacking fellow Moslems who were making their pilgrimage to Mecca. At the same time, the Turks, focused on the Balkans and expanding westward in the Mediterranean, did little to actively improve the lot of their Arab subjects, who at the beginning of the twentieth century remained a fierce, backward, semiliterate people. The long-standing policy of the Ottoman Empire to formally relegate any of its subjects who were not ethnic Turks to the status of second-class citizenship did nothing to abate Arab hostility, of course, and the Young Turks' willingness to embrace the doctrines of "Ottomanism" only made the problems worse. Uprisings broke out repeatedly, based in mountain strongholds and remote regions that were unreachable by the Ottoman Army, while the tribes habitually defied census registration, refused to pay taxes, and attempted to disrupt construction of the Hejaz Railway, which had finally connected Damascus with Medina in 1908.

In the summer of 1910, Druze Arabs living in the province of Transjordan began to raid Ottoman towns and villages as a preliminary to a full-scale uprising, and the CUP, as part of its effort to shore up its popular support among the Turks, sent in troops to put down the rebellion. Commanded by Farouk Sami Pasha, the troops found success in their campaign, and a year later Farouk was sent on a similar mission to deal with a similar uprising by Bedouins in the same region. Within a year he had brought a semblance of peace to the province. Farther south, in Asir and Najd, which were ruled by the Saud family, the efforts of the regime in Constantinople were somewhat more successful, mainly through an increased military presence and a strengthened administration, coupled with the loyalty of local chieftains, such as Ibn Rashid of Najd and Sherrif Hussein of Mecca, who were fighting against the Sauds.

In Yemen, at the southernmost tip of the Arabian Peninsula, Ottoman rule was little more than notional. Just as the Druze rebellion flared up, the hereditary ruler of the region, Imam Yahya, declared a holy war against the Ottoman Empire, a revolt that his Shi'ite followers wholeheartedly embraced. The Three Pashas reacted immediately by sending a corps of Turkish troops to the region, and in a campaign that lasted the better part of two years, the two sides eventually fought each other to a military draw, and a peace of sorts was concluded. In practice the "peace" amounted to yet another defeat for the Turks, for Imam Yahya was allowed to retain his autonomy and was given significant financial concessions as well. Not surprisingly, then, when the Ottoman Empire declared war on the Allies in November 1914, the whole of the Arabian Peninsula, as well as much of Palestine and Syria, was waiting for another opportunity to break out in revolt.

The Arabian province to which T. E. Lawrence found himself posted in October 1916, the Hejaz, held a special significance among all of the provinces in the Arabian Peninsula, as it was home to the two holy cities of Islam, Mecca and Medina. For almost a thousand years, the most powerful figure in this region was the Sherrif of Mecca, the chief of the sherrifs who represented the Prophet Mohammad's family, the Hashim, and who was the traditional steward of the two holy cities. In 1517, after the Ottoman sultan Selim II conquered Syria and Egypt, the Sherrif of Mecca acknowledged the spiritual authority of the caliph in Constantinople but retained, as did his successors, a large degree of local autonomy. Whatever the nominal jurisdiction of the Ottoman governors, the true rulers of Hejaz province were the Hashemite grand sherrifs.

In November 1908, as part of the reforms that immediately followed in the wake of the Young Turks' revolution, Sayyid Hussein ibn Ali was appointed the new Sherrif of Mecca. Initially, Hussein cooperated with the Ottoman military and civilian administration, ingratiating himself with the Sultan and the CUP alike and helping to suppress the rebellions of the Arab princes ibn Saud and Idrisi of

Asir. This was disingenuous on the part of Hussein, for his ambition was not to see a consolidation of Ottoman authority in Arabia but to establish sovereignty in the Hejaz, of which ibn Saud and Idrisi stood in the way. By the autumn of 1914, as Enver's alliance with Germany appeared to be dragging the empire into the Great War, the situation in Hejaz province seemed to be almost tranquil, and the Turks took the unnatural quiet to be a sign that their belated efforts in winning over the allegiance of the Arabs was succeeding. The truth of the matter was that Sherrif Hussein was playing a waiting game, biding his time until he deemed the moment right for his own move to throw the Ottoman Turks out of the Hejaz and restore control of its holy cities to the Arabs.

Not everyone in Constantinople or the local administration in Hejaz was fooled by Hussein's charade. Col. Vehib Bey, who was both provincial governor and commander of the military district of Hejaz, repeatedly warned the Three Pashas, and specifically Talaat, the minister of the interior, that Hussein was working toward allying the Arab tribes under the banner of an Arab caliph (who would then supplant Caliph Mehmet Resad as Sheikh-ul-Islam and caliph—spiritual leader—of all of the world's Moslems), with himself as the temporal leader of a revived Arab nation. Vehib was uncompromising in the language of his reports, stating explicitly that Hussein "desired the downfall of the state" and "would not forgo the smallest opportunity to cooperate with the enemy if there was a hostile attack against the Red Sea coast."

That Vehib had not been talking through his fez became clear after November 14, 1914, when Mehmet Resad issued his call to jihad against the Allies. Hussein refused to endorse it, saying, "The Holy War is doctrinally incompatible with an aggressive war, and absurd with a Christian ally, namely Germany." For Arab Moslems, the Sherrif's declaration was sufficient for them to feel absolved of any responsibility to obey the call to holy war or indeed any obligation of service to the Ottoman Turks. Nonetheless, Hussein repeatedly assured Constantinople of his loyalty to the Ottoman regime, even going so far as to send his son Faisal to Damascus in the spring of 1915, there to meet with Djemal Pasha, who had just returned from his disastrous Suez expedition. Faisal, following Hussein's instructions, assured Djemal that the Sherrif was prepared to defend the holy cities and fight for the empire as necessary.

Djemal, still stinging from his humiliation at Suez, was at this time indulging in what amounted to a reign of terror in Damascus and throughout the Levant.

Summary arrests and executions of anyone who offered the slightest suspicion of disloyalty to the empire became commonplace, and Arabs were made particular targets of Djemal's wrath. He, along with Enver and Talaat in Constantinople, found Hussein's affirmations of loyalty reassuring. They had no idea that at the same time he was proclaiming his fealty to the Turks, Sherrif Hussein was secretly corresponding with the British high commissioner in Egypt, Sir Henry McMahon. Djemal in Damascus and Colonel Basri, the governor of Medina, had their suspicions that Hussein was preparing to double-cross them but lacked sufficient proof to act on them. Hanging the odd Marionite priest or a handful of Beruiti students was one thing; trying to indict someone possessed of Hussein's political and spiritual stature among the Arabs was something else entirely. It could well have provoked the very rebellion the Turks were hoping to avert. So Hussein continued to negotiate with Sir Henry, who was exploring the possibilities of opening a new front against the Turks in Palestine. Terms of alliance were eventually agreed on, and on January 1, 1916, the Arab Revolt was openly declared.

Djemal reacted quickly but cautiously, ordering his divisional commanders at Damascus and Medina, Basri Pasha and Fahreddin Pasha, respectively, to take up defensive positions around the cities and protect the railway but to take no action against the Arabs that might be provocative. He hoped that the Arabs would fire the first shot, providing the Turks with a justification for whatever repressive measures they might take in putting down the revolt. Hussein's Arabs proved obliging, attacking the outposts around Medina on the night of May 23–24. A few days later, they attacked the city of Jiddah, on the Red Sea, with artillery support from Royal Navy gunboats. Within a week, Jiddah had fallen to the Arabs.

The Turkish garrison at Medina was reinforced on May 31, and Fahreddin took command of the "Hejaz Expeditionary Force," some fourteen thousand strong. Arrayed against it was Hussein's "Army," for the most part made up of desert nomads more loyal to their tribal leaders than to Hussein himself, of around fifty thousand men. They had fewer than ten thousand firearms among them, some of which dated back to the late eighteenth century. For the most part, the Arabs who lived in the cities had little or no use for Hussein's pretensions. Nevertheless, with British political backing and financial support, Hussein was able to take a number of coastal cities from the Turks. In retaliation, Enver, Talaat, and Djemal agreed that the time had come to go over to the offensive, their first objective being the capture of Mecca, which was currently held by Hussein's forces. Increasing British pressure in southern Palestine forced them to redeploy their units, and in September 1916 the plan to take Mecca was abandoned.

It was shortly after this that Captain Lawrence was presented to Hussein and began working with the Arab insurgents. He soon demonstrated a remarkable array of talents, both diplomatic and military. His experience at Carchemish stood him in good stead, for unlike many a young European in similar circumstances he had not simply dismissed the Arabs among whom he lived as mere "wogs" to be utilized for local labor and nothing more. Instead, he had learned the subtle complexities of Arab social and familial relationships, which, coupled with his own charismatic personality, established for him a position of leadership among Hussein's followers. Captain Lawrence understood that culturally, Arabs were more drawn to personal loyalty than to ideological motivation. (Writing in 1915 of the Arabs in Syria, Lawrence observed, "There is no national feeling among them. Their idea of nationality is the independence of tribes and parishes, and their idea of national union is episodic combined resistance to an intruder." A year later, in Basra, he wrote a report for Cairo in which he commented that the local nationalist party was "about twelve strong.") Nonetheless, Lawrence's insight into the Arab character allowed him to convince Hussein's sons Faisal, Ali, and Abdullah, who were leading the actual fighting, to coordinate their actions against the Turks with British strategy.

El Aurens proved to be skilled at conventional warfare, as he demonstrated in December 1916, when the Turks attacked the city of Yenbo. He carefully coordinated the tactics of his Arab forces with the artillery support of Royal Navy gunboats to turn back the Ottoman attack. Lawrence's outstanding talent, however, was his gift for irregular operations. Acknowledging that Hussein's Arabs were poorly organized, trained, and armed, Lawrence knew they could not hope to defeat the Turks in a straightforward, stand-up fight—Hussein was planning an attack on Medina—so Lawrence convinced the Sherrif that the Arabs would be best employed in hit-and-run raids along the length of the Hejaz Railway. The intent was not to demolish the railway but to repeatedly damage it, allowing the Turks to keep it working after a fashion but never to full capacity. The raids would inflict minor damage at remote points, halting traffic for a few days each time until repairs were made. As a consequence, the Turkish force at Medina was essentially left stranded and impotent, as the railway was never working long enough to either withdraw the garrison or reinforce it. At the same time, the Turks were compelled to deploy a multitude of troops in endless patrols in search of and pursuing the raiders, while their limited numbers of railway construction units would be committed to repairing tracks damaged in the raids, rather than improving existing lines or building new ones.

The first step in Lawrence's strategy was the capture of the coastal city of Wejh, which was ideally sited to be the base for attacks on the Hejaz Railway. On January 3, 1917, Faisal began moving northward along the Red Sea coast with 10,400 men—5,100 mounted on camels, 5,300 men on foot—along with pieces of light artillery, 10 machine guns, and 380 baggage camels. While the garrison at Wejh, numbering some 800 strong, prepared for an attack from the south, the Royal Navy landed 400 Arabs and 200 British sailors to the north of Wejh, which they then attacked on January 23, taking the city in little more than a day. By this time, Sherrif Hussein's followers numbered about 70,000, of whom 28,000 were armed with modern rifles, the rest making do with swords and spears. Using Wejh as a base, they began to relentlessly harass Ottoman communications, capturing supplies and cutting up isolated units of Turks patrolling the railway.

These actions, though small in scale and not at all decisive in and of themselves, were of critical value to the British in Cairo, who were planning a major offensive into Palestine in 1917, with Damascus as its ultimate objective. The raids kept the Turks off balance and served to disguise British intentions, as the vulnerability of the garrison at Medina always made it appear to be an attractive target for an attack. Lawrence and his desert irregulars were far from the whole of the Arab Revolt, and there was considerable conventional support for Hussein provided by the British and the French (including a battalion of camel-mounted Gurkhas). Even a few regiments of Arab "regulars" were raised, organized, and equipped along British lines, although their usefulness was marginal; Lawrence's irregular desert warriors remained the most effective arm of Sherrif Hussein's revolt.

The summer of 1917 saw what would be remembered as El Aurens's most legendary achievement, the capture of the port city of Aqaba, the only remaining Ottoman port on the Red Sea. Taking Aqaba was a strategic necessity: the Turkish garrison there would pose a serious threat to the right flank of Allies' newly formed Egyptian Expeditionary Force when it began to advance across the Sinai and into

Palestine, plus the city would serve as a major supply base once the British advance began. The considered opinion of the British commanders in Cairo was that a successful landward attack on Aqaba was impossible, given the difficult terrain around the city, an opinion shared by Hussein and his sons. Determined to prove them all wrong, Lawrence took his personal retinue into the desert on May 9, having decided to use other Arab tribes, rather than Hussein's followers. Making a wide circuit inland through the desert, he met with Auda ibu Tayi, the leader of the Howietat Arabs, regarded by many as the fiercest—and most fiercely independent—of the northern Bedouin tribes. Auda agreed to form and lead a raiding force in an attack on Aqaba under Lawrence's direction. Before departing, Lawrence informed Cairo of his plans and then vanished into the desert. Cairo expected to eventually learn that the young officer had died somewhere in Palestine or the Negev.

Nonetheless, on July 6, after a four-week trek across the desert, those Arab forces captured Aqaba, suffering only a handful of casualties. Lawrence then made the 150-mile journey to Suez by camel in less than three days (but not in the twenty-nine hours he would later claim to have done) to arrange for the Royal Navy to supply his Arabs in Aqaba and eventually take over the city. When General Allenby began his offensive against the Turkish defenses of the Gaza-Beersheba defensive line later that year, Aqaba would provide a secure base for the harassing raids the Arabs would stage in support of Allenby's attacks.

Infinitely more valuable to Allenby than any of El Aurens's raids on Turkish troop trains or attacks on Turkish outposts, however, was the intelligence that Lawrence's Arab irregulars were able to collect about Turkish deployments and defenses. Even here, though, the record of just how much credit belongs to Lawrence and how much should be accorded to others is, like so much of anything Lawrence touched, unclear and sometimes contradictory. The intelligence war against the Turks was, appropriately enough, an extraordinarily Byzantine business, one that to this day remains impossible to fully unravel.

Lawrence's Arabs were Allenby's most important source of information about the Turks in Palestine but not his only source. An obscure agronomist living in the village of Zichron Yaakov, on the slopes of Mount Carmel in Palestine, who at the time was known only among his colleagues for his botanical discoveries, was also supplying the British with what is said in some circles to have been the most crucial intelligence about Ottoman defenses in the Levant. His name was Aaron Aaronsohn.

Born in Romania in 1876, Aaronsohn went to Palestine in 1882, along with his brother, Alexander, and his sister, Sarah, when their parents emigrated. He grew up into a tall, stout, almost Teutonic-looking adult, at once earthy and methodical in character. Agriculture was almost mother's milk for young Aaron, for his father had been a farmer in Romania, and he continued to be one in Palestine. Aaron's fascination with growing things led him into agronomy, however, and in 1906 he discovered wheat growing wild on Mount Hebron that was a hybrid strain of the first form of wheat ever cultivated by humanity. The discovery was of intense interest to botanists, archaeologists, and anthropologists but was little remarked on outside those academic circles. Yet in addition to becoming a botanist, Aaronsohn had also become a devout, even fanatical, Zionist.

In many ways, there is very little more that can be said about Aaronsohn with absolute certainty. His actions during the war have become so enmeshed in Zionist hagiography that biographers have found it all but impossible to distinguish between what is fact, fiction, and mere burnishing and embellishment. Aaronsohn did control an espionage ring called NILI (Netzach Israel Lo Ishaker— "The Glory of Israel will not deceive," from I Samuel 15:29), which used his Jewish Agriculture Experiment Station on the coast of Palestine as a base. The core of his organization consisted of members of his family, who acted as spies and couriers. His sister, Sarah, was arrested by the Turks and taken to Damascus, where she was brutally tortured and eventually committed suicide in 1917. Aaronsohn did have contacts with British intelligence in Cairo and traveled to Britain and the United States, where he worked to muster support for Zionist goals in Palestine, which is where he exerted his greatest influence.

Yet to borrow a phrase that Lawrence used to describe his own operations, this was merely "a sideshow within a sideshow": Lawrence's Arabs were able to gather far more information than could Aaronsohn's NILI. The sheer ubiquity of the Arabs allowed those who were working for Lawrence a degree of "invisibility" that Aaronsohn's people could never attain. The Turks were more suspicious of Jews than they were of Arabs, who were fellow Moslems, and watched Jews more closely, a factor that played a major role in Sarah Aaronsohn's arrest. In the end, it was the intelligence provided by Lawrence's Arabs that proved to be more valuable to the British, which Aaronsohn knew and resented. He once described Lawrence as "a little snot," found him to be "overbearing," and accused him of being anti-Semitic, a charge that has been rejected by Jewish historians. Although it hardly seems justified, Aaronsohn's antagonism grew out of a sense that even as he was attempting to parlay the role of NILI into political support within the British government for the goals of Zionism, Lawrence's successes seemed to diminish whatever influence Aaronsohn was developing. The agronomist's attitude was unfortunate—what Lawrence thought of him is unknown—for there was no reason why the two men could not have cooperated in their efforts. Both were working for the same immediate goal—the ejection of the Turks from Palestine. Given Aaronsohn's prickly personality and Lawrence's high-strung nature, however, cooperation would have probably been impossible in any event.

El Aurens and his Arab irregulars would advance alongside General Allenby's forces during the rest of the war, culminating in their triumphal entry into Damascus on October 3, 1918, just two days after the Australian Light Horse Regiment liberated the city. (Lawrence, attempting to burnish the reputation of the Arabs in anticipation of the inevitable peace conference, tried to claim that his Arabs were the first Allied forces to enter Damascus, a myth that he vigorously promoted and that persists to this day.) The Arab desert campaign would become a textbook example of the best use of irregular forces in support of a conventional military campaign, and Lawrence, through both his own self-promotion and the sensationalist efforts of American journalist Lowell Thomas, would emerge from the war as "Lawrence of Arabia," a larger-than-life figure of newspapers, books, and eventually film.

Yet Lawrence's great legacy was not what he accomplished but, rather, what he almost accomplished, yet ultimately failed to do: redrawing the map of the Arab Middle East. In his dealings with Sherrif Hussein and his sons, Lawrence proposed that the Ottoman provinces in Mesopotamia, the Levant, and Arabia be partitioned into a patchwork of new states, including four kingdoms—one each to be awarded to Hussein, Faisal, Abdullah, and Ali. The borders he drew were curious, although not without a certain logic. One of the new Arab kingdoms would have corresponded to roughly the eastern half of modern Iraq, and in fact it is labeled on one map Lawrence drew up as "Irak." (The region's name, which Lawrence spelled phonetically, has deep-rooted traditions in the Arab world, with some traditions suggesting that it dates back to Sumeria; in colloquial Arabic, it means "fertile land.") Another would have included most of the western half of modern Iraq, as well as modern Syria and Jordan, along with a slice of Saudi Arabia. The Arabian

Peninsula would have been split into two separate kingdoms. An independent Armenian homeland in southeastern Anatolia would be created, as would a Kurdish state to the north of Mesopotamia, near the Caucasus, sharing a border with Russia. Palestine was to be a separate province, as was the Lebanon, while the Sinai Peninsula would have been added to Egypt.

What remains impossible to establish with absolute certainty is how much of this geopolitical tinkering was solely Lawrence's ideas and how much of it had been approved or even conceived by the Arab Bureau of Britain's Foreign Office, as all parties involved were keeping separate (and sometimes multiple) sets of books, as it were. Technically, legally Lawrence had no right to give such assurances to Sherrif Hussein or his sons, but he fully believed that the British government, when presented with what amounted to a fait accompli once the majority of the territory in question had been liberated with the active assistance of the Arabs, would ultimately back him, however grudgingly. What he hadn't counted on, and of which he had no knowledge, were the workings—machinations might be a more fitting description—of three men: Sir Mark Sykes, François Georges-Picot, and Arthur Balfour.

The first two gentlemen, both of them minor diplomats, rather than policymakers in their respective governments, were the coauthors of the Sykes-Picot Agreement, which was concluded on May 16, 1916. The agreement was a secret compact between the governments of Great Britain and France, to which imperial Russia assented. It assumed as its starting point that in the wake of the defeat of the Central Powers, the Ottoman Empire would be broken up. It then attempted to define what would be each of the three Great Powers' respective spheres of influence in the former Ottoman territories. It was intended to be a trade agreement, one that would eliminate the sort of expensive and sometimes abrasive commercial competition that had been the source of a number of diplomatic crises in the late nineteenth and early twentieth centuries in parts of Africa and South America. Several of its provisions had unexpected consequences, however.

Under the terms of the agreement, when the Ottoman Empire was partitioned, Great Britain would be given control of an area that included the southern half of modern Iraq, modern Jordan, and a small area around Haifa allowing access to the Mediterranean. Southeastern Anatolia, northern Iraq, Syria, and Lebanon were to go to France. Russia was to get Constantinople, the Turkish Straits, and the Armenian provinces. Nothing was said about separate homelands for the Armenians or the Kurds, and no mention was made of establishing any autonomous Arab states, while Palestine was to be subject to an international administration. One specific provision of the agreement did, however, reserve to Britain, France, and Russia the right to determine national boundaries within each power's respective sphere of influence. In effect, it gave the three Allies the authority to set up any client states they wished within their own bailiwicks.

Some historians have argued that the Sykes-Picot Agreement was the first step taken in formalizing the process that the three Allies had been anxious to begin from the previous century, namely, carving up the Ottoman Empire. The war and the assumption that the Allies would be victorious, so the story goes, provided the final impetus needed for France, Russia, and Great Britain to openly acknowledge their national ambitions. All three powers had spent the last half of the nineteenth century in what had been an international death watch, waiting for "the Sick Man of Europe" to finally expire so that the corpse could be portioned out. The Ottoman Empire had refused to be so cooperative, lingering on far longer than anyone had imagined possible, and now the death watch had turned into a lynching party, but the result would still be the same. The Sykes-Picot Agreement, then, or so it is explained, was simply a continuation of pre-war expansionist policies and imperialist desires that the governments involved were finally being permitted to openly acknowledge and act upon.

That interpretation gives the agreement, as written, far more weight and authority than it deserves. Neither Sir Mark Sykes nor François Georges-Picot had ever been (or would ever be) a senior official in his respective foreign ministry. They were not the sort of men who were entrusted with drawing up solemn agreements that fundamentally changed national policies without supervision or guidance from their superiors. The entire agreement has all of the appearances of being a half-baked proposal that middling-level diplomatic officers concoct in the hope of attracting the attention of more senior diplomats, with an eye toward advancing the authors' careers. It was not the stuff of serious national policy, and only through a combination of accident and ambition would it become such.

Most pointedly, no one in the British government could have taken the Sykes-Picot Agreement very seriously. When examined through the two prisms of historical British foreign policy and the strategic situation in France and the Eastern

Front at the time it was drawn up, it begins to appear as a sop offered by the British to the French and the Russians to boost the Allies' sagging national spirits. At the time the agreement was being drawn up, the French were mired eyeball-deep in hell at Verdun (where more than 350,000 Frenchmen would eventually die), while in the fall and the early winter of 1915 the Russians had lost more than 400,000 men and been forced to retreat more than 300 miles in the wake of the Battle of Gorlice-Tarnow. The morale of both nations was wavering, and in that light the terms of Sykes-Picot make sense: as incentives to continue the fight against the hated Huns, the French were being offered a tremendous postwar addition to their overseas empire, while Russia was promised the fulfillment of the centuries-old dream of the tsars—possession of Constantinople and the Straits of the Bosporus and the Dardanelles.

Yet how could such promises have been made by any responsible British government? It had been a cornerstone of Great Britain's conduct of her foreign affairs since the eighteenth century to support the Ottoman Turks as a check to Russian expansionism by keeping the tsar's navy bottled up in the Black Sea—the concept had ceased to be merely a policy and became something approaching a doctrine. The Cabinet had even vetoed any Russian participation in the naval action at the Dardanelles for fear that if the Russian fleet gained possession of Constantinople, it would never relinquish it. To expect Great Britain to completely reverse such a long-held and determined commitment to such a doctrine bordered on the absurd. There was no guarantee, whatever ententes had been established with Russia in the decade before the Great War, that once peace returned there would be no reversion to former international ambitions and frictions between the British lion and the Russian bear.

The real obstacle that the Sykes-Picot Agreement created for the implementation of Lawrence's promises to the Arabs was that it sowed confusion about exactly how the question of ordering and organizing the former Ottoman territories would be resolved. It would require, in the finest traditions typical of the political mediocrities who were then governing Great Britain and France, further diplomatic dithering and obfuscation. It cannot be fairly said and should not even be implied that such were the motives or intentions of Sir Mark Sykes or François Georges-Picot. In fact, had it not been for another piece of diplomatic tomfoolery on the part of a greatly experienced politician who should have known better, any confusion created by the Sykes-Picot Agreement might have been easily brushed aside when the belligerents finally sat down to work out the terms of the peace.

Instead, Arthur Balfour, the British foreign secretary, issued a statement on November 2, 1917, that would become known to posterity as the Balfour Declaration. It committed Great Britain to support the establishment of a Jewish homeland in Palestine, a long-held ambition among Zionists and, in doing so, because of (perhaps intentionally) ambiguous wording, created insoluble problems that, mutated and multiplied, plague Palestine to this day.

The declaration itself was a simple, apparently straightforward document, a letter written by Foreign Minister Balfour to Walter Rothschild, Second Baron Rothschild, the most prominent figure in Britain's Jewish community. The original was typed out, then signed by Balfour, and read,

FOREIGN OFFICE,
NOVEMBER 2ND, 1917.

Dear Lord Rothschild,
I have much pleasure in conveying to you, on behalf of His Majesty's Government, the following declaration of sympathy with Jewish Zionist aspirations which has been submitted to, and approved by, the Cabinet:
"His Majesty's Government view with favour the establishment in Palestine of a national home for the Jewish people, and will use their best endeavours to facilitate the achievement of this object, it being clearly understood that nothing shall be done which may prejudice the civil and religious rights of existing non-Jewish communities in Palestine, or the rights and political status enjoyed by Jews in any other country".
I should be grateful if you would bring this declaration to the knowledge of the Zionist Federation.

Yours sincerely
Arthur James Balfour

Like the Sykes-Picot Agreement, the Balfour Declaration was something of a propaganda ploy. But whereas, when it was drafted, Sykes-Picot was meant to provide incentive to wavering Allied governments that were suffering tremendous military setbacks to keep fighting, Balfour's note to Lord Rothschild was intended primarily for public consumption. In late 1917 Great Britain was growing increasingly war-weary. The moral fatigue of more than three years of fighting and the cost—almost a million British soldiers, sailors, and airmen dead—had begun to corrode the spirit of the British people, as the likelihood of the Allies actually winning the war seemed to diminish with each passing day. Russia was clearly a spent force: having suffered nigh-incalculable casualties, with a succession of revolutionary governments lurching ever further to the left (although no one knew it when Balfour signed the note to Lord Rothschild, the Bolshevik Revolution was only five days away), it was merely a matter of time before Russia simply gave up. The French Army had been wracked by a series of mutinies in the summer of 1917, after the abattoir of the Neville Offensive in the spring had cost the lives of nearly a half-million French soldiers. And Britain herself had in the fall just gone through the muddy horror of Passchendaele, a fiasco, for which the sitting government, as much as the generals, were responsible and where an expenditure of some three hundred thousand Tommies produced a gain of barely seven hundred yards.

Although the government continued to make optimistic noises, especially now that the United States had joined the fight (the Americans had declared war on Germany in April, but as yet very few of their soldiers had reached the Western Front), a pessimism began to settle over the hearts and minds of the British public. The war had been going on so long that it seemed to have become a self-perpetuating way of life, and any sense of why the war was being fought, why Britain had gone to war in the first place, began to fade. Awkward questions about how and why the war was being waged were given voice in the lobbies and the cloakrooms of the Commons, and it would not be long before they were heard within the House itself. Measures had to be taken, measures that would rally the people, or sections of them, ideas and aims that would impart a sense of the tangible and worthy to the immense national exertions that the war effort was demanding. Consequently, late 1917 was a time when the British government was making promises to almost anyone who was willing to listen to them. The fundamental concept of the Balfour Declaration was one such, but its consequence would lie as much in what it did *not* say as in what it did.

Tying Great Britain's determination to defeat the Turks to the idea of creating a Jewish homeland possessed tremendous potential, for Britain's Jewish community, Zionist and anti-Zionist alike, was highly influential in the realm of international finance, as well as in the press. Rallying them to renewed support for the war in the hope of fulfilling the dream of Jews the world over—a Jewish homeland in Palestine—would be a masterstroke, because the religious, cultural, and family ties that had allowed the Jews to retain their identity as a people for so many centuries were international, and so would be the effect of the Balfour Declaration. That this was a carefully calculated objective for the declaration was made explicitly clear by Balfour himself, who, at a War Cabinet meeting on October 31, 1917, flatly stated that a declaration favorable to Zionist aspirations would allow Great Britain "to carry on extremely useful propaganda in Russia and America."

Predictably—and understandably—the Jewish communities in Europe and the United States were ecstatic when the Balfour Declaration was made public. Yet the day would not be long in coming when both Jews and Arabs would come to regard it as an instrument of betrayal. Lord Rothschild and Edwin Samuel Montagu, the secretary of state for India (and an *anti*-Zionist Jew), believed that the phrase "a national home for the Jewish people" was a tacit commitment by Great Britain to foster and support a Jewish *state*. For his part, Sherrif Hussein, when presented with a copy of the declaration, believed that it violated the promises made in 1915 by Sir Henry McMahon, the British high commissioner for Egypt. McMahon, writing in his official capacity, had assured Hussein that all Arab lands, with the exception of "portions of Syria" lying to the west of "the districts of Damascus, Homs, Hama and Aleppo," would be Arab controlled.

Hussein pointed out that Palestine lay well to the south of these areas and wasn't explicitly mentioned. To him, the declaration was a means by which Arabs already living in Palestine would be arbitrarily dispossessed in favor of Jews who had never yet set foot in that land. In that Palestine was a very small portion of the territories that were being promised to Hussein and his sons, it might have seemed that the Sherrif was overreacting. Yet given the convoluted and sometimes prickly nature of the Arab code of honor, Hussein felt that his anger was justified, as the Balfour Declaration represented, to him, a violation of solemn agreements—something that dishonored both Great Britain and himself.

Enter David Lloyd George, Great Britain's prime minister from 1916 to 1922, the evil genius of early-twentieth-century British politics and possibly the most ambitious and unscrupulous individual ever to reside at No. 10 Downing Street.

Born into a Welsh family that had barely escaped working-class status, he was a cunning charmer, and his Celtic roots had blessed him with a capacity for spell-binding eloquence that he dexterously employed to advance himself, as well as the interests he represented. In 1912 he would be openly accused of corruption, although he managed to avoid formal charges.

In 1916, when sharp and sustained criticism began in the House of Commons of Prime Minister H. H. Asquith for his government's conduct of the war, Lloyd George, who was Chancellor of the Exchequer and the number-two man in Asquith's Cabinet, saw an opportunity to take his place. The deal the Welshman struck with the Conservative opposition that removed Asquith from office and made Lloyd George prime minister essentially destroyed the Liberal Party, a detail that caused him little concern, then or later. Lloyd George would amply demonstrate for the rest of his time in office that principles no longer greatly signified for him; he was eventually forced to resign in 1922 because a House of Lords investigation revealed that he had been involved in the sale of peerages and Honours.

Because Balfour was Lloyd George's foreign minister, statements coming from the Foreign Office carried by implication the prime minister's imprimatur. Yet instead of stepping forward to clarify for all concerned precisely what the declaration promised, Lloyd George assiduously avoided the issue, apparently hoping that some deus ex machina would present itself when the time came to fulfill the mutually contradictory pledges made by Britain or possibly even believing that the responsibility for doing so would fall on his successor, whoever that might be. The result of the hue and cry raised on all sides over the meanings and implications of the Balfour Declaration was predictable. The British, in attempting to thrash out some sort of workable compromise, would dither and continue to do so until Arab and Jew would decide to take matters into their own hands and try conclusions, a process that is still going on today.

Yet all of that was in the future when Lawrence and his horde of Howietat camel riders captured Aqaba in July 1917. With the fall of the Red Sea port, the war in the Middle East was entering its endgame, as the British were preparing to drive up the Tigris-Euphrates Valley in Mesopotamia and capture Baghdad, while at the same time striking northward in Palestine, through Jerusalem and into Damascus. For the Turks, the long death watch was coming to a close: the Ottoman Empire was going to die at last.

CHAPTER NINE
THE ROAD TO DAMASCUS

The month of August 1916 was a watershed for the Ottoman Empire. It saw the second, and last, effort of the Turkish Army to seize control of the Suez Canal, the Turks' final attempt to tip the overall strategic situation in the Middle East decisively in their favor. It also marked the end of a remarkable era of martial prowess, one that had begun with Osman himself when he created the Ottoman Empire six hundred years earlier, for this attack on the Suez would be the empire's final attempt at conquest.

After the Turks' first attack on the Canal was repulsed in early 1915, and despite the distractions of the Gallipoli campaign and the attack up the central valley of Mesopotamia, the strategic initiative in Egypt and Palestine seemed to be firmly in the grasp of the British. They had maintained a force of at least thirty thousand troops in eastern Egypt, dedicated to defending the waterway, and when the ANZACs were withdrawn from Gallipoli in early 1916, some of them were posted to the Western Front in France, but the majority were returned to Cairo, where the British Army maintained its Middle East Command headquarters. There they caught the eye of Gen. Sir Archibald Murray, who was drawing up plans to advance across the Suez Canal and the Sinai Peninsula into Palestine, with his ultimate objective being the city of Damascus.

Murray was hardly an old desert hand, and events would prove him to be a very average combat general, but he was a born organizer, and his work in preparing the Egyptian Expeditionary Force to move across the Sinai and the Negev was remarkably thorough and would prove invaluable to his successor. Taking a cue from the Turks' first Suez offensive, in January 1915, where they had constructed an elaborate chain of supply dumps across the Sinai as they advanced, Murray did them one better. He included plans for a rail link and a fresh-water pipeline to be brought up with his troops as they moved eastward. Murray's first objective was the construction of a defense line roughly 100 miles (160 km) east of the Canal. While he was preoccupied with this work, however, his Turkish counterpart—actually, the German general Kress von Kressenstein—was contemplating a second attack on the Suez Canal in the summer of 1916.

At the time and ever since, the Turks have attempted to place the blame for the failure of the first attempt to capture the Canal squarely on von Kressenstein's shoulders, although the evidence strongly supports the view that the overambitious plan was in truth Djemal's brainchild. This time around, the Turks' German adviser would have his way and the plan to be followed was his own, essentially the one that he would have tried to put into motion had Djemal not overruled him eighteen months previously. As conceived by von Kressenstein, this time the Turks would simply occupy the east bank of the Canal and rely on heavy artillery to interdict and disrupt the passage of shipping through the waterway. It was a far less ambitious and at the same time more realistic undertaking than their first attempt at the Canal, a plan well-suited to the strategic and logistic realities of the Turks' situation, for it recognized that the Ottoman Empire lacked both the manpower and the firepower to seize both sides of the Canal. Von Kressenstein gathered a mixed Turkish-Arab force roughly sixteen thousand strong at the edge of the Sinai Desert in June 1916. There he waited for almost six weeks for the arrival of machine guns, antiaircraft units (the British were becoming particularly adept at using strafing airplanes to disrupt Turkish columns, hitting hard at Turkish morale in the process, in addition to any casualties they caused), and the vital heavy guns.

Friedrich Kress von Kressenstein was one of the very few of the Ottoman Empire's senior officers during the Great War who would be remembered as an outstanding military commander, although he didn't exactly burnish his reputation in the attempts to take the Suez Canal. Born in 1870 in city of Nürnberg in the Kingdom of Bavaria, he was a career artillery officer who found himself attached to Liman von Sanders's military mission to Constantinople in early 1914. Originally posted as an officer of engineers, when the war began in October he was reassigned to the headquarters of Djemal's Fourth Army, based in Damascus, as chief of staff. After the first attempt on the Suez Canal was repulsed, Djemal rather hurriedly returned to Damascus, leaving von Kressenstein in local command in Palestine, a role that suited the German officer perfectly. Biding his time, watching Murray's gradual advance, von Kressenstein moved into the Sinai and waited just east of the Egyptian settlement of Romani, some twenty-five miles (forty kilometers) east of the Canal.

Very early in the morning of August 4, von Kressenstein began his attack. With surprise on their side, the Turks quickly overran the forward British positions and began moving into the town of Romani itself, but their momentum was lost in the face of unexpectedly heavy artillery fire. Fighting continued in the village and on the hills around Romani throughout the day, halting during the night, and resuming the following morning. By this time the Turks were running short of water and ammunition, and the British forces, particularly the mounted Australian units, the Light Horse, were pressing them hard. A few hours after dawn the entire Turkish force was in retreat, and by the time von Kressenstein was able to disengage, his army had lost more than half of its strength, leaving behind almost 5,000 dead and wounded, along with another 4,000 taken as prisoners of war. British casualties totaled a little more than 1,100.

Von Kressenstein led his remaining force back across the Sinai, moving sixty miles (one hundred kilometers) to El Arish, where in an attempt to boost morale at home and at the front the Turkish authorities promptly announced a victory. The Ottoman soldiers on the spot knew better, of course. The Turkish "Suez Expeditionary Force" had shot its bolt and, in doing so, had carried out the last Turkish attack of the war, although no one realized the latter to be the case at the time. General Murray continued his methodical advance across the Sinai, arriving at El Arish in early December 1916 and capturing it quite handily, in the process clearing any remaining Turkish forces from the whole of the Sinai Peninsula.

For the British the next step was, obviously, to move into Palestine itself; the objective was to drive north and capture the city of Damascus, which would not only force any remaining Turks out of Palestine, but would also cut off the Ottoman forces in Mesopotamia. Von Kressenstein, his battered command having been considerably reinforced by units from Damascus to a strength of some eighteen thousand soldiers, almost all of them Turks, had established a strong defensive position along a series of ridges between Gaza and Beersheba, blocking the only passable route into Palestine. General Murray delegated the task of dislodging the Turks to his immediate subordinate, Gen. Sir Charles Dobell, who, with some twenty-two hundred British and ANZAC troops under his command, should have been able to muster a local superiority of numbers and force a breakthrough somewhere along the Turkish position that had quickly become known as the Gaza Line. It was not an inspired command decision on Murray's part, and it began the process that would eventually lead to his relief and replacement.

Sir Archibald Murray was an "old soldier," though at the age of fifty-seven in 1917 he hardly qualified as old by Great War standards. A major general, he commanded a division of the British Army when the war began in August 1914. He gave up that post to serve as chief of staff to Field Marshal Sir John French, the commander in chief of the British Expeditionary Force, when the BEF went to France. It was not a happy appointment, for although Murray and French were friends, they did not work well together, and when the opportunity came to give Sir Archibald command of the Egyptian Expeditionary Force (EEF), the War Office in London acted with almost obscene haste in packing him off to Cairo.

His organization of the EEF was exemplary, and rarely would supply difficulties seriously plague its British and ANZAC units for the whole of the Palestine campaign. But Murray was an administrator, not a fighting soldier: twice he would attempt to force the Gaza Line, and twice he would fail. His failure, it has to be admitted, was not entirely his fault, for the Gaza position would demonstrate that Kress von Kressenstein had a talent for defensive warfare that bordered on genius.

In any event, after an almost eight-month-long slog across the Sinai, the first British attack on the Gaza Line went in on March 26, 1917. The First Battle of Gaza was a confused and confusing affair, with both sides standing on the brink of imminent victory or defeat during the course of the day. Von Kressenstein, still smarting from his repulse at Romani, at first overestimated the strength of the British force and believed it impossible to hold the Gaza position, so informing Djemal in Damascus by telegraph. Djemal, for his part, insisted that von Kressenstein make a stand at Gaza, and von Kressenstein, being a good soldier, determined to do his best to obey his orders.

Dobell opened the battle with an encircling movement by some of his mounted units on his left flank, threatening to cut off the four thousand or so Turks defending the town of Gaza proper. An infantry assault in the center held the Turks pinned in their lines and it appeared to von Kressenstein that the British were about to turn his flank and roll up the entire Gaza Line. Not wanting to throw away more troops to what seemed to be a lost cause, in mid-afternoon he canceled the orders for reinforcements coming from Beersheba. Yet at almost the same moment, Dobell was calling off his own attack, withdrawing the encircling Light Horse regiments because he believed that the infantry attack in the center had failed and the Turks were repositioning to face the mounted Australians. The next day, when Dobell tried to renew the attack on Gaza, he found that von Kressenstein had put the night hours to good use, reinforcing the garrison in the town and improving the defensive positions. Local counterattacks by the Turks erased the earlier British gains, and a lack of water finally compelled Dobell to bring the attack to a halt.

This time it was the British who falsely claimed a victory. Dobell's Tommies and ANZACs had suffered four thousand casualties, against a loss by von Kressenstein's Turks of twenty-four hundred. Given that the losses by an attacking force are almost always greater than those of the defender, and given the overall numerical superiority possessed by the British, these numbers were neither disproportionate nor excessively high. But Dobell and Murray made the mistake of deliberately exaggerating Turkish casualties, trebling their numbers, in the official reports made to Cairo and London. Taking these reports at face value and believing that the Turks were on the verge of collapse in Palestine, the War Cabinet ordered Murray to attack Gaza yet again, anticipating that when the Turkish line broke, the Tommies and the ANZACs could then march virtually unopposed into Jerusalem. When he struck at Gaza on April 17, however, von Kressenstein was waiting for him.

Once again, command of the actual attack was delegated to General Dobell, who this time eschewed any attempt at maneuver and resorted to the sort of brute-force tactics that were proving to be so costly and ineffective for the British Army on the Western Front. The Second Battle of Gaza opened with an artillery bombardment that employed gas shells for the first time in the Middle East. Dobell's three over-strength infantry divisions outnumbered von Kressenstein's eighteen thousand Turks by more than two to one and were supported by eight heavy Mark I tanks. But Dobell was no more successful than were the British generals in France: von Kressenstein had used the three weeks between the first and second assaults on Gaza to good advantage, constructing a formidable defense in depth, lavishly equipped with heavy machine guns. Despite their courage and determination, the Tommies and the ANZACs gained little ground but suffered heavily: 6,444 killed or wounded, with Turkish losses less than a third of that number.

As more than one historian has observed, Johnny Turk (the sobriquet bestowed with genuine admiration by the ANZACs on their Turkish foes) didn't need the Germans to teach him how to fight—the Turks had been waging war for eight hundred years—he simply needed to be taught how to wage a modern war. Once again, the same phenomenon that had manifested itself on the Gallipoli Peninsula and in Mesopotamia at Kut appeared at Gaza. The Turks, properly led and equipped, though outnumbered, had once again fought the British to a standstill. Von Kressenstein, after watching Dobell's attack grind to a halt, saw an opportunity to launch a counterattack. He would not, he knew, be able to throw the British back to the Suez Canal, but it might be possible to seriously disrupt their supply lines and the preparations for any further advance into Palestine. Djemal, still safely ensconced in Damascus, overruled him, and so von Kressenstein settled for confidently preparing for the inevitable—another British attack on Gaza. Attempting to keep the British off balance, he devised a series of local counterattacks at several points along the Gaza-Beersheba line. As the British appeared to lapse into inactivity, the number and frequency of their attacks declined. By mid-summer they had ceased altogether. Von Kressenstein remained alert, however, and in September Berlin recognized the skill with which he had defended Gaza in April by awarding him the Pour le Mérite, Germany's highest decoration.

Meanwhile, Murray relieved the hapless Dobell but in turn was sacked himself just days after the Second Battle of Gaza, when the War Cabinet in London turned a critical eye on his lackluster handling of the offensive into Palestine. At first glance, his replacement, Gen. Sir Edmund Allenby, hardly appeared to be an improvement—his reputation at that point was one of a tactically inflexible martinet. But the decision to give him Murray's command proved to be one of the wisest and best choices made during the entire war on any front.

The British general whose name would become inseparably linked with Britain's war in the Middle East and as famous as Sir Ian Hamilton's would be notorious, Edmund Henry Hynman Allenby, born on April 23, 1861, began his military career as a cavalryman. He was educated at the Royal Military Academy at Sandhurst and commissioned in the Inniskilling Dragoons in 1882. Prior to the Great War, most of his service experience had been in southern Africa; by the end of the Boer War in 1901, he had attained the rank of brevet colonel. He was given command of the cavalry division of the BEF when it was sent to France in August 1914. The skill he displayed in his handling of the unit led to his being appointed commander of the entire Cavalry Corps four months later and given command of the Third Army in early 1915. Yet he failed to distinguish himself in that post, and a long-standing friction with Field Marshal Sir Douglas Haig, the commander in chief of the BEF, led to his replacement by Gen. Sir Julian Byng in early 1917. Murray's vacated command was intended to be a backwater posting, as London, which had mustered great expectations of Murray and been disappointed, now expected little from Allenby.

Allenby was a strict disciplinarian, a trait that didn't particularly endear him to the boisterous, freewheeling Australians, who soon nicknamed him the "Bloody Bull." An undeserved reputation as a martinet is still assigned to Allenby in some circles. However much they may have resented his demands for proper military courtesy and a measure of "spit and polish," they quickly appreciated that he was a far different commander from Murray. Almost immediately after he arrived in Cairo, he packed his headquarters off to a position just a few miles behind the lines in Palestine (Murray had tried to direct the campaign from the comfort of the Egyptian capital) and was soon a frequent visitor to the front lines, examining the ground and the tactical situation for himself. It soon became clear that he was an intelligent, professional soldier who had no intention of wasting the lives of his own soldiers.

Six months were to pass between Murray's second attempt at taking Gaza and Allenby's first offensive. They were months of preparation, as Allenby gathered reinforcements, eventually bringing his troop strength to eighty-eight thousand. He also brought in additional artillery, a supply of gas shells for the new guns, and a collection of tanks and aircraft. But he wasn't inclined to simply deploy men and material in a repetition of the "brute force" tactics that had failed Dobell in April—and were so badly failing the BEF in France that summer. His intention was to deceive the Turks, catching them off balance and out of position to stop a truly decisive attack on the Gaza-Beersheba Line.

Arrayed against the EEF this time were the Turkish Seventh and Eighth Armies, with a strength of just thirty-five thousand men stretched out along a twenty-five-mile (forty-kilometer) line. But as the Turks had demonstrated at both the First and the Second Battles of Gaza, they knew how to hold a position, and their defenses were dense and well-sited. Anticipating that the British would once more try to take Gaza directly, von Kressenstein weighted his deployment more toward that town, rather than toward the other end of the line, Beersheba.

Beersheba, though, was the key to Allenby's plan for breaking the Gaza Line. Inevitably in the Middle East, the availability of water was critical to the success of any operation, and the six wells at Beersheba were the first objective of Allenby's plan. First, however, he had to convince the Turks and von Kressenstein that his eye was firmly fixed on Gaza alone.

What followed next was one of the great deceptions in the history of warfare. A huge tent city was erected behind the British lines south of Gaza, inhabited by only a few hundred men who would dash about like beavers whenever a Turkish reconnaissance plane flew overhead, giving the impression that the camp was home to thousands of British soldiers. Fifteen thousand canvas dummy horses were built; false wireless messages to nonexistent units were transmitted; teams of horses dragging huge harrows raised enormous dust clouds that simulated the movements of infantry columns or cavalry regiments; daily, long caravans were seen advancing toward Gaza, while at night they would be redirected eastward, to a position a few miles south of Beersheba. (The legend that a British intelligence officer deliberately planted false and misleading documents on the Turks was just that, however—a legend.) Von Kressenstein and the Turks took all of this at face value and on October 27 sent out a reconnaissance in force, with an all-out attack meant to disrupt the British preparations scheduled to follow on October 31.

Allenby beat von Kressenstein to the punch, however, as that was the same day scheduled for his attack on Beersheba. Having massed more than forty thousand troops, including the whole of the Australian Light Horse Division, against just four thousand Turkish defenders, Allenby sent in the attack with firm instructions to take the vital wells before the Turks could destroy them. The attack climaxed with a mounted charge by two regiments of Light Horse—a unique incident, for normally the Light Horse utilized their horses to move into battle, where they would dismount and fight as conventional infantry. It was the last mounted action by any forces of the British Empire, and it took the town and the wells by coup de main.

With the Gaza position now broken, the Turks began falling back toward Jerusalem under constant heavy pressure from Allenby's forces. At the same time, the Ottoman command structure in Palestine underwent a complete change, as the fall of Gaza marked the end of Djemal's rather sorry military career. He had long ago delegated actual battlefield command of the Turkish Seventh and Eighth Armies to his German advisers but had retained nominal command of the Ottoman forces in Palestine. Now, humiliated much as Enver had been after Sakiramish, he gave up even that pretense and left Damascus for Constantinople. On November 7, the same day that Gaza was abandoned, von Kressenstein was recalled to Berlin, his place taken by Gen. Erich von Falkenhayn, who, seeing no chance of stopping Allenby's advance short of the holy city, began preparing defensive positions in and around Jerusalem.

Von Falkenhayn had something of a mixed reputation as a senior officer. He had been the German minister of war from June 1913 to January 1915; that duty briefly overlapped his tenure as chief of the German General Staff, a post he held from September 1914, when he replaced the hapless Helmuth von Moltke ("von Moltke the Younger"), until he was forced to resign that post in August 1916. He had been the mastermind behind the Battle of Verdun: when his plan failed to break the French Army and cost the Germans casualties as great as those suffered by the French, he was dismissed by the Kaiser. Yet he had talent as a military commander. When Romania entered the war in August 1916, von Falkenhayn was given command of the Central Powers' troops in Transylvania and immediately took the offensive against the Romanians, driving deep into their territory. By Christmas, Bucharest had enough and Romania asked for an armistice. Von Falkenhayn was then sent to Constantinople, where Enver, demonstrating a definite lack of confidence in Djemal's martial talents, gave him overall command of the Ottoman forces in Palestine.

Allenby tried to move around von Falkenhayn's defensive line, which stretched from Jerusalem to the sea, in much the same way he had done to von Kressenstein but without the advantage of the strategic deception that had so thoroughly misled the latter. Moving eastward through the Judea Hills, he tried to swing wide of the holy city, but von Falkenhayn initiated a string of local counterattacks that slowed Allenby's movements and forced him to consolidate his forces.

Both commanders were operating under strict instructions from their respective capitals to avoid fighting within the limits of Jerusalem itself, a stricture that they observed with extraordinary care. In the end, this restriction was more of a hindrance to the Turks than to the British, for once Allenby had consolidated his strength, he was able to strike at the Ottoman forces around Jerusalem where and when he chose. An attack went in on the morning of December 8, and the city fell the same day when the Turks withdrew to positions north of Jerusalem; Allenby formally entered the city three days later.

It was a carefully staged entrance, with the British general passing into Jerusalem through the Jaffa Gate, the traditional portal used by the city's captors. Allenby was careful to not present himself as a conqueror, however, but as a pilgrim: he chose to pass through the gate on foot, rather than enter the city mounted. It was a distinction that was not lost on Jerusalem's populace, nor was the significance of the proclamation Allenby entered once inside the city walls:

TO THE INHABITANTS OF JERUSALEM THE BLESSED AND THE
PEOPLE DWELLING IN ITS VICINITY:

The defeat inflicted upon the Turks by the troops under my command has resulted in the occupation of your city by my forces. I, therefore, here now proclaim it to be under martial law, under which form of administration it will remain so long as military considerations make necessary.

However, lest any of you be alarmed by reason of your experience at the hands of the enemy who has retired, I hereby inform you that it is my desire that every person pursue his lawful business without fear of interruption.

Furthermore, since your city is regarded with affection by the adherents of three of the great religions of mankind and its soil has been consecrated by the prayers and pilgrimages of multitudes of devout people of these three religions for many centuries, therefore, do I make it known to you that every sacred building, monument, holy spot, shrine, traditional site, endowment, pious bequest, or customary place of prayer of whatsoever form of the three religions will be maintained and protected according to the existing customs and beliefs of those to whose faith they are sacred.

Guardians have been established at Bethlehem and on Rachel's Tomb. The tomb at Hebron has been placed under exclusive Moslem control.

The hereditary custodians at the gates of the Holy Sepulchre have been requested to take up their accustomed duties in remembrance of the magnanimous act of the Caliph Omar, who protected that church.

[signed]
Allenby

The capture of Jerusalem was greeted with a mixture of jubilation and relief in the Allied capitals, being taken as a sign that the Allies actually *were* winning the war. The news from all of the fronts had been uniformly bad for the British, the French, and the Russians in the autumn and the early winter of 1917. The United States had come into the war with the Allies in April of that year, but fear was beginning to grow in London, Paris, and Rome that the war could be lost before any significant American reinforcements reached France. (Italy, once suitably induced with promises of great swaths of Austrian territory once the war was won, had joined the Allies in the spring of 1915.) Russia, with her armies collapsing along with her economy, was negotiating a separate peace with the Central Powers at the Polish town of Brest-Litovsk. An end to the fighting in the east would release more than a hundred German divisions to be transferred to the Western Front, giving the Germans numerical superiority over the Allies for the first time since 1914. The Italian Army had suffered crippling losses at Caporetto, the French Army was only slowly recovering from a string of mutinies by troops at the front that had crippled it during the summer months, and the BEF had been decimated by the Passchendaele campaign: the British had suffered so many losses in more than three years of war that within another three months, the British Army would run out of replacements for its battered divisions. Even the cost of Allenby's victory was something of a relief: it had been relatively cheap—fewer than eighteen thousand British and ANZAC casualties. These were set against losses to the Turks that numbered more than twenty-five thousand, nearly two-thirds of the Turkish forces in Palestine—losses the Ottoman Army could ill afford.

One of the unanticipated consequences of Allenby's victories was the opportunity they offered the War Cabinet in London to alter strategic priorities in the Middle East. A few weeks prior to the fall of Jerusalem, the imperial General Staff had issued orders that effectively ended offensive action by the British forces in Mesopotamia. Now with the Holy City in Allied hands, London was able to impose a halt on the Egyptian Expeditionary Force as well.

Earlier, after the disaster of Kut-al-Amara, the British government in London had been forced to revise its view of the Mesopotamian Front. Up to that point, the War Office in London had been content to let the Indian government "run the show" in Mesopotamia, given that the preponderance of units in that theater were drawn from the Indian Army. After Townshend's surrender, that willingness dissolved, and the imperial General Staff, at the insistence of chief of staff Gen. William Robertson, insisted that Britain's Middle East strategy would henceforth be directed from London. One of Robertson's first actions was a thorough reorganization of the British command structure in Mesopotamia, sending the unfortunate and unpopular Gen. George Gorringe packing in July 1916. Coincidentally, on the other side of the lines, the Turks were reshuffling their own officers, with Khalil Pasha, the victor of Kut, being given command of all Turkish forces in the whole of the Mesopotamia.

Khalil understood that in desert warfare, merely occupying ground cannot be decisive. Decision comes with taking and holding specific geographic features and locations and, in so doing, providing opportunities to destroy the enemy's forces. During the lull in operations in the summer of 1916, Khalil drew his troops back from the positions immediately below Kut, shortening his lines and forming a reserve that offered the possibility of an offensive into Persia, driving at the vital British oil fields. In the event, long before the Turks' preparations for that attack were completed, the new British commander in Mesopotamia had begun another offensive toward Baghdad.

Gen. Sir Frederick Stanley Maude would eventually be recognized as one of the two best commanding officers on either side in the whole of the Middle East theater (Allenby being the other). A youthful (by First World War standards) fifty-two years old when he was tapped to be Gorringe's successor, he'd been born into a military family (his father held the Victoria Cross) and educated at Eton and Sandhurst, then distinguished himself as a junior officer, before serving as military secretary to the Governor-General of Canada, and taking a General Staff posting in London in 1904.

August 1914 saw Maude sent to France with the BEF, first on the staff of III Corps, then in command of the Fourteenth Brigade. He was seriously wounded in April 1915 and while recuperating in England was promoted to major general and sent to Gallipoli, where he took command of the 13th Division during its withdrawal from Suvla. He stayed with the division when it was later transferred to Mesopotamia and took overall command of the British and imperial forces there after Gorringe's dismissal. Known as Systematic Joe for his reputation as a careful and methodical commander, Maude and his command style seemed perfectly suited for the strategy that the imperial General Staff wanted to follow along the Tigris and Euphrates. Essentially, London let Maude know that all that was expected of him and the "Tigris Corps" was that he hold the existing British position and do nothing that would require additional men, material, or supplies.

Manpower had been a constant headache for the British in Mesopotamia: more soldiers were being laid low by disease, particularly typhus, than by enemy action. No sooner had Maude assumed command than he began reorganizing the supply and services structure for the entire region, with a particular emphasis placed on improving the work of the medical corps. By October 1916, due in no small part to those efforts, the troop strength of the Tigris Corps was up to 150,000 effectives, enough to let Maude feel confident that he could secure his supply lines while still being strong enough to take the offensive against the Turks before the winter floods began.

As Maude developed his plans, it was impossible to keep them entirely secret from the Turks; given the open, flat terrain, the movements of large bodies of troops were impossible to conceal. Karabekir Bey, the local Turkish commander who had succeeded Khalil Pasha on the latter's promotion, had some forewarning, then, of what was to come. Despite being outnumbered three to one, Karabekir felt confident that by drawing on the tactical skill of his German advisers, he could stop any British advance. That summer, at the River Somme in France, the Germans had all but perfected the art of the defense, developing ruthlessly lethal patterns of interlocking rifle, machine-gun, and artillery fire from well-sited, deeply entrenched positions, and it was this expertise that Karabekir meant to put to good use along the Tigris. At the same time, aware of the perils of overconfidence, he asked Khalil for reinforcements. Khalil, however, was absorbed with his own plans for the offensive into Persia and denied Karabekir's request, citing a lack of manpower to be able to accomplish both.

Maude's attack went in on the night of December 13–14, 1916. Attacking on both banks of the Tigris, two British corps, fifty thousand men, moved against the Turks. Admonished by London to avoid unnecessary casualties, Maude used a plan of attack that was methodical and slow but ultimately successful. It would require ten weeks before the whole of the Turkish position above Kut was cleared, but the British were able to systematically eliminate the Turkish strongpoints, often bringing them under direct fire from the Royal Navy's gunboat flotilla, which dominated the river and against which the Turks were never able to deploy an effective counter. Karabekir skillfully executed the retreat from Kut, using his machine guns to hold the pursuing British cavalry at bay, even as his infantry columns were being harassed by wild Arabs who murdered and pillaged stragglers and isolated detachments from either army with abandon. The way to Baghdad was open.

By the end of February, the British attack finally lost its momentum some sixty miles (one hundred kilometers) north of Kut, but its tenacity and duration had forced Khalil to first postpone and then abandon his plans for a Turkish drive into Persia, as well as recall an entire corps of infantry from the Russian frontier. For its part, the Tigris Corps was ready to push on to Baghdad after a week-long halt to rest and refit. That short breathing space gave Khalil an opportunity to shake the defenses of Baghdad into order: he was badly outnumbered, with no more than fifteen thousand effective troops at hand, but he was determined to hold the eastern terminus of the Berlin-to-Baghdad Railway, the Ottoman Empire's critical east-west axis. He had reason for confidence, because he knew that twenty thousand additional infantry were on their way from the Caucasus. The question was whether they would arrive before the British did.

Yet in a situation which required decisive action, Khalil uncharacteristically dithered. Initially deploying to defend Baghdad at Ctesiphon (where the Turks had first stopped the British in November 1915), he then decided while the defenses there were still incomplete to instead make a stand outside of Baghdad itself, shifting his troops and redirecting their work accordingly. Khalil's hesitation made the whole issue of holding Baghdad moot: however methodical General Maude might be, he was not about to permit Khalil the time to recover from such a blunder. On March 5 Tigris Corps resumed its advance on Baghdad, and by the evening of March 10, after five days of maneuver and countermaneuver, the Turks were evacuating the city to the north; the following morning, March 11, 1917, Indian infantry entered the city from the south.

The fall of Baghdad, though not as symbolic to the Allies as would be the capture of Jerusalem at year's end, resonated throughout the Middle East far more strongly than would the fall of the Holy City, signifying that the fabric of the Ottoman Empire itself was beginning to unravel. Baghdad had for centuries served as a sort of "eastern capital" for the Turks, a symbol of Ottoman power in the Arab world. In the late nineteenth and early twentieth centuries, it had become symbolic to the West as well, as the far terminus of the Berlin-to-Baghdad Railway project, itself meant to be the emblem of waxing Ottoman power as the empire gradually revived itself. The fall of Baghdad also illuminated, with unremitting clarity, how swiftly the Turks' remaining strength was waning. Constantinople had no reinforcements whatsoever to send to Khalil, however vital holding the city may have been. Every division the Ottoman Army possessed was deployed against the British or along the empire's frontiers, the army's reserves were exhausted, and replacements were impossible to come by. Whatever strength the divisions in the field possessed would be all that was left to them. It was the beginning of the end for the Turks, not only of the war, but of the Ottoman Empire itself.

Ironically, on the other side of the lines, Maude's successes were playing hob with the strategic plans of the imperial General Staff. After taking charge of the operations in Mesopotamia, London had been hoping to have a scaled-back Tigris Corps simply hold its positions, while some of its troops could be sent to the hard-pressed Western Front in France. The major thrust against the Turks in the Middle East, meanwhile, was to be carried out in Palestine. The victorious drive up the river instead compelled the War Office to continue to reinforce Tigris Corps in order to maintain it at its fighting strength of 150,000 infantry and cavalry, along with the Royal Navy contingents manning the gunboats on the two rivers.

For all his deliberate, careful, "Systematic Joe" image, Maude possessed a quality that was rare among Great War generals, regardless of nationality: the capacity to know when to allow a campaign to have its head, letting its momentum carry it as far forward as possible, without the restraints of timetables, frontal boundaries, phase lines, and the like. As Tigris Corps entered Baghdad, Maude sensed that it was good for one last lunge and so, rather than stop in the city to consolidate and reinforce, he barely paused there before directing his divisions northward once more, this time toward Samarrah, 80 miles (130 km) distant. Samarrah was the last railhead in Mesopotamia still in Turkish hands; taking it would force all of the Turkish forces in the region to retreat westward into Anatolia and compel them to do it on foot.

Khalil Pasha still had the remnants of the Baghdad defenders, ten thousand troops, under his immediate command, while two divisions pulled back from the Persian border were now converging on Samarrah. Khalil expected to have thirty thousand infantry at hand to defend Samarrah when Tigris Corps arrived, and given the need to protect his lengthening supply lines and communications, it was unlikely that Maude would be able to muster even a two-to-one superiority in troop strength. Nor could he count on moral superiority to make up some of the deficiency. Long gone were the days when the British and Indian soldiers fighting in the Tigris-Euphrates Valley disparaged the skill of "Johnny Turk." The Turks might be bullied out—or blown out or maneuvered out—of their positions, but there wasn't a soldier in Tigris Corps who expected the Turks to simply throw down their rifles and quit.

As the march on Samarrah developed, the Turks did put up one of their best fights of the entire Mesopotamian campaign. Circumstances forced Maude to adopt a rather complex plan that had four separate but interlocking parts, a plan that would require almost six weeks to carry out. First came a series of short, sharp attacks up the Tigris River toward Samarrah, to keep the pressure on the main objective and force Khalil to commit what few reserves he had to holding the railhead. Second was a series of maneuvers meant to push the Turks off the banks of the Euphrates River and so prevent them from trying to deliberately flood the neighboring plains, which would have hopelessly bogged down Maude's divisions. The third part was to move a blocking force to the northeast of Samarrah to prevent the two Turkish divisions under Ali Ishan Bey that had been recalled from the Persian border from linking up with Khalil. The last part of Maude's plan was to prevent the arrival of any reinforcements from the west. (Maude was not to know that there were *no* such reinforcements to be had anywhere in the empire.)

The four parts of Maude's plan methodically fell into place, although the Turks fought with courage and determination at every point. As usually happened in the battles in Mesopotamia and Palestine, British superiority in artillery, both in numbers and in weight of guns, proved decisive. The quick capture of Fallujah on March 19 was pivotal, as it forestalled any attempt at flooding the plains of the Euphrates. At Dogameh two weeks later, a long and bloody battle developed when Ali Ishan's two infantry divisions tried to bull their way through the British lines to link up with Khalil's forces. The British and Indian lines held, but each side lost more than three thousand dead and wounded. The defeat at Dogameh was the last straw for the Turks, and on April 23 they abandoned Samarrah.

General Maude's Tigris Corps had advanced more than 175 miles (280 km) in fewer than seven months and, in doing so, broke the back of Ottoman power in Mesopotamia. But success had come with a price: eighteen thousand British and

Indian soldiers were dead and a further forty thousand wounded or laid low by disease. Because of poor record keeping and the destruction of large numbers of documents during the retreat, as well as later, Turkish casualties would never be known.

After Samarrah fell, there was a lull in the action in Mesopotamia. It wasn't until the end of September that Maude felt Tigris Corps had regained sufficient strength to once again take the offensive against the Turks. An attack against the town of Ramadi on September 28 was a memorable success, as it marked the first use of armored cars in desert combat, allowing the British to literally run circles around the Turkish defenders. This action set the stage for the capture of Tikrit, the Allies' last significant offensive move in Mesopotamia.

When Gen. Alexander Cobbe was dispatched with two divisions of infantry and one of cavalry to strike at the Ottoman defenses north of Samarrah, the Turkish commander quickly withdrew to the town of Tikrit, which sits on the west bank of the Tigris River, 80 miles (130 km) north of Baghdad. Cobbe followed and on November 5, 1917, attacked, pitting his 15,000 infantry and cavalry against 4,000 Turks. The Turkish infantry fought tenaciously, yielding their positions only after suffering heavy casualties and inflicting serious losses on the British. Cobbe's troops entered the city of Tikrit itself the following morning, the Turks having evacuated during the night.

Whatever plans General Maude might have had for following up on this latest success were never put into action, for on November 18 he died suddenly of food poisoning. His death stunned the officers and the other ranks of Tigris Corps. At the same time, the necessity of posting a successor to Maude's command gave the War Office an opportunity to slow the tempo of Tigris Corps's operations, by ordering it to consolidate its gains and assume a defensive posture. This allowed for a dramatic reduction in the numbers of replacements that had to be sent to Mesopotamia, as well as permitted the withdrawal of most of the British divisions in order to redeploy them on the Western Front.

Events outside of the Middle East suddenly were making themselves felt throughout the region to a degree that they never had up to this point in the war. The Egyptian Expeditionary Force's advance northward through Palestine was halted just days after General Allenby had entered Damascus, and six of his ten infantry divisions were recalled to France. The British Army's manpower crisis was looming ever larger with each passing week, at the same time that the Allies' strategic situation was rapidly deteriorating. Just as it began to seem as if the final collapse of the Ottoman Army, and with it the Ottoman Empire, was imminent, the very real possibility that the Allies could lose the war materialized.

In February 1917, when revolution forced the tsar from the throne of imperial Russia, the Provisional Government in St. Petersburg avowed its intent to continue the war against the Central Powers. But another spring and summer of desperate fighting had exhausted the last strength of the Russian Army and sapped Russian morale to the breaking point. In November the Bolsheviks toppled the Provisional Government and began negotiating a separate peace with Germany and Austria-Hungary. It was self-evident to the French and the British that once a treaty was concluded, the Germans would transfer the majority of their troops currently serving on the Eastern Front to the Western, giving Germany an absolute superiority in manpower that it hadn't enjoyed since late 1914. The only questions were where the Teutonic hammer blow would fall and when. Every battalion that could be scraped together would be needed on the Western Front if the Allies were to have any chance of stopping the coming juggernaut.

The Germans launched their offensive on March 21, 1918—they called it variously the *Siegesturm*, the Stroke of Victory, or the *Kaiserschlact*, the Kaiser's Battle—but they were ultimately stopped short of a decisive triumph against either the French or the British. It was a close-run thing: on April 11, the commander of the BEF, Field Marshal Sir Douglas Haig, declared in a famous Order of the Day that the British Army was fighting with its "back to the wall." The German drive on Paris wasn't stopped until it had approached to within forty miles (sixty-four kilometers) of the French capital. The Germans' failure was due to a combination of British and French tenacity and courage, the timely arrival of American reinforcements, and the German High Command's inept execution of its offensive plans. Yet they came perilously close to success, and until it was clear that there would be no German breakthrough on the Western Front, all available Allied strength had to be directed to France. So it was not until early summer that Allenby began to receive the manpower and the supplies that would allow him to resume his advance on Damascus. In the meantime, Allenby tried to keep some sort of pressure on the Turks with a pair of cavalry attacks across the Jordan River. Both were turned back, although the British were able to hold a small bridgehead across the Jordan, north of the Dead Sea.

In that interim, the command of Turkish forces in Palestine changed yet again. In Damascus, Djemal carefully focused the blame for the defeats at Gaza and Jerusalem on Gen. Erich von Falkenhayn, the commander of the Yilderim Army Group, which consisted of the Seventh and Eighth Armies, with a nominal troop strength of approximately 150,000. While Djemal was agitating for his replacement, von Falkenhayn did little to bolster his position, having made himself unpopular with his Turkish subordinates with his open displays of favoritism for the German members of his staff. At the same time, his repeated demands for Ottoman withdrawals to shorten the Turkish lines in order to save manpower were poorly received in Damascus, as the Turks viewed them as demoralizing to their own soldiers and at the same time undermining Ottoman authority within the territory they still held. Djemal's intrigues finally succeeded in February 1918, when von Falkenhayn was replaced by Otto Liman von Sanders, who had won the Turks' admiration and respect for his role in defending the Gallipoli Peninsula in 1915. Von Sanders immediately halted any further withdrawals and began encouraging local counterattacks to keep the British off balance while the Turks constructed new defensive positions north of the Dead Sea. He knew that his Turks no longer possessed the strength to take the offensive against the British, but he was confident that they could stop any further enemy advances.

During the summer, five of the six infantry divisions that had been taken from the EEF were replaced with units from the Indian Army. The Turks were kept preoccupied by regular units of Sherrif Hussein's newly formed Arab Army, while the Arab irregulars under Lieutenant Colonel Lawrence continued to harass Turkish communications and troop movements. By the beginning of September, Allenby judged that the time had come for what he meant to be the decisive attack against the Turks: his objective was not merely to drive them out of Palestine, but to trap and destroy the Ottoman Army in the process.

Reprising the deceptions that had worked so well before the Third Battle of Gaza, Allenby focused the Turks' attention on the eastern end of his line, in the Jordan Valley, while he massed his infantry and cavalry for a breakthrough in the west, along the coast. Von Sanders positioned nearly all of his troops in the front lines, his only reserve being two regiments of German infantry (part of the so-called Asia Korps, a melange of artillery, signals, and engineer units supported by a handful of infantry battalions that had been originally sent to assist the Turks in 1915) and an under-strength division of Turkish cavalry. Sickness and lack of supplies had been eroding his soldiers' morale, with desertion becoming a steadily increasing problem that left many of his units sharply undermanned, and this led von Sanders to create a classic "crust" defense, in the hope of stopping the British attack before it got well and truly going. He lacked confidence in his soldiers' ability to fight a battle of maneuver and abandoned all hope of conducting a defense in depth.

Allenby's attack began early on September 19, 1918, in the middle of a storm, when 385 medium and heavy guns opened up a furious artillery barrage on the Turkish positions around Mount Megiddo, the key position in the Turkish defensive line, some fifteen miles inland from the Mediterranean Sea. Within hours the Turkish line was breached, with the British cavalry riding hell for leather northward to cut off the Ottoman line of retreat. Von Sanders had no choice but to order a full-scale withdrawal of the entire Yilderim Group. Continuously harassed from the air by Royal Air Force bombers and fighters and on the ground by Lieutenant Colonel Lawrence's Arab irregulars, all the while pressed hard by the steadily advancing British infantry, the Turks' Seventh and Eighth Armies ceased to exist as viable military forces within a week, and the retreat became a rout.

For ten days, British and Australian mounted troops were kept busy rounding up large numbers of demoralized and disorganized Turkish troops—the final total was some seventy-five thousand Turkish prisoners of war. Not all of the Turks who wanted to surrender got the chance to do so, however; as they retreated, a handful of Turks turned on the local inhabitants, committing dreadful atrocities of rape and murder. In return, the Arab irregulars refused to take prisoners. On September 27, near the village of Tafas, an entire Turkish brigade (along with a few hundred German and Austrian advisers) was massacred; the next day the Arabs did the same to another Ottoman unit, killing more than five thousand Turks in the two actions, at a cost of a few hundred Arab dead.

As the Turkish armies disintegrated, British infantry moved north along the coast toward Beirut, and Indian divisions marched up the Beqaa Valley, capturing the last of the Turkish supply depots. Meanwhile, Allenby ordered the 5th Mounted Division and the ANZAC Mounted Division to cross over the Jordan River, take the Golan Heights, and drive toward Damascus. Djemal Pasha fled before the Australians were able to completely encircle the city, leaving a local magistrate in charge. At dawn on the morning of September 30, the Australian Third Light

Horse regiment passed through the city and cut off all roads leading out of Damascus; they were shortly followed by three more regiments of Light Horse and a brigade of Indian cavalry. Trapped, the Turkish garrison, twelve thousand infantry, formally surrendered a few hours later. Not long afterward, a column of Lawrence's Arab irregulars charged noisily into the city and almost immediately began fostering the myth that they alone had captured Damascus. The following day, acting on the promises that Lawrence had made to them almost two years earlier, the Arabs proclaimed Faisal ibn Hussein the king of Syria.

The capture of Damascus essentially brought an end to the war in Palestine, although sporadic fighting would continue in parts of the province of Syria for another four weeks. But it was the fall of Damascus that well and truly took the heart out of the Turks. Allied columns were racing across Syria and northern Palestine, and the Ottoman Army had ceased to exist in all but name. When an Allied offensive began advancing out of Macedonia, where the Allies, the Turks, and the Bulgars had spent almost three years in masterful mutual inactivity, on the same day that Damascus fell, the new Sultan, Mehmed VI (his brother, Mehmed V, had died of old age on July 3), reasserted imperial authority and dismissed Enver in disgrace from his post as war minister. When Allenby's troops captured the city of Aleppo on October 26, the Turks had had enough: the Young Turk leadership and especially Talaat Pasha, now the Grand Vizier, conceded that the war was lost. The Cabinet resigned en masse on October 8, and at the Sultan's direc019 Marshal Ahmet Izzet Pasha, who had no ties to the Young Turk regime, formed an interim government, which immediately asked General Townshend, who had been captured at Kut, to serve as an emissary to request an armistice with the Allies. When the Allies agreed, Mehmed VI designated his new minister of marine, Raouf Bey, who just four years earlier had been anticipating his new command as captain of the dreadnought *Sultan Osman I*, to be his chief negotiator. Raouf met with British admiral Somerset Arthur Gough-Calthorpe aboard HMS *Agamemnon* in the harbor of the Greek island of Mudros (ironically, the site of Gen. Ian Hamilton's headquarters during the Gallipoli campaign) and on October 28 they signed the cease-fire.

The terms of the armistice were harsh, but the Turks had little choice other than to accept. The Allies would occupy the forts that guarded the Straits of the Dardanelles and the Bosporus; control of all ports and railways would be turned over to the Allies; Turkish forces had to withdraw to the interior of Anatolia, and all Ottoman garrisons outside of Anatolia were to surrender outright; the Ottoman Army was to be immediately demobilized; and the Allies would reserve the right to occupy any Turkish territory "in case of disorder." Constantinople itself would be occupied, and implicit within the terms of the armistice was the assurance that the Ottoman Empire would eventually be partitioned among the victorious Allied powers. Though two more years would pass before the funeral rites would be completed, the message was clear: the Sick Man of Europe had finally expired. The Ottoman Empire had fallen at last.

CHAPTER TEN

THE FALL OF THE SULTAN'S REALM

When the Turks decided to quit on October 28, no one in any of the Allied capitals could claim it was unexpected; the only real surprise was that the Turks had held on so long. After all, the whole edifice of the Central Powers' alliance was crumbling before the eyes of the world. Even as Raouf Bey and Admiral Gough-Calthorpe were sitting down in HMS *Agamemnon*'s wardroom, the Dual Monarchy of Austria-Hungary had already begun disintegrating, bringing an end to nearly five hundred years of Hapsburg rule in Central Europe. Bulgaria had quit a month earlier, signing an armistice with the Allies on September 29. Only the Germans fought on, but even they would reach the end of their strength before another week had passed. Berlin asked for an armistice on November 8; three days later it was signed and became reality.

For a week, perhaps ten days, the whole world seemed to stop and collectively take a deep breath as it began to assimilate the reality of peace, recognize how fundamentally the world had changed (understanding would require decades), and assess the costs of the conflict. The Great War had left all of the great European powers physically and morally exhausted, emotionally and financially drained. One, Russia, had collapsed under the strain and quit completely in early 1918 and even now was dissolving in the chaos of civil war. An entire social order, along with all of its virtues as well as its vices, had been swept away in the carnage, as three of Europe's ruling houses were toppled, taking their empires with them—the

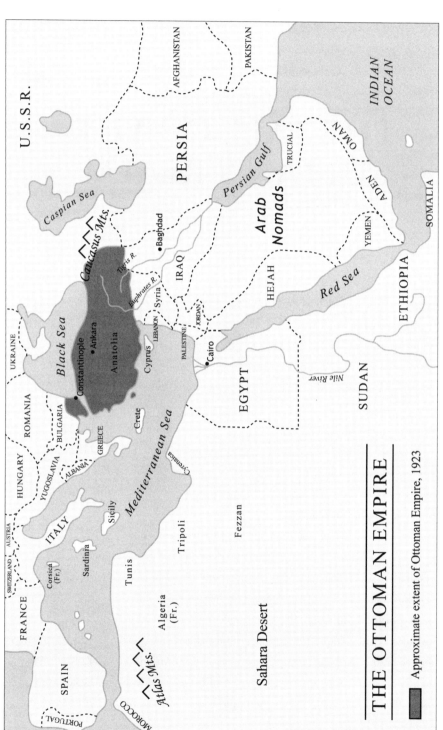

THE OTTOMAN EMPIRE

■ Approximate extent of Ottoman Empire, 1923

Chad Blevins

Romanovs, the Hapsburgs, and the Hohenzollerns. There was little cause for optimism that a fourth, the House of Osman, wouldn't join them in oblivion.

True, there didn't seem to be much left over that a sultan and his government could rule. If the other Great Powers had been exhausted by the war, the Ottoman Empire had been devastated; proportionately, the Turks had sacrificed as greatly as did their German and Austrian allies. If the Ottoman Empire had collapsed so much more completely than did imperial Germany or the Dual Monarchy—and it had—it was because the Sultan's realm had begun so far below the levels of its allies in the first place. While there was widespread hunger (and cases of genuine starvation) in Germany and Austria-Hungary, at least they were spared the worst of the agonies that the Turks would endure in the years that immediately followed the end of the war. By the time the armistice was signed, food, clothing, and medical care had become almost nonexistent anywhere in the empire; typhus and cholera were beginning to spread within the army and reach out into the civilian populace, while malaria and scurvy started to appear as well. Once-prosperous farms were reduced to arid tracts of barren soil or vistas of weeds and scrub, as there was hardly a draft animal able to pull a plow to be found anywhere—the government had commandeered almost every horse, mule, and ox in the empire. The Turks' meager rail net, pathetically sparse by European standards before the war, was in tatters, the rails and the rail beds themselves in disrepair, while what little rolling stock remained was worn out and all but worthless. Apart from a handful of government-owned automobiles in the capital, there was virtually no other motor transport anywhere in the empire.

Long before the armistice, the Ottoman economy had ground to a halt, as inflation reached 400 percent in the last months of the war. Not unexpectedly, a thriving black market appeared in Constantinople. The middle class had for all practical purposes ceased to exist as the merchants, the businessmen, and the professionals, most of them from ethnic or religious minorities, either had been driven from the empire or had fled during the war. Apart from the two ammunition factories in the capital, manufacturing of any kind had all but ceased everywhere in Anatolia. And even had there been working factories and shops in Constantinople, there was no one to man them: the able-bodied workers they would have employed had long since fled to the countryside to avoid military service.

Desertion from active duty, along with outright evasion from conscription, had been a problem for the Ottoman Army from the beginning of the war, but as the conflict progressed it had grown to epidemic proportions. By October 1918, the whole of the Turkish Army numbered barely a hundred thousand men, scarcely 15 percent of its peak strength in early 1916. Much as Russian soldiers had done in 1917, tens of thousands of Ottoman soldiers, mostly Arabs and Kurds but also Turks, "voted with their feet" and deserted at the first available opportunity. Some sources estimate that in the last year of the war, four hundred thousand men either simply walked away from their units or took to the hills when called up to serve in the army. "Took to the hills" was exactly what they did, vanishing into the huge empty spaces of Mesopotamia or Arabia, the mountains of northern Anatolia, or the rugged countryside of Palestine or the Turkish steppe. There they blended in with the local populace, who, having little sympathy for the Young Turks and feeling no loyalty to the Sultan, almost always willingly protected them. The terms of the armistice had dictated that the Ottoman Army be demobilized and disbanded, but for all practical purposes the army, fatally weakened by these desertions, had already dissolved after the fall of Damascus. As it did, almost all central authority in what had been the empire had vanished.

There wasn't much hope that the Ottoman Empire would be allowed to continue to exist in any form, however truncated. In the final three months of the war, as it became increasingly obvious that the Central Powers were going to finally lose the conflict, the Allies had issued a succession of steadily more severe conditions that had to be met before they would agree to any armistice, and among them had been demands for the Kaiser in Berlin and the emperor in Vienna to give up their thrones. While the American president Woodrow Wilson had made a guarantee of the integrity of Turkish Anatolia as a Turk homeland part of his peace proposal, which became known as "The Fourteen Points," no mention was made of what form of government would be acceptable to the Allies. Instead, during the course of the next four years, the Ottoman Empire was transformed into the Republic of Turkey, and what had been the Sultan's realm was reshaped into what the world would come to know as the modern Middle East. How that came about was determined by three interrelated events: the occupation of Constantinople, the partition of what had been the Ottoman Empire, and the negotiation of the Treaty of Sèvres.

On November 12 the first Allied troops, a French infantry brigade, entered Constantinople; the next day they were followed by several British battalions; later that same day, the Allied fleet sailed into the Bosporus. Within a month, an Allied administration of military occupation had been set up, and sections of the city were assigned to the various Allied garrisons posted there. The most symbolic event came in February 1919, when the French general Franchet d'Espèrey rode into the city astride a white horse, a deliberate echo of Mehmed the Conqueror's triumphal entrance into Constantinople in 1453. A melodramatic gesture, to be sure, but every Turk understood its meaning.

Not unexpectedly, Enver, Talaat, and Djemal were wanted by the Allies as war criminals, as were all of the former ministers of the wartime Cabinet. So thoroughly had that unhappy triumvirate discredited themselves among their own countrymen, they could not even count on the protection of their fellow Turks. Even before the armistice was signed at Mudros, Enver had fled the capital, together with Talaat and Djemal, aboard one of the last German merchant ships to leave Constantinople. All three ultimately wound up in Berlin for a brief period of time; all three would come to unhappy ends within four years.

Under pressure from the Allies, Mehmed VI had set up special courts-martial to try Talaat, Enver, and Djemal, along with their fellow Cabinet members, in absentia. They were charged with being "mired in an unending chain of bloodthirstiness, plunder and abuses" and drawing the Ottoman Empire into the Great War "by a recourse to a number of vile tricks and deceitful means." Their indictment also declared that "The massacre and destruction of the Armenians were the result of decisions by the Central Committee"—that is, the Three Pashas—and went on to accuse them of attempting to "pile up fortunes for themselves" through "the pillage and plunder" of the Armenian victims' possessions. Although the "trial" was little more than a thinly disguised kangaroo court, the defendants were all safely out of reach in Germany, Switzerland, or Scandinavia, and so the inevitable verdict of "guilty" was returned on July 5, 1919: to no one's surprise, the Three Pashas were condemned to death. The Turkish embassy in Berlin went through the motions of requesting that the trio be extradited to Constantinople, but the German government, which had only just persuaded the Allies to allow Germans accused of war crimes to be tried by German courts, were in no mood to hand anyone over. They threw up a legal smokescreen that blocked the extradition, while Talaat, Enver, and Djemal once again indulged in their mutual passion for intrigue.

Talaat was the first to go. He spent the better part of two years after leaving Constantinople attempting to stir up rebellion among the Moslem populations in the southern regions of the newly formed Soviet Union, using Berlin as his base of operations. He knew he was a marked man and feared assassination by Armenians seeking revenge, so he changed his address frequently. But his luck ran out on March 15, 1921, as he was strolling arm in arm with his wife down a street in the Berlin suburb of Charlottenburg. A young Armenian named Soghomon Tehlirian stepped in front of the couple, greeted Talaat by name, then drew a revolver and put a bullet through the Turk's brain.

Djemal tried to create a new role for himself in the diplomatic world, serving as liaison officer in talks between the newly established Soviet Union and the postwar Turkish government. Later Djemal went to Central Asia, where he became an adviser to the Afghan Army. Careful to maintain his ties to the new Soviet regime, he was sent as Moscow's representative to Tbilisi, in the Georgian Soviet Socialist Republic, where he was assassinated on July 1, 1922, by an Armenian nationalist, in reprisal for his part in the Armenian massacres.

The Armenians never got to Enver. Hardly had he arrived in Berlin than he reverted to type and resumed his perpetual intriguing. Meeting with German radicals, he tried, unsuccessfully, to establish some sort of cooperation between the Russian Bolsheviks and the German communists in a harebrained scheme to return the Young Turks to power in Constantinople. From Berlin he went to Moscow, where he was introduced to Lenin, who gave him a minor post in the new Soviet government's Asiatic Department. While working for the Bolsheviks, he still dreamed of playing a role in shaping the future of the now-disintegrating Ottoman Empire and approached the Turkish Nationalists, offering them his services, but was sharply rebuffed. In November 1921 he was sent by Lenin to Bukhara in the Turkistan Autonomous Soviet Socialist Republic to help suppress a revolt against the Bolshevik regime in Moscow. Enver being Enver, he sensed a chance to further his own fortunes by throwing in with the rebels instead and within a year was actually leading the rebellion. But on August 4, 1922, his headquarters was attacked by a brigade of Red Army cavalry. Enver had only his personal guard, thirty strong, with him, and he died in a burst of machine-gun fire as he was leading his men. He was forty years old.

In Constantinople, Adm. Somerset Arthur Gough-Calthorpe, who had signed the armistice with Raouf Bey, was appointed military governor in January 1919. One of his first tasks was overseeing the arrest, as war criminals, of people who had held senior government posts during the war. Calthorpe was sending a message to the Sublime Porte, and while the other Allies refused to endorse Calthorpe's action, the Sultan and his government understood it perfectly: the House of Osman and its lackeys remained, wielding what little power they did, only at Allied sufferance. In February 1919 the Sultan informed the Allies that his government was prepared to fully cooperate with the occupation forces in every way.

The detainees were sent to the island of Malta, where they were held until their "trials" in Constantinople before the same tribunal that had convicted Enver, Talaat, and Djemal. The court sat for nearly a year, from April 1919 through March 1920, although it became clear after just a few months that the tribunal was simply going through the motions. The judges had conveniently condemned the first set of defendants (Enver, et al.) when they were safely out of the country, but now, with Turkish lives genuinely on the line, the tribunal, despite making a great show of its efforts, had no intention of returning convictions. Calthorpe protested to the Sublime Porte, took the trials out of Turkish hands, and removed the proceedings to Malta. There an attempt was made to seat an international tribunal, but so badly or so well, depending on the point of view, had the Turks bungled the investigations and mishandled the documentary evidence that nothing of their work could be used by the international court. After Calthorpe was replaced by Adm. John de Robeck in August 1920, the proceedings were halted, and de Robeck informed London of the futility of continuing the tribunal with the remark, "Its findings cannot be held of any account at all."

While Calthorpe was in Constantinople, he kept a sensitive finger on the pulse of events in what was left of the Ottoman Empire, and very early on he grew concerned about the actions of the recently appointed inspector general of the Ottoman Army (such as it was and what remained of it), Mustafa Kemal. The British remembered Kemal well from the defeat he had handed them at Gallipoli, and he was widely regarded as the most astute officer in the Sultan's service. Believing that Kemal had larger designs than simply reforming and reorganizing the Turkish Army, as his post required, Calthorpe wanted him dismissed, but Kemal had become a national hero to the Turks after Gallipoli, and he had a large number of friends and sympathizers within the government. They worked out a compromise with Calthorpe whereby the post of "inspector general" was given no authority to command troops. Still, his skepticism unallayed by this maneuver, Calthorpe for-

warded to the Foreign Office a report of his suspicions about Kemal and his association with the growing Turkish Nationalist movement. Calthorpe was recalled to
London in mid-summer, while his worries, along with similar concerns expressed
by other officers, were downplayed by Whitehall. As events would turn out, that
may have been the best thing that could have happened for the Turks.

Adm. John de Robeck replaced Gough-Calthorpe as "Commander in Chief,
Mediterranean, and High Commissioner, at Constantinople" on August 5, 1919. If
Calthorpe had been worried by Kemal, de Robeck found himself as seriously con-
cerned by another situation that was simmering uneasily in the Ottoman capital.
De Robeck couldn't help but be aware of a rising resentment of the Allies in the
Ottoman parliament, and he soon grew suspicious of its growing ties with the
nascent Turkish Nationalist movement. Rumors were rife in Constantinople that
Turkish revolutionaries were building sizable stockpiles of arms and ammunition,
and in a warning letter to London, de Robeck pointedly asked, "Against whom
would these resources be employed?"

De Robeck had cause for alarm, for there *was* a rising bitterness in the Turks'
attitude toward the Allies. It was rooted in the reports from the Paris Peace Conference of the terms of the peace treaty that would be imposed by the Allies, coupled
with the arrogance with which the British and the French were carving up Turkish
Anatolia and partitioning the provinces of the empire. Adding to the tension was
the apparent readiness of the Sultan, who everyone knew remained on his throne
at the Allies' pleasure, to sit idly by as his realm was dismembered.

The partition was, of course, a consequence of the wartime agreements that
the Allies had made among themselves, although they were at times openly contradictory. The centerpiece of these was the Sykes-Picot Agreement, which had
divided Mesopotamia and the Levant between the British and the French, but the
"spheres of influence" and the areas of outright control delineated by the agreement conflicted with the ambitions of Arab nationalists, who had clung to the
promises London had made to Sherrif Hussein while the British had still been in
the Sinai.

Ultimately, the British decided that they would retain control of Mesopotamia and the southern half of the Ottoman province of Syria, specifically Palestine
and Jordan. The northern half of Syria, including the city of Damascus, would be
transferred to French control. This was in direct contravention of the assurances
given to Hussein's son Faisal, who had established the "Kingdom of Syria" in

Damascus in October 1919, the boundaries of which were to include Jordan and Palestine. Regardless, the British withdrew and the French moved in, and they soon dissolved Faisal's government.

In an effort to convince Paris and London to change their positions, Faisal had traveled to the Paris Peace Conference. There he hoped to gain the support of the president of the United States, Woodrow Wilson, who had made national self-determination one of the cornerstones of America's entry into the Great War on the side of the Allies. But Faisal was outmaneuvered by the British prime minister, who prevented any substantial contact between Faisal and Wilson, and the would-be Arab monarch returned to Syria empty-handed. In the meantime, the French, ignoring Faisal completely, had gone ahead and named Gen. Henri Gouraud as a high commissioner in their newly styled province of Syria-Cilicia, giving him near autocratic power. After attempting to assert himself as "King Faisal I of Greater Syria," the would-be monarch was expelled by the French in August 1920. He spent a year in exile in Great Britain, then returned to the Middle East where, after a rigged, British-sponsored plebiscite, he was crowned Faisal I of Iraq, with perhaps enough power and authority to change his palace guard without first seeking British permission.

Faisal hadn't been without allies, for in June 1919 the American King-Crane Commission arrived in Syria, created by the United States Congress to determine how successfully Allied policies were in responding to the wants and needs of the peoples in the former Ottoman territories and provinces. The commission's report made it clear that the Arab populace in Syria was adamantly opposed to the presence of the French, the repudiation of the promises made to Hussein and Faisal, and the Balfour Declaration. Yet when President Wilson attempted to press the commission's conclusions, they were angrily rejected by France and studiously ignored by Britain.

In the meantime, farther to the south, the British recognized the primacy of Sherrif Hussein ibn Ali over what had been the Ottoman province of Hejaz, thereby honoring at least one of their wartime promises and fulfilling Hussein's long-standing ambition to become both de facto and de jure ruler of the region. To the east, the House of Saud had been given control of the heartland of the Arabian Peninsula, the Nejd, while the independence of the Caliphate of Yemen and the Sultanate of Oman, on Arabia's southern coast, remained unaffected. In the process of all of these territorial shifts, however, borders were being drawn more or less arbitrarily, with little reference to historical precedent or, in the case of the Arabs, religious factions, traditional tribal boundaries, and dynastic claims.

The French response to Faisal's claims is understandable, given that the power of France had been in a slow but steady decline since the end of the Napoleonic Wars. After the horrifying casualties the French had suffered during the Great War (one of every three Frenchmen between the ages of eighteen and forty had been killed or wounded), it was inevitable that France's decline would only accelerate, and the French wanted something to show for the price they had paid. The acquisition of new territory, even at the expense of an erstwhile ally, would serve as some degree of compensation, so France was quick to seize whatever she could. As the French saw it, they had not been party to the pledges made to Hussein and so were not bound by them, and in any event, they believed, the Sykes-Picot Agreement took precedence.

Yet the British reaction is far more difficult to fathom. Great Britain had paid a price for victory nearly as terrible as that of France: more than ninety years later, the bodies of British soldiers are still being unearthed from soil in Belgium and France that had once been part of the Western Front. But Britain had gone to war because the government—and the nation—felt honor-bound to abide by the treaty guaranteeing the neutrality of Belgium. Now, in the Middle East, while solemn pledges made to the Arabs in the name of the British government and people weren't actually being trampled, they were being dismissed as irrelevant. This was no small consideration, for in 1914 then foreign secretary Sir Edward Grey had argued before the House of Commons that if Great Britain did not abide by its promise to defend Belgium should that nation be attacked, the integrity of Great Britain's word in future international agreements would become suspect, giving other nations cause for mistrust and undermining Britain's power and moral authority in world affairs. Yet it was precisely this situation that now obtained in the Middle East after the Turkish armistice.

The personage behind this policy was the British prime minister, David Lloyd George, who at the Paris Peace Conference demonstrated to the world his preference for accruing and exercising power, rather than accomplishing the ends that the use of that power could achieve. He attempted to present himself to the world as the consummate statesman, the voice of reason trying to balance the aims of

French prime minister George Clemenceau, who was demanding harsh, punitive terms in any peace treaty with Germany, and American president Woodrow Wilson, who was advocating moderation as the best means of ensuring a lasting peace. The result, which became the Treaty of Versailles, was predictable: its terms were severe enough to leave the German people embittered and susceptible to rabble rousers and hate-mongers preaching betrayal and revenge, while at the same time lacking the punitive power to prevent them from ultimately rearming and attempting to extract that revenge. Lloyd George had been openly contemptuous of the idealistic Wilson and the militant Clemenceau—he once compared working with them to "being seated between Jesus Christ and Napoleon"—but unlike them he had no coherent policy of his own to advocate. He had promised the British people that Germany would pay in full the material and monetary costs of the war but went to the Paris Peace Conference without having concocted a workable plan that would accomplish that goal. The terms of the Treaty of Versailles as ultimately signed were a hodge-podge of half-hearted half-measures that throttled Germany's postwar economy without bringing any meaningful benefit to that of Great Britain. After the treaty was signed, in a rare moment that was equal parts frankness and prescience, Lloyd George admitted that it was a failure that in twenty years' time would lead to another European war.

The British prime minister was equally lacking in having a coherent plan for the lands partitioned off from the Ottoman Empire. Although he was far from unaware of the various and competing agreements and promises made by Great Britain regarding the postwar Middle East, he gave no attention to their consequences. He paid lip service to British promises made to the Arabs, in particular the so-called McMahon-Hussein Correspondence, and declared them to be "treaty obligations." The correspondence was a series of letters exchanged between Sherrif Hussein and Sir Henry McMahon, the British high commissioner in Egypt, from 1914 to 1916. In it, the British government promised Arab self-determination and autonomy in the Ottoman regions of Mesopotamia, Syria, Palestine, and Arabia.

However inconvenient it might be, such an explicit commitment was something Lloyd George could not simply pretend did not exist. Nor could he claim that these were pledges made by the Asquith Government that had been rendered null and void by subsequent events. On January 11, 1918, a Foreign Office letter (known as the Hogarth Message, after the British officer who delivered it) was sent to Hussein stating the official position of the British government to be that "the Entente Powers are determined that the Arab race shall be given full opportunity of once again forming a nation in the world. This can only be achieved by the Arabs themselves uniting, and Great Britain and her Allies will pursue a policy with this ultimate unity in view."

Yet when Lloyd George finally met with Clemenceau and Wilson (along with Prime Minister Vittorio Orlando of Italy) in March 1919 to settle the partition of the former Ottoman territories, the British prime minister's focus was on settling the Allies' differences over the specifics of the Sykes-Picot Agreement, which allowed for neither Arab self-determination nor Arab autonomy. The decisions regarding boundaries, borders, and spheres of influence to which the four leaders finally agreed would become formalized in the next three years by the creation of a series of territorial "mandates" by the League of Nations, which assured that the paramount authorities in the region would be France and Great Britain. This did not greatly trouble the French, but for the British the upshot was precisely that of which Sir Edward Grey had warned should Great Britain not honor its diplomatic commitments. The British, although they continued to be respected or at least feared throughout the region were also never again fully trusted anywhere in the Arab world.

How the Allies dealt with the Arabs, however, was of little concern to the Turks. The increasing tension that Admirals Gough-Calthorpe and de Robeck had reported to London was the consequence of the Allies' equally high-handed behavior toward what remained of the Turkish homeland. At the same time that the French and the British were setting up their spheres of influence in Mesopotamia and Syria, they were also carving up Anatolia, or "Turkey," as it was becoming known in popular parlance, which had been the Turks' homeland for more than a millennium.

All of the Ottoman territory on the north, or European, side of the Bosporus and the Dardanelles was to be given to Greece, save for the land immediately surrounding Constantinople. Along with this went a large tract on the Aegean coast that in ancient times had been known as Ionia, as well as the Turks' remaining Aegean islands. The Straits were to be completely demilitarized, as was Constantinople. The eastern quarter of Turkey would be divided between the newly created (and soon to be short-lived) Democratic Republic of Armenia and a contemplated

Kurdish state. Most of what remained to the Turks, barely three-fifths of Anatolia, was to be divided into French, British, and Italian spheres of influence.

All of this was first determined at the Paris Peace Conference; the details were worked out by the British, the French, and the Italians at the Conference of London in February, then further refined at the San Remo Conference two months later. Rumors and rumblings began flying around the Ottoman capital within days of their formulation, but the details of how the Turkish homeland was to be divided and subdivided weren't made public until August 10, 1920. That was when the peace settlement between the Allies and the Ottoman Empire was presented to the Sultan's representatives, at the French town of Sèvres, outside of Paris.

The Treaty of Versailles, the peace settlement executed between Germany and the Allies a year earlier, has become synonymous with harsh and unfair peace settlements, although, as such documents go, there have been far worse. The German-dictated Treaty of Brest-Litovsk in March 1918, for example (where the Germans used the same tactics that the Allies employed fifteen months later—they simply handed over the terms and showed the Russian delegation where to sign), was far more punitive. The Treaty of Sèvres, as the peace settlement between the Allies and the Ottoman Turks would be called, followed in broad strokes the example of Versailles but was much harsher in its details. As with Germany, Austria, and Hungary, the Turks had not been allowed to participate in any negotiation of the terms of the treaty. The Allies regarded the Central Powers as "defeated" nations that had lost their rights to negotiate. The Turks were simply informed of the treaty's contents and instructed to sign it. And like the Versailles document, the Treaty of Sèvres would evoke a violent reaction from the defeated nation, although more quickly and ultimately with far more palatable consequences.

In short, the treaty confirmed the partition of the empire's provinces between the Allied powers, as well as the division of Anatolia and the ceding of parts of the Turkish homeland to the Greeks, the Armenians, and the Kurds. The Ottoman Army was to be limited to fifty thousand officers and other ranks, the navy reduced to a flotilla of light warships, and an air force absolutely forbidden in any form. Persons who were deemed responsible for "barbarous and illegitimate methods of warfare . . . [including] offenses against the laws and customs of war and the principles of humanity" were to be turned over to the Allies. The Bosporus, the Dardanelles, and the Sea of Marmara were to be internationalized, open to navigation by all merchant traffic as well as warships, regardless of what flag they flew or whether or not the Turks were at peace or at war at the time of their passage.

All of these were terms that could have been realistically expected by the Sultan, the handful of Turkish officials who still pretended that they were running an empire, the remnants of the Ottoman Army, and even the Turkish people. However galling the knowledge may have been, what could not be denied was that the Turks were beaten, and inevitably the victors' terms would be severe. Yet the further provisions of the treaty went far beyond anything that had been imposed on Germany or the other Central Powers. They were openly humiliating to the Turks, who were infuriated when the terms were announced and regarded them as nothing less than an attempt by the Allies to reduce what remained of the Ottoman Empire to a state of permanent vassalage to Great Britain, France, and Italy.

Under the conditions set forth by the treaty, the Allies would be given absolute authority over the empire's finances, first by assuming control of the Ottoman Bank, the empire's central financial institution, which would allow them to control the national currency. They would also have the power to draw up the national budget and write financial laws and regulations. The national debt would be restructured so that all monies paid to its relief would go only to the British, the French, and the Italians, who would also be the recipients of import and export duties levied at Turkish ports. All business enterprises owned by German, Austrian, Hungarian, or Bulgar interests were to be liquidated, along with any private property owned by citizens of the former Central Powers; the monies resulting from these liquidations were to be turned over to the Allies. Taxes, customs collection, international loans, and commercial concessions would all be subject to the approval and oversight of an Allied financial commission. The only good news for the empire was the mandatory abolition of all internal tariffs in Turkey.

One provision of the settlement was ironic when the treaty was passed down to the Turks: the empire's electoral system was to be reorganized in order to allow for proportional representation in the Ottoman parliament of all of the ethnic groups living in Turkey. The irony came from the fact that the Turkish parliament had been abolished by Admiral de Robeck five months before the treaty was published, on March 18, 1920. There was nothing ironic, however, about how that abolition came about.

No sooner had the Allies marched into Constantinople in November 1918 than they made it clear that none of the members of the sitting Ottoman parliament were politically acceptable to them. Given the chaos within the empire, organizing new elections took time, and it was not until December 1920 that voting for a new Ottoman parliament took place. When the returns came in, an overwhelming majority of the newly elected members belonged to the Association (or Society) for the Defense of Rights for Anatolia and Roumelia (Anadolu ve Rumeli Müdafaa-i Hukuk Cemiyeti). The association, under the indirect leadership of Mustafa Kemal, was dedicated to safeguarding the honor of the Ottoman Turks at the same time that it preserved as much of the empire as possible. Kemal, as inspector general of the army, remained in Angora (modern Ankara), in the heart of Anatolia, where he was trying to reassemble the ragged remnants of the Ottoman Army into something that resembled a proper military force. It was this activity by Kemal, coupled with his influence over the new parliament, that caused Admiral Gough-Calthorpe such concern: no one knew what, if anything, Kemal was planning to do with the Turkish Army.

The last Ottoman parliament opened on January 12, 1920; it would last just sixty-six days. It was led by the new Grand Vizier, Ali Rizat Pasha, who had been hand-picked by the Allies, and its power was sorely limited. Before they were seated, its members were informed that they could only pass laws that were acceptable to, or specifically ordered by, the British; to be valid, any legislation that did pass had to be countersigned by the Allied military governor, as well as by the Grand Vizier. It was an impossible situation for any legislative body with any measure of integrity. Instead, the last Ottoman parliament acted with courage: its sole accomplishment was to pass a body of resolutions that collectively went down in Turkish history as the Misak-i Millî, the Nation's Oath. This would become the cornerstone of the Turkish republic. Of it, Kemal would declare, "It is the nation's iron fist that writes the Nation's Oath which is the main principle of our independence to the annals of history."

Six resolutions made up the Misak-i Millî, five of them addressing the disposition of Ottoman territory, the assurance of Anatolia as a Turkish homeland, the security of the Bosporus and the Dardanelles, the determination of ethnic homelands, and the security of Moslem minorities in predominantly Christian or Jewish territories. Yet the heart and soul of the Misak-i Millî was the sixth resolution, for it was completely incompatible with the fate that the Allies were determined to impose on the Ottoman Empire. It read, "In order to develop in every field, the country should be independent and free; all restrictions on political, judicial and financial development will be removed."

This, of course, was utterly unacceptable to the Allies, and on the night of March 15, 1920, British soldiers began to occupy the parliament buildings in Constantinople, arresting five members in the process. There was open resistance from the Turkish garrison, with some loss of life on both sides; the exact number of dead would remain unknown. When the parliament met three days later, before an order could arrive from Admiral de Robeck permanently dissolving the institution, it drafted a letter of protest to the Allies, declaring the arrest of its members to be a violation of its sovereign rights. De Robeck's order was followed up by the arrest of as many members of parliament as could be found, nearly one hundred in all, who were then sent to Malta, where they were held on various pretexts in the hope of coercing their cooperation in implementing the terms of the forthcoming treaty. (None of the arrested parliamentarians were ever tried, for none of them had actually committed a crime. Although some would remain incarcerated for nearly two years, all would eventually be released.)

In the absence of a parliament, the Sultan, Mehmed VI, became the only legitimate remaining Ottoman authority. In endorsing de Robeck's abolition of parliament, he reduced himself to the status of an Allied puppet, although Mehmed himself didn't see the situation that way. For him, nothing mattered but the continuity of the House of Osman, so he was prepared to accept any terms or conditions from the Allies that allowed him to remain on the Ottoman throne. Surrounded by sycophants who assured him that the only "real" Turks were those who remained loyal to him and obeyed his orders, the Sultan became completely detached from the developing reality in what was left of his realm. That was why, when he was privately informed of the draft terms of the Treaty of Sèvres on June 5, 1920, Mehmed VI instructed his representatives to sign without protest when it was presented to them.

No one was more outraged by the treaty and Mehmed's meek acceptance of it than was Mustafa Kemal. Kemal had emerged from the war as the Turks' only true national hero, and it was almost inevitable that if there were to be any Turkish resistance to the Allies, their occupation, and their dictation of the peace terms, it would coalesce around him. Kemal was a very different kettle of fish from the sort of Turks with which Mehmed had surrounded himself. Kemal was a Turkish patriot, who held a core-deep belief that the entire edifice of the Sultanate had become a millstone on the neck of the Turkish people. He had joined the Committee of Union and Progress and supported the Young Turks because he believed in the need for the empire to undergo drastic and dramatic reform. The events in the Ottoman capital since the armistice only further confirmed the validity of his belief.

Kemal returned to an occupied Constantinople exactly two weeks after the armistice, on November 18, 1919, just in time to watch the French and British troops march into the Ottoman capital. He had been able to withdraw the remnants of the Turks' Seventh and Eighth Armies, perhaps twenty thousand infantry accompanied by a handful of cavalry units with little artillery, out of the Damascus debacle and post them around the city of Angora in the heart of Anatolia, hoping to use them as the nucleus of a resurrected Turkish Army. His ambition was furthered when the Sultan named him inspector general of the army. Some accounts suggest that Mehmed made this appointment as a sort of bribe to purchase Kemal's allegiance, while other evidence strongly suggests he did this to get Kemal out of Constantinople, away from where this potentially troublesome general might prove an inconvenience.

Once back with the army, Kemal sent word out that any remaining Turkish units should begin moving to Angora, bringing as much of their equipment with them as possible. He was from all appearances still loyal to the Sultan and the Ottoman parliament, but as time passed and it became more evident that Mehmed VI had become an Allied puppet and parliament his mouthpiece, Kemal's allegiance shifted. Or rather, it might be more accurate to say that his allegiance never changed, but the institutions to which it was given did. Kemal was a proud man, the Turks a proud people, and the timidity with which Mehmed complied with every Allied whim was an affront to that pride. The resentment it engendered simmered all across Anatolia.

By the spring of 1919, Kemal had established links to most of the nascent groups that would become the core of the Turkish Independence Movement. These exchanges came to the attention of Admiral Gough-Calthorpe in Constantinople and had formed the basis for his attempts to marginalize Kemal or have him dismissed from his post altogether. They also were the root of the tension that had so concerned Admiral de Robeck. The correspondence led to the drafting of the document known as the Amasya Circular, which was made public on June 11 in

Amasya. Signed by Kemal, Raouf Bey, Refet Bele, Bekir Sami Bey, Ali Fuat Cebesoy, and Kazim Karabekir (who had forced Townshend's surrender at Kut), the six principal leaders of the Independence Movement, its publication is regarded as the event that put the Turkish War of Independence in motion.

The Amasya Circular was nothing less than a call for the eviction of the occupying powers and the creation of not only a Turkish homeland, but a Turkish nation state. It was brief, pointed, and, to the Turks, rousing:

> The unity of the motherland and national independence are in danger.
>
> The Constantinople government is unable to carry out its responsibilities.
>
> It is only through the nation's effort and determination that national independence will be won.
>
> It is necessary to establish a national committee, free from all external influences and control, that will review the national situation and make known to the world the people's desires for justice.
>
> It has been decided to hold immediately a National Congress in Sivas, the most secure place in Anatolia.
>
> Three representatives from each province should be sent immediately to the Sivas Congress.
>
> To be prepared for every eventuality, this subject should be kept a national secret.
>
> There will be a congress for the Eastern Provinces on July 1. The delegation from the Erzurum Congress will depart to join to the general meeting in Sivas.

Sivas was a modest trading center two hundred miles east of Angora, where from September 4 to 11, 1919, the leaders of the Independence Movement met and hammered out a strategy for reasserting Turkish autonomy and authority over the whole of Anatolia, which in common parlance was becoming known as "Turkey." One of the first acts of the Sivas Congress was to formalize the Independence Movement under the name of the "Association (or Society) for the Defense of Rights for Anatolian and Roumelia." Elections for the Ottoman parliament were already scheduled for December, and it was agreed that the movement should present a full slate of candidates, a shrewd move that would impart a measure of legitimacy to the movement. At the same time, a "Representative Committee" was created, which in practice was a shadow Cabinet ready to step in as a function-ing government should the Sultanate cease to function for any reason. Overriding everything was Kemal's emphatic insistence on two principles: independence and integrity. He was not going to permit a return to the corrupt ways of the Sultans, nor would he allow the Turks to fall into the chaos of civil war, which at that mo-ment was wracking neighboring Russia.

When Admiral de Robeck's decree abolished parliament, Kemal acted swiftly. On March 18, 1920, he announced that a new Turkish legislative body, the Grand National Assembly, would convene in Angora, where it would assume sovereignty for the Turkish nation. All of the members of the now-defunct parliament who were able to evade British arrest made their way to Angora, where they joined with deputies elected by local assemblies around the country. On April 20, 1920, the new assembly gathered for the first time, assuming for itself full governmental power and naming Mustafa Kemal as its first prime minister, as well as the first speaker of the Grand National Assembly.

Mehmed VI was quick to react. Echoing the actions of his brother at the be-ginning of the Great War, acting in his spiritual role as caliph, he issued a fatwa declaring that faithful Moslems should not support the Nationalist movement in any way. At the same time that the fatwa was announced, the Sultan pronounced a death sentence in absentia on Mustafa Kemal and the Nationalist leadership. No sooner was this done than the mufti of Ankara, Rifat Börekçi, issued a fatwa of his own, declaring that with Constantinople under Allied control, Mehmed VI was under foreign coercion, deprived of the ability to rule independently. Therefore, his decrees as both Sultan and caliph were invalid. It was a careful distinction, for the Nationalists were at pains to make it clear that while they opposed the Sultan's government, nominally at least they remained loyal to the Sultan.

For their part, the Allies, and particularly the British, were unimpressed by the Nationalists at this point. It was their considered opinion that for all of his military accomplishments, Mustafa Kemal simply lacked the resources to pose a serious danger to the Allied occupation of Constantinople or their plans for parti-tioning Anatolia. The Ottoman Army had been too badly disorganized at the end of the war and suffered from too many shortages of weapons and equipment to be regarded as any genuine threat. It was the opinion of the commander of the British garrison in Constantinople that Kemal's forces could be contained and defeated using irregulars loyal to the Sultan's government, provided they were properly supported, and backed if needed by Allied troops.

Yet Kemal was as aware as the Allies of the weaknesses of the Nationalist forces. Even while the Grand National Assembly was organizing itself, he initiated contact with the nascent Soviet Union. The new regime in Moscow had no more love for the Allies than did the Turkish Nationalists, and by August, 60 artillery pieces, 30,000 shells, 180,000 grenades, 10,000 mines, and 3.5 million German, Austrian, and Russian rifles were on their way to Turkey. More supplies and equipment were coming from French and Italian arms merchants who refused to let minor considerations such as their respective governments' policies get in the way of good business. Motivated by the Grand National Assembly's appeal to the Turks' loyalty to the idea of a Turkish homeland, rather than to a distant and ineffectual Sultan, combined with Kemal's competent leadership, and decently equipped at last, the Turkish Nationalists were ready to face the threats that were encroaching on Turkey from the east, the west, and the south.

The initial contact between Moscow and the Nationalists had been made when Kemal met with a Bolshevik delegation headed by Col. Semyon Budyenny in April 1919. The Bolsheviks were trying to annex all of the territories that had once been part of imperial Russia, including the newly created Democratic Republic of Armenia. The republic's borders had initially been drawn in the Treaty of Brest-Litovsk, which with the collapse of imperial Germany had become a dead letter. Now the Bolsheviks were casting covetous eyes on as much of the Caucasus as they could reach. They also saw a revived Turkish state as a buffer insulating the fledgling Soviet Union from the capitalist West or even as a potential ally and were prepared to offer up Armenia to accomplish this. Kemal wasn't prepared to go so far, however, and carefully rebuffed Budyenny by declaring, "Such questions must be postponed until Turkish independence is achieved."

The issue of the fate of the Republic of Armenia, however, remained. In Paris, the Allies were still trying to agree on the borders of the new Armenian state, which would eventually be incorporated into the terms of the Treaty of Sèvres. Nearly a year would pass, spent in petty bickering and diplomatic posturing on the part of bit players in the larger drama of the fate of Armenia. The Armenians were focused on absorbing the provinces of Van and Bitlis into their new republic, something the Turkish Nationalists, who envisioned a "Turkey" that was defined by the geography of Anatolia, rather than by ethnic boundaries, flatly refused to consider.

It wasn't until the summer of 1920 that the Armenians felt strong enough to make an overt move toward finally consolidating their position. In June a small Armenian Army formally annexed the disputed district of Oltu, an action that was the trigger for a bitter little three-month war between the Turks and the Armenians. At the beginning of September the local Turkish commander, Kazim Karabekir, took Oltu away from the Armenians and began moving toward the city of Kars a few weeks later.

Kars had once been a trading center of some significance in the Ottoman Empire, and it was still predominantly Moslem, though not ethnically Turk. This was enough for the Armenian Army to begin a purge of the populace of Kars, however, while at the same time pleading for aid from the French and the British. The French had already had enough Armenian problems of their own in the province of Cilicia and turned a deaf ear to the Armenian Republic, while the British were preoccupied with suppressing rebellious Arab tribes in Iraq. The Armenians then turned to the Soviet Union, which opportunistically agreed to give her support against the Turkish Nationalists, although the Armenians had no idea that the Soviets were prepared to use the agreement as a pretext for occupying the Armenian Republic once the Turks had been driven back.

Yet the promised Soviet support proved meaningless, as Karabekir, whose army outnumbered the Armenian forces by better than two to one, drove his troops forward and split the Armenian Republic in half. By the middle of November 1920 the Turks had occupied every major strategic position in Armenia, and on November 18 they offered a cease-fire that the Armenians had no choice but to accept. As the two sides were negotiating a peace settlement, the Soviets made their move, invading the Armenian Republic from the east on November 29. Hoping to salvage something from the wreck, the Armenian government immediately agreed to the terms offered by the Turkish Nationalists, formalized in the Treaty of Alexandropol, even though this meant surrendering almost half of the Armenian territory to the Turks. Ultimately, it did the Armenians no good, as fewer than two weeks later, the Soviets toppled the Democratic Armenian Republic and replaced it with the Armenian Soviet Socialist Republic, which in October 1921 would sign a treaty of "brotherhood and friendship" with the Soviet Union that in effect incorporated Armenia into the USSR. Seven decades would pass before an independent Armenia would reappear on the maps of the world. There would never be an accurate accounting of the casualties suffered by either side in the Turkish-Armenian War.

Although Karabekir's victories in the east, together with a diplomatic settle-ment with the Soviet government after the demise of the Armenian Republic, gave the Turkish Nationalists an unexpected degree of legitimacy, the Allies continued to consider the Sultanate the "true" Turkish government. Kemal and his followers were still regarded as little more than a band of brigands and rebels. A minor clash at the village of Izmit was the catalyst that transformed the Turkish Independence Movement into the Turkish War of Independence. At Izmit, near Constantinople on the Sea of Marmara, Nationalist troops faced off against the government's ir-regulars, which were backed by two battalions of British infantry. Though the Na-tionalists were ultimately forced to retreat, it was the Tommies who defeated them, the irregulars having fled. Though inconclusive in itself, the clash at Izmit showed the Nationalists to be a better disciplined and organized fighting force than previ-ously believed and compelled the Allies to confront the Nationalist movement as a genuine threat to their plans for the remnants of the Ottoman Empire, one that only properly trained and equipped troops—regulars—would be able to defeat.

But could the Allies do it? After reviewing the situation in Turkey, it was the studied conclusion of Marshal Ferdinand Foch, France's senior soldier and the of-ficer who had been the Allied generalissimo in the final year of the Great War, that a minimum of twenty-seven infantry divisions would be required to suppress the Nationalist movement. The problem was that between them, the French and the British didn't have twenty-seven divisions on hand. They had demobilized their huge wartime armies, and the war-weary populations of France and Great Britain weren't prepared to fight yet another war so soon after the end of the last one. In London, Lloyd George attempted to make a great show of coercing the Turks, but the Conservatives in the House of Commons, which made up the largest part of the prime minister's governing majority, made it clear that they would not support any military adventures in Turkey. Still, the British and the French understood that the Nationalists would not be defeated by anything less than disciplined, well-trained forces.

Fortunately for them, as they saw it, the Greek Army was at hand. The Greeks, whose enmity with the Turks had endured for more than a millennium, had already been promised the Ottoman province of Adrianople in Europe, the Turkish Aegean islands, and the province of Smyrna (ancient Ionia, the home of Troy) in Anatolia, which had a large ethnic Greek population. These pledges had been made in return for Greece joining the Allies during the war; the government of Prime Minister Eleftherios Venizelos was anxious to redeem them. The Greeks needed little encouragement, then, to send troops across the Aegean to take possession of Smyrna.

The Greeks had occupied most of Smyrna in late May and early June 1919, in accordance with the division of Anatolia already worked out at the Paris Peace Conference that would be incorporated into the Treaty of Sèvres. There the situation remained for the better part of a year, until the Greeks began moving down the coast to prevent what was little more than a bare-faced land grab by the Italians, who were hoping to transform their sphere of influence in Anatolia into an out-and-out colony. By the end of the summer of 1920, the Greeks held most of western Turkey, and in response to urgings from Lloyd George, who wanted to bring as much pressure to bear on the Turks as possible to accept the Treaty of Sèvres, they launched offensives into the mountains of central Anatolia.

Knowing that they possessed a better-equipped army than Kemal's, as well as having numerical superiority over the Turks, the Greeks anticipated forcing a crushing defeat on the Nationalists and ending their pretensions. But in a display of military skill equal to anything he had shown at Gallipoli, Kemal conducted a series of fighting withdrawals, buying time for his army to rearm and to move the troops who had fought against the Armenians westward to face the Greeks. On January 11, 1921, the Turks made a stand in the First Battle of Inönü, stopping the Greek advance in its tracks. Ten weeks later, in the Second Battle of Inönü, the Greeks were stopped yet again and within days were retreating back into Smyrna.

The Greeks resumed the offensive in June, once more driving into the Anatolian heartland, thrusting directly at Angora, intent on striking a crippling blow against the Turks. The result was the Battle of Sakarya, which literally raged for twenty-one days, from August 23 to September 13, 1921. At the end, both armies were exhausted, and the Greeks, operating at the end of a badly overextended supply line, were forced to retreat to their starting positions at the end of September.

A year-long stalemate ensued, as both sides lacked the strength for further attacks. The Turks finally launched an offensive of their own on August 26, 1922, and in fewer than three weeks drove the Greeks completely out of Turkey. Called the Greco-Turkish War, it had been a bloody and brutal conflict. Both Greeks and Turks would be accused by the other side of committing atrocities against soldiers and civilians alike, and the evidence confirms that there is truth to the charges. That it was so vicious should have come as no surprise, given the animosity between Turks and Greeks that had endured for centuries. By its end, the war had claimed more than 24,000 Greek dead, along with 20,000 Turks killed in action; 40,000 Greeks were wounded, as were 30,000 Turks; the Greeks reported 18,000 missing, and the corresponding Turkish figure would never be known.

Yet the ferocity with which the Turks fought had an unintended and unexpected effect on the British, the French, and the Italians. After the Second Battle of Inönü, the Italians, who understandably had no real stomach for fighting the Turks, began scurrying back toward the city of Antalya, on the southern coast of Anatolia. The British and the French realized that their Greek cat's paw wasn't going to defeat the Turkish Nationalists after all and decided to wash their hands of the entire Anatolian mess. Acknowledging that the Treaty of Sèvres as written would never be ratified by the Turks, they called a conference in London where, unlike the Paris Peace Conference, the Turks were invited to participate, both the Turkish revolutionaries and the Sultan's government being represented. The purpose of the conference was to rework the Treaty of Sèvres into something that would be acceptable to all parties.

The British were, of course, desperately overstretched by the demands of keeping their empire secure. The only major troop commitment they could sustain in the Middle East was their campaign to pacify the more belligerent Arab tribes in Iraq; they had no strength to spare for action against the Turkish Nationalists. The French, who were preoccupied with Syria, had already tried—and failed—to fight the Turks by proxy. In 1916 they had overseen the formation of the "Armenian Legion," a unit of expatriates created to fight the Turks in Anatolia and eventually serve as the nucleus of an Armenian national army. It had served without any particular distinction in Palestine under General Allenby, and when the French occupied Syria, the Armenian Legion was employed as part of the garrison force. The Armenians made their first attempt at creating an independent Armenian state in what had been the Ottoman province of Cilicia, which bordered Syria on the north and which the French initially regarded as part of their Syrian "mandate."

Cilicia was separated from Syria proper by the Taurus Mountains, which the Turkish Nationalists regarded as vital to establishing secure borders for Turkey, making the idea of an Armenian homeland there intolerable. By this time the Armenian Legion's conduct, an unbroken record of banditry, indiscipline, and attacks on the Moslem population of the region, had become an embarrassment for the French, who disbanded the unit in early 1920. Concentrating on colonizing Syria at the same time that they were trying to suppress the widespread Arab protests there, the French lacked the strength to fight the Turks in Cilicia, and with the Franco-Turkish Agreement, signed on October 20, 1921, they acknowledged the Turks' sovereignty over the province of Cilicia and settled the boundary between Turkish Anatolia and Syria.

Privately, French officials in the Middle East blamed the British for not taking stronger measures of their own against the Turkish Nationalists. Had they done so, the French believed, it would have dispersed the Turks' strength to the point where they would have been unable to both stop the Greeks advancing out of Smyrna and crush the embryonic Armenian state in Cilicia at the same time that they were facing a British advance southward from Constantinople. However the blame sorted out, though, the result was that the Turks had compelled the Allies to return to the negotiating table.

Not that the British and the French simply threw up their hands after the Greeks were driven out of Anatolia. But they really had no choice other than to negotiate with Kemal and the Nationalists: the defeat of the Greeks revealed the reality of the power shift in Turkey that made the Grand National Assembly the de facto government and Angora its capital. The Sultanate and Constantinople had been marginalized to the point where they no longer possessed even a symbolic value. At the same time, the people of France and Great Britain had made it clear to their own governments that they were no more willing to support yet another war than they had been two years earlier, especially one fought to enforce a treaty that was little known or understood on the streets of Paris or London, and that seemed to involve neither the vital interests nor the national honor of either country.

There was one moment of crisis in mid-September when the British refused a Turkish demand to withdraw the troops that had been posted, ironically, near Gallipoli in order to ensure the neutrality of the Dardanelles. Lloyd George attempted to bluster the Turks into backing down, threatening to declare war, but his bluff fell apart when Australia and Canada, for whom he had presumed to speak along with Great Britain, informed the British prime minister that they had no intention of taking part in any such conflict. (When the House of Commons likewise refused to back Lloyd George's play, the incident would lead directly to the prime minister's fall from office a month later.) Common sense finally asserted itself, and an armistice between the Nationalists, Italy, France, and Britain was signed in Mudanya, a town on the south coast of the Sea of Marmara, on October 11, 1922; the Greeks acceded to the armistice three days later.

The terms of the armistice effectively scrapped the Treaty of Sèvres. The partition of the Ottoman Empire's non-Turkish territories was accepted as a fait accompli by the Turks, who really did not want them anyway. Almost all of the European territory that was to have been ceded to Greece was returned to the Turks, while Turkish sovereignty over Constantinople as well as the Bosporus and the Dardanelles was reaffirmed, although the waterway would remain effectively internationalized. There was no mention this time of separate Armenian or Kurdish states or spheres of influence for the Allies. These concessions by the French and the British provided the basis for the negotiations of a new peace treaty between the Ottoman Turks and the Allies at the Conference of Lausanne, held in Lausanne, Switzerland. The Italians, militarily feeble and politically fragile, had no real choice but to go along with the concessions.

Ismet Inönü, the commander in chief of the Turkish Army and Kemal's deputy, was the head negotiator for the Turks, while Lord Curzon, the British foreign secretary, filled the corresponding role for the Allies; Eleftherios Venizelos represented Greece directly. The conference opened on November 20, 1922, and although there was little doubt that the negotiations would lead to a peace treaty, it was not a cut-and-dried affair. It took eight months before a treaty acceptable to all parties was finally drafted. There were numerous protests by the Turks over what they regarded as high-handed conduct on the part of the Allies. At one point the Turks actually walked out of the conference, while the French announced that they regarded the final draft of the treaty as nothing more than "the basis for further negotiation" and initially refused to sign.

The conference wasn't without its touches of humor. The pattern for the negotiations was simple: Inönü would present the Turkish position and then sit back and wait while Lord Curzon (who was something of a windbag) would respond with a seemingly interminable refusal. Inönü, who was partially deaf, would in turn switch off his hearing aid until Curzon finally wound down, then would simply repeat his original demand as if Curzon had never spoken. In the end the Turks' stubbornness won out, and on July 24, 1923, the Treaty of Lausanne was signed, and the Great War between the Ottoman Empire and the Allied Powers officially came to an end.

The treaty guaranteed the independence, autonomy, and territorial integrity of Turkey and clearly defined the Turkish boundaries with Greece and Bulgaria, along with the borders with Iraq and Syria. (The Turkish borders in the Caucasus with the Soviet Union were, obviously, beyond the Allies' jurisdiction and so were not addressed in the treaty.) The Turks surrendered all claims on the Dodecanese Islands, which Italy had seized in 1911; they also recognized as de jure the de facto authority the British had exercised over Cyprus, Egypt, and the Sudan since 1882. For the time being, the fate of the province of Mosul was left unresolved. The British, who had discovered oil in the province just before the war ended, were adamant that Mosul be incorporated into their mandate in Iraq, while the Turks insisted that because they had held the province at the time the Armistice of Mudros was signed, it was still Turkish territory. The treaty formalized an agreement between the two nations to allow the League of Nations to arbitrate a final determination; in 1926 the League would, perhaps predictably, finally assign the province to Iraq.

The most controversial part of the Treaty of Lausanne was the provision written to simultaneously protect the ethnic Greek minority in Turkey and ethnic Turks in Greece, which in practice translated into a massive exchange of population between the two nations. In fact, most of the ethnic Greeks living in Turkey and the Turks in Greece had already been deported under the "Convention Concerning the Exchange of Greek and Turkish Populations," which Greece and Turkey had signed at Lausanne on January 20, 1923. Some 1.5 million Greeks were forcibly removed from their homes and transported to Greek territory, while a half-million ethnic Turks in Greece suffered the same fate in reverse; the Greeks also seized on the terms of the convention to rid themselves of several hundred thousand other minorities as well. Although there was a coldly reasonable rationale motivating the convention—both nations were freed of potentially troublesome minorities at a time when each was attempting to restore order to its own house—the deportations created bitterness among Turks and Greeks that would last for generations.

Having finally achieved an acceptable peace and secured Turkish independence, there was one final detail to which the Grand National Assembly was required to attend: the fate of the House of Osman. The lands that had once been the empire were no longer of any concern to the Turks; they were the Allies' problem now.

The French faced a turbulent, sometimes violent future in their mandate in Syria—the former Ottoman province would even become a battleground for a sort of civil war during the Second World War, between Frenchmen loyal to the Vichy regime and those who gave their allegiance to the Free French. The British, of course, would have their hands full with their own mandates, as the Arab tribes continually bickered among themselves—when they weren't shooting at Englishmen. Egypt and Palestine would be the sources of endless grief in Whitehall: Egypt because as long as there was a British Raj in India and an empire in the Far East, Great Britain had to maintain control of the Suez Canal, whatever the cost; Palestine because the British had made promises to the Arabs and the Jews that they could not keep and that in the end were mutually exclusive.

More than any other single factor, the Balfour Declaration propelled the intolerance and shortsightedness on both sides that has perpetuated the conflict between Arab and Jew that for more than three generations has symbolized the Middle East for the rest of the world. Both peoples felt it to be a betrayal. The Jews believed that by promising them a Jewish homeland, the British were guaranteeing them a Jewish state; the Arabs came away convinced that the British had lied to them all along and that in "giving" Palestine to the Jews, they had robbed Arabs of their birthright. It is impossible to say what would have happened had there been swift, deliberate action by David Lloyd George, first to clarify the meaning of the Balfour Declaration on its publication, and then, after the armistice with the Turks, to honor the pledges made to Sherrif Hussein and his sons. It was a region already filled with turmoil and the potential for provocation, and perhaps it might have become an international powder keg in any case. Yet because Lloyd George was too much the politician and too little the statesman, the world will never know.

None of that would have concerned Mustafa Kemal, Ismet Inönü, or any of the members of the Grand National Assembly even had they known of it. What was pressing business to them was the final resolution of the Ottoman Empire. For centuries, the Sultan and the Sultanate had become ever more distant and detached from the Turkish people. Both had ceased to command the loyalty, let alone the affection, of the Mehmet laboring in his field or the Hammid toiling in his shop long before the catastrophe of 1914–18. There was no reservoir of affection for the Sultan's throne such as the average Briton felt for the Crown. They had ceased to think of themselves as "Ottoman Turks"—they were simply "Turks" now. The

House of Osman, and with it Constantinople, had ceased to have any useful purpose, had lost even its symbolic value—and its relevance. The time had come, in the considered opinion of the new Turkish government, for a clean slate, if Turkey was to become a truly modern nation-state and not some lingering relic from the Middle Ages.

The Sultanate was officially abolished on November 1, 1922, even before the Conference of Lausanne was convened. Fifteen days later the last Sultan, Mehmed VI, was stripped of his authority as caliph as well. On October 13, 1923, the Grand National Assembly transferred the seat of Turkish government from Constantinople to Angora; on October 29, 1923, the assembly formally dissolved the Ottoman Empire, installing in its place the Republic of Turkey. For the next quarter-century, Kemal would be its president, an office to which he was elected by acclamation when the republic was formalized and which he held until his death in 1938.

The energy, vision, and dedication with which Kemal alternately pushed, dragged, cajoled, persuaded, and led his people to transform Turkey from a medieval, semitheocratic autocracy into a dynamic, sometimes turbulent, but always progressive secular republic was almost superhuman. He would ultimately be accorded the surname "Atatürk"—"The Father of the Turks"—so great would the people of Turkey believe to be their debt to him. How Kemal guided the transformation of the Turkish nation is one of the most fascinating stories of the twentieth century—but it is also a story for another time. . . .

At long last the Ottoman Empire, for six hundred years the epicenter of so much world-shaking and -shaping history, itself passed *into* history. Yet Europe, preoccupied with its own burden of grief, and the rest of the world, focused on Europe in morbid fascination, barely noted its passing: the empire would not be mourned—it would be scarcely missed.

In the decades to come, whenever historians turned their attention to the Great War—it would soon become known as the World War, and ultimately events would compel humanity to even assign it a number—their gaze would remain fixed on the abattoir of the Western Front. Entire libraries would be written in justification or condemnation of particular generals who commanded there, along with the strategies they employed. It was as though if enough words were written about the Somme or Verdun or the Chemin des Dames or Passchendaele, then the expenditure of a generation's worth of blood and treasure for a few square miles of muddy, crater-pocked, stump-strewn land could ultimately be justified. And if the volume of ink spilled were to equal the volume of blood shed, then slaughter could be transformed into strategy and stalemate into decision.

As this search for justification grew and became self-perpetuating, the Ottoman Empire, its role in shaping the course of the First World War, and its eventual collapse and demise were continually pushed to the rear of the stage. The exception was the Gallipoli Campaign, which was recognized as simply a microcosm of the Western Front and so deserved to be similarly rationalized. That it was the Ottoman Turks' decision to leap into a war in which they had no quarrel and which fundamentally altered the grand strategic equation of the war was ignored or minimized. Had they only chosen a different path, they would have reaped immeasurable benefits by thoughtfully standing to one side while the Allies and the Central Powers tried conclusions. To wit, once the Turks had joined the Central Powers, by closing the Straits of the Dardanelles they, however unintentionally, drove Allied strategy both east and west. Russia, denied access to the resources of, and resupply by, France and Great Britain, would struggle to hold off relentless German offensives until the army and the nation reached a breaking point. The western Allies, in turn, struggled valiantly to succor their faltering eastern ally, both by direct action—Gallipoli—and indirectly, by attempting to divert German strength from the east with offensives of their own in the west.

If Constantinople had never closed the Straits, had never declared war on the Allies, the entire history of the twentieth century would have been changed beyond recognition. Arguably, there would have been no Russian revolution, no Russian civil war, no Soviet Union, no Cold War. Quite likely, there would have been no Second World War, or if there were, it would have been fought without a Waffen-SS, a Gestapo, or a Final Solution. Indeed, the war almost certainly would have ended—in an Allied victory—without the United States having ever become involved, with all of the implications that eventuality would have held for the world's postwar political and economic structure. The Great War may well have ended as early as the summer of 1916, with a negotiated peace between the Great Powers, who would have still been great, before the bitterness and hatred spawned by the last two years of the war poisoned the souls of all of the nations who were fighting.

Yet events took a path that led the Ottoman Empire, finally at the end of its strength, to play a more profound and pivotal role in shaping the world than it had even at the height of its power and glory under Suleiman the Magnificent. And when it was over, the empire would vanish like a puff of smoke or a shadow at noonday.

Istanbul (the name of the city was officially changed from Constantinople in 1930) is, ironically, much like Vienna, its great imperial rival for four centuries. It is a city living in—and on—its past. A visitor to Istanbul is always aware of the city's immense antiquity, its vast depth of culture, its incredible historical stature. Yet while Istanbul is in its way vibrant and dynamic, it is unquestionably an old city, where people are more inclined to look backward in time than forward. Ankara looks and feels much more modern and progressive, more attuned to what is to come than to what has been—it always seems to be noon in Ankara. Inevitably, perhaps, Ankara (once Angora, it, too, had its name changed in 1930) is very much the city of Mustafa Kemal Atatürk. Equally inevitable, Istanbul—Constantinople— is and always will be the city of the Sultan. And it is there that at sunset, when the shadows grow long, it will always be possible to find the shadow of the Sultan's realm.

AUTHOR'S NOTE

The Ottoman Empire is experiencing a revival of sorts in the twenty-first century. Or rather, interest in the empire is undergoing a revival. More accurately, there has been a renewed interest in its demise. Unhappily, much of that interest is peripheral or secondary, extending only as far as the fall of the empire relates to another subject. Most prominent among those subjects are the creation of the modern Middle East, the origins of the region's perpetual Arab-Jewish conflict, and the history of the nation-state of Iraq, all of which have their origins in the fall of Ottoman Turkey. There have been historians who have presented the collapse of the Sultan's realm as little more than a backdrop for the Great Powers' political maneuverings and machinations as they divvied up the empire's territories. Certain ethnic groups have appropriated it as the setting for airing and promoting their cultural grievances and political agendas. A whole new generation of scholarship that is focused on the First World War—the Great War—devotes whole chapters of its work to the Gallipoli Campaign and the British drive up through Palestine in 1918 but relegates most of the rest of the war in the Middle East to a handful of pages. And overarching all of this is a sense that the Ottoman Turks themselves were little more than spectators in the destruction of their empire, standing thoughtfully to one side while the Allies gleefully dismantled what had once been one of the world's most colorful, powerful, and dynamic realms.

This is unfortunate, for the story of the last days of the Ottoman Empire is one that deserves to be told for its own sake. In the middle of the sixteenth century, while feudal Europe was still coalescing into true nation-states, the empire had reached its apogee, as the dominant military, economic, cultural, and religious power in the world. In the second decade of the twentieth century, after almost three hundred years of decline had reduced the Ottoman realm to such an enfeebled status that it was known as "the Sick Man of Europe," it was still able to rise up a final time in one great act of defiance and confound the strategies of the Great Powers, demanding a measure of respect it had long since been denied, and challenging the combined military power of Russia, France, and the British Empire. And when the Ottoman Empire finally died, it did so not because it had been a mere spectator while British and French diplomats, politicians, and generals plotted its destruction. It was the Turks themselves who were the agents of the empire's demise: the Ottoman Empire expired as a consequence of a series of self-inflicted wounds. This was the story that I hoped I have told in *Shadow of the Sultan's Realm*.

I had a lot of help in being able to tell it. First and foremost, I'm pleased to acknowledge the assistance of Mr. Nabi Ôensoy, the Ambassador of the Republic of Turkey to the United States, along with Dr. Yücel Güçlü, who is a first counselor at Turkish Embassy, and Mr. Hakan Tekin, the Consulate General Los Angeles. All three gentlemen were gracious enough to provide contacts and introductions within the Republic of Turkey, as well as at Ankara University and Istanbul University. They made available their knowledge of just who knew what in his homeland and who might have answers to specific questions about Ottoman history. I am also endlessly grateful to the American Research Institute in Turkey, especially Dr. Elif Denel, the director of the Institute's Ankara office, and Dr. Antony Greenwood, the director of the Istanbul office.

I've said on more than one occasion that library and archive staffs are the best professional allies that any historian can hope to have, and I'll gladly say it again. I want to extend my thanks for the assistance given to me by the librarians, the archivists, and the staff pages of the following libraries, museums, and institutions: Hope College's Van Wylen Library, in Holland, Michigan; the libraries of Grand Valley State University, in Allendale, Michigan; the libraries of the University of Southern California and the University of California, Los Angeles, in Los Angeles, California; the Library of Congress, in Washington, D.C.; the Imperial War Museum, the British Museum, and the National Archives (formerly the Public Records Office), in London, England; the Istanbul University Library, in Istanbul and the Ankara University Library and Documentation Center, in Ankara, Republic of Turkey.

As can be expected, some of the usual suspects showed up during the research and the writing of this book. Trish Eachus came through once again in her stalwart role as proofreader and advance editor—and was as determined as ever to cure me of my run-on sentences, however hopeless a task that may be. Leonard Crabtree was tireless as a researcher, always ready, willing, and available to help. I also want to thank my friend Chris Luna, who was unhesitating in his willingness to make available the resources I needed to finish this book. And finally, I have to most emphatically state my particular gratitude to Elizabeth Demers, my editor at Potomac Books, for her infinite patience.

In closing, let me reiterate my gratitude to all of the institutions and the individuals I've mentioned. In the case of specific persons, although my opinions did not always agree with theirs, not one of them ever made any qualification to their assistance as a consequence of our disagreements; this was true professionalism. While nearly every author at some point will state that they are personally responsible for the ideas and the opinions expressed in his or her work, in this case, because some readers may take exception with some of my comments and observations, I will state even more emphatically than usual that all of the conclusions and the opinions found in *Shadow of the Sultan's Realm* are mine alone. As always, I wouldn't have it any other way.

CHAPTER SOURCE NOTES
AND CITATIONS

(Complete information on cited works can be found in the bibliography.)

CHAPTER ONE—THE SULTAN'S REALM

Several excellent general histories of the Ottoman Empire have been written in the last two decades, and they benefit from having abandoned the smug sense of superiority that was characteristic of most Western writing about the Ottoman Turks. Especially useful to this work were Caroline Finkel's *Osman's Dream: The Story of the Ottoman Empire, 1300–1923*; Colin Heywood's *Writing Ottoman History: Documents and Interpretations*; Colin Imber's *The Ottoman Empire, 1300–1650: The Structure of Power*; Carter Findley's *The Turks in World History*; Patrick Kinross's *The Ottoman Centuries: The Rise and Fall of the Turkish Empire*; Jason Goodwin's *Lords of the Horizons: A History of the Ottoman Empire*; and M. Sükrü Hanioglu's *A Brief History of the Late Ottoman Empire*. In addition, *History Derailed: Central and Eastern Europe in the Long Nineteenth Century* by Tibor Iván Berend and *Subjects of the Sultan: Culture and Daily Life in the Ottoman Empire* by Suraiya Faroqhi provide valuable background information—political, social, and economic—as a context for the larger history. Likewise, *An Economic and Social History of the Ottoman Empire, 1300–1914*, by Halil Inalcik et al., though massive, is worth the time spent on exploring it. For a more "traditional"—that is, Western imperialist—view of the Ottoman Empire, see Sir Edward Shepherd Creasy's *History of the Ottoman Turks: From the Beginning of Their Empire to the Present Time*.

CHAPTER TWO—THE EVE OF WAR

The rise of the Young Turks and the 1908 revolution, as well as the problems confronting the CUP, are presented in useful detail in *The Making of Modern Turkey* by Feroz Ahmad, as well as his earlier *The Young Turks: The Committee of Union and Progress in Turkish Politics, 1908–1914*. Also especially useful are M. Sükrü Hanioglu's *Preparation for a Revolution: The Young Turks, 1902–1908* and David Kushner's *The Rise of Turkish Nationalism, 1876–1908*. The relationship between the Ottoman Turks and their subject peoples is dissected in Hasan Kayali's *Arabs and Young Turks: Ottomanism, Arabism, and Islamism in the Ottoman Empire, 1908–1918*. Stanford J. and Ezel Kural Shaw's *History of the Ottoman Empire and Modern Turkey Volume 2, Reform, Revolution, and Republic: The Rise of Modern Turkey 1808–1975* provides the "big picture" of the causes and consequences of the 1908 revolution, while a personal view of the Young Turks and the Three Pashas is found in Ahmed Djemal's *Memoires of a Turkish Statesman: 1913–1919. Istanbul: The Imperial City*, by John Freely, offers valuable portraits of the Three Pashas and gives deserved attention to how Enver's Germanophile leanings warped the triumvirate's regime. A distinctly Turkish and very useful perspective can be found in *Rise of the Bourgeoisie, Demise of Empire: Ottoman Westernization and Social Change*, by Fatma Müge Göçek. *Imperial Classroom: Islam, the State, and Education in the Late Ottoman Empire*, by Benjamin C. Fortna, and *The Politicization of Islam: Reconstructing Identity, State, Faith, and Community in the Late Ottoman State*, by Kemal H. Karpat, are solid presentations of Ottoman society and in particular the role of Islam under the Young Turk regime.

"The Turkish people, after their thirty years of despotism, are like a two-year-old infant that can't walk firmly and is somewhat inarticulate. They are very raw and the Government as such is none too strong."—G. R. Berridge, *Gerald Fitzmaurice (1865–1939), Chief Dragoman of the British Embassy in Turkey*, p. 114.

"Lacked responsible leaders of position," and "a collection of good-intentioned children."—Francis Harry Hinsely, *British Foreign Policy under Sir Edward Grey*, p. 150.

"We desire the integrity of the Ottoman Empire and we wish Tripoli always to remain Turkish."—Donald Quataert, *The Ottoman Empire*, p. 265.

CHAPTER 3—OPENING MOVES

Any study or research into the Ottoman Army at the beginning of the First World War must begin with Edward J. Erickson's excellent *Ordered to Die: A History of the Ottoman Army in the First World War*. Mesut Uyar's *A Military History of the Ottomans: From Osman to Atatürk*, while more general than Erickson's work, gives perspective on how the Ottoman Army reached the state it was in by 1914. Volumes 1, 2, and 3 of *Source Records of the Great War*, edited by Charles F. Horne, provide a distinct primary source setting for how the conflict spread from the Balkans and engaged the rest of Europe. Taken together, Edward R. Kantowicz's *The Rage of Nations*, Niall Ferguson's *The War of the World: Twentieth-Century Conflict and the Descent of the West*, Martin Gilbert's *The First World War: A Complete History*, and John Keegan's *The First World War* provide a comprehensive picture of the strategic military and political events that led to the Three Pashas' decision to join the Central Powers. *Istanbul: The Imperial City*, by John Freely, recounts the process in detail. The British side of how the British and Ottoman Empires blundered into war with each other is well presented in Cedric James Lowe and Michael L. Dockrill's *The Mirage of Power: Volume Two: British Foreign Policy 1914–22*, as well as *The Last Lion, Winston Spencer Churchill, Volume I, Visions of Glory*, by William Manchester.

"*Wohltäter des Türkenvolkes*," "the benefactor of the Turkish peoples."—William Manchester, *The Arms of Krupp 1587–1968*, p. 205.

"The 300 million Moslems scattered across the globe can be assured that the German emperor is, and will at all times remain, their friend."—R. Michael Feener and Terenjit Sevea, *Islamic Connections: Muslim Societies in South and Southeast Asia*, p. 112.

"The reason I love Germany is not sentimentality but the fact that they are not a danger to my beloved country; on the contrary, our two countries' interests go hand-in-hand."—Feroz Ahmad, *The Young Turks: The Committee of Union and Progress in Turkish Politics, 1908–1914*, p. 166.

"The German flag will soon fly over the fortifications of the Bosporus."—John Lowe, *The Great Powers, Imperialism, and the German Problem, 1865–1925*, p. 210.

"We cannot put this country on its feet with our resources. We shall therefore take advantage of such technical and material assistance as the Germans can place at our disposal. We shall use Germany to help reconstruct and defend the country until we are able to govern the country with our own strength. When that day comes, we can say good-bye to the Germans within twenty-four hours."—Henry Morgenthau, *Ambassador Morgenthau's Story*, p. 21.

"Speak very loudly and brandish a big gun."—Barbara Tuchman, *The Guns of August*, p. 7.

"Von Wangenheim had in combination the jovial enthusiasm of a college student, the rapacity of a Prussian official, and the happy-go-lucky qualities of a man of the world."—Morgenthau, *Ambassador Morgenthau's Story*, p. 5.

"All the weak spots of the Turkish military organisation."—Alan Moorehead, *Gallipoli*, p. 51.

"We paid the last installment (700,000 Turkish liras). We reached an agreement with the manufacturer that the ships would be handed over on 2 August 1914. Nevertheless, after we made our payment and half an hour before the ceremony, the British declared that they have requisitioned the ships. . . . Although we protested, nobody paid attention."—Robert K. Massie, *Castles of Steel: Britain, Germany, and the Winning of the Great War at Sea*, p. 49.

"In case of war, Germany will leave her military mission at the disposal of the Ottoman Empire. The latter, for her part, assures the said military mission an effective influence on the general conduct of the army, in accordance with the understanding arrived at directly between His Excellency the Minister of War [Enver] and His Excellency the Chief of the Military Mission [Liman von Sanders]."—Charles Francis Horne, ed., *Source Records of the Great War*, vol. 2, p. 165.

"Turkey is today without any question worthless as an ally. She would only be a burden to her associates, without being able to offer them the slightest advantage." —Morgenthau, *Ambassador Morgenthau's Story*, p. 10.

"Force the Ottoman Empire, even against their will, to spread the war to the Black Sea against their ancient enemy, Russia."—Massie, *Castles of Steel*, p. 39.

"As early as today or tomorrow."—Morgenthau, *Ambassador Morgenthau's Story*, p. 63.

"The military authorities at the Dardanelles have been instructed to let Austrian and German war-ships enter the Straits without hindrance. Grand Vizier fears, however, that if use is made of this privilege before the relations with Bulgaria have been settled, an acceleration of developments not desired at the present time by Germany or Turkey might be the result."—Morgenthau, *Ambassador Morgenthau's Story*, p. 64.

"In a manner suitable for the establishment of a link with the Muslim peoples of Russia."—Horne, *Source Records of the Great War*, vol. 2, p. 167.

"With the concurrence of Turkey or against her will."—Ahmad, *The Young Turks*, p. 187.

"We heard the clanking of the portcullis descending before the Dardanelles."—Martin Gilbert, *The First World War*, p. 41.

"May inspire [the Turks] with temerity for the most extreme steps."—Luigi Albertini, *The Origins of the War of 1914*, vol. 3, p. 622.

"Not to fasten any quarrel upon Turkey during the present war. . . . It would become very embarrassing for us, both in India and in Egypt, if Turkey came out against us. If she did decide to side with Germany, of course there was no help for it; but we ought not to precipitate this. If the first great battle, which was approaching in Belgium, did not go well for the Germans, it ought not to be difficult to keep Turkey neutral."—Viscount Grey of Fallodon, *Twenty-Five Years*, vol. 2, p. 163.

"The objective before us was therefore twofold: (1) to delay the entry of Turkey into the war as long as we could, and at all costs till the Indian troops were safely through the Canal on their way to France; and (2) to make it clear, if the worst had to come, that it come by the unprovoked aggression of Turkey."—Grey, *Twenty-Five Years*, vol. 2, p. 166.

"When the Turks invade Egypt, and India is set ablaze with the flames of revolt, only then will England crumble. For England is at her most vulnerable in her colonies."—Gilbert, *The First World War*, pp. 81–82.

"Fomenting rebellion in the Islamic territories of our enemies."—Wolfgang G. Schwanitz, ed., *Germany and the Middle East, 1871–1945*, p. 7.

"I shall crush the Russian Black Sea fleet."—Gilbert, *The First World War*, p. 104.

"I have well and truly thrown the Turks onto the powderkeg."—Gilbert, *The First World War*, p. 105.

CHAPTER 4—ALARUMS AND EXCURSIONS

The campaigns in the Sinai and Mesopotamia are recounted in broad terms but with an excellent eye toward context, in Gilbert, Keegan, and Ferguson. More detail is found in *The World War One Sourcebook*, by Philip J. Haythornthwaite. There are several websites, notably www.firstworldwar.com and www.worldwar1 .com, that cover the campaigns, the armies, the weapons, and the personalities in detail. In *Gallipoli*, Alan Moorehead provides an excellent background and context of the larger war in the Middle East. Erickson, in *Ordered to Die*, details the immense obstacles faced by, as well as the accomplishments of, the Turkish Army in the Suez attack and the defense of the Mesopotamia. David Fromkin's *A Peace to End All Peace* provides details from the British side of the defense of the Suez, as well as the rationale for the attacks up the Tigris-Euphrates Valley.

"A brilliant future awaits the Armenians."—Martin Gilbert, *The First World War: A Complete History*, p. 108.

"The Young Turks had got their country into a war which was much too big for them. They were small gamblers in a game of very high stakes, and, as it usually happens in such cases, their presence was hardly noticed by the other players for a while. They watched, they waited, they made their anxious little bids, they tried desperately to know which way the luck was going, and they put on an air of being at quite at ease which was far from being the case."—Alan Moorehead, *Gallipoli*, p. 33.

CHAPTER 5—GALLIPOLI

There is an immense library of works about Gallipoli, some of it excellent, much of the rest of it written with greater or lesser degree of bias. Fortunately, the more recent scholarship has worked hard at balance, and most of the hagiography has fallen by the wayside. For a detailed examination of the military aspects of the campaign, an excellent starting point is Philip J. Haythornthwaite's *Gallipoli 1915, Frontal Assault on Turkey*, followed by Robert Rhodes James's *Gallipoli: A British Historian's View*, Les Carlyon's *Gallipoli*, and Kevin Fewster's *Gallipoli: The Turkish Story*. Again, Edward J. Erickson's *Ordered to Die* (the title comes from an order issued by Mustafa Kemal at Gallipoli) is essential. Mustafa Kemal's role in the defense of Gallipoli and his emergence as the Turks' most dynamic commander are presented in Emil Lengyel's *They Called Him Atatürk* and Andrew Mango's *Ataturk: The Biography of the Founder of Modern Turkey*. For one of the best accounts of the human experience of the Gallipoli Campaign, Alan Mooreheard's *Gallipoli* has never been surpassed. Worthwhile online resources include www.eyewitnesstohistory .com/gallipoli.htm, www.diggerhistory.info/pages-battles/ww1/anzac/gallipoli .htm, and www.anzacsite.gov.au.

"There are not six men in the Committee of Union and Progress who care for anything that is old. We like new things."—Alan Moorehead, *Gallipoli*, p. 65.

"All telephone wires were cut, all communications with the forts were interrupted, some of the guns had been knocked out. . . . In consequence the artillery fire of the defense had slackened considerably."—Robert Rhodes James, *Gallipoli*, p. 156.

"I do not expect you to attack, I order you to die! In the time which passes until we die, other troops and commanders can take your place!"—Edward Erickson, *Ordered to Die: A History of the Ottoman Army in the First World War*, p. xv.

"The British allowed us four good weeks of respite for all this work before their great disembarkation. . . . This respite just sufficed for the most indispensable measures to be taken."—Luigi Albertini, *The Origins of the War of 1914*, vol. 3, p. 130.

"You have got through the difficult business, now you have only to dig, dig, dig, until you are safe."—Moorehead, *Gallipoli*, p. 130.

"Those heroes that shed their blood and lost their lives . . . you are now lying in the soil of a friendly country. Therefore rest in peace. There is no difference between the Johnnies and the Mehmets where they lie side by side here in this country of ours. . . . You the mothers who sent their sons from far away countries, wipe away your tears. Your sons are now lying in our bosom and are in peace. Having lost their lives on this land they have become our sons as well."—Mustafa Kemal Atatürk, at http://www.anzacsite.gov.au/2visiting/walk_03anzaccove.html.

CHAPTER 6—KUT

The general background of the Mesopotamian Campaign is set forth in the First World War histories by Gilbert, Keegan, and Ferguson, while David Fromkin, in *A Peace to End All Peace*, recounts the military operations and the political maneuverings there. In *Arabs and Young Turks*, Hasan Kayali gives an insight into the tensions that existed within the Ottoman Army between Turks and non-Turks and explains the increasing unreliability of the army's Arab elements. Once again, both www.firstworldwar.com and www.worldwar1.com provide useful details. The friction between London and New Delhi over how to pursue the war in Mesopotamia is examined in Cedric James Lowe and Michael L. Dockrill's *The Mirage of Power: Volume Two*.

"Of those who go to the Jihad for the sake of happiness and salvation of the believers in God's victory, the lot of those who remain alive is felicity, while the rank of those who depart to the next world is martyrdom. In accordance with God's beautiful promise, those who sacrifice their lives to give life to the truth will have honor in this world, and their latter end is paradise."—Timothy J. Paris, *Britain, the Hashemites and Arab Rule, 1920–1925: The Sherifian Solution*, p. 22.

"The Holy War is doctrinally incompatible with an aggressive war, and absurd with a Christian ally, namely Germany,"—T. E. Lawrence, *Seven Pillars of Wisdom*, p. 50.

CHAPTER 7—ARMENIAN AGONY

The Armenian Massacres (or Armenian Genocide) are a minefield for any historian attempting to determine what actually happened to the Armenian people from 1915 to 1918. The sheer volume of propaganda generated by both sides, Armenian and Turk, is almost overwhelming, bias is pervasive, and there is a disturbing amount of outright fabrication in what are proclaimed to be "balanced" accounts. More to the point, the extraordinary efforts to which Armenian expatriates have gone in the United States and the United Kingdom to suppress any presentation of a Turkish rebuttal or refutation is unsettling, to say the least. That something horrible happened to the Armenians in those years is unquestioned, and the eyewitness account of their suffering presented by Father Johannes Lepsius in *Deutschland und Armenien 1914–1918, Sammlung diplomatischer Aktenstücke* (*Germany and Armenia 1914–1918, Diplomatic Document Collection*) cannot be denied. After that, things become less clear-cut, as the questions of exactly what happened and why and whether or not what took place was actually genocide do not lend themselves to simple, black-and-white answers. *The Memoirs of Naim Bey: Turkish Official Documents Relating to the Deportation and the Massacres of Armenians, compiled by Aram Andonian*, one of the cornerstones of the Armenian case, has been persuasively labeled a forgery. Two publications by Henry Morgenthau, Sr., the American ambassador to Constantinople, *Ambassador Morgenthau's Story* and *The Murder of a Nation*, while given wide circulation and credence by Armenian expatriates, are clearly works of wartime propaganda. The best examinations of the Armenian massacres, though no unanimous conclusions, are found in Taner Akçam's *A Shameful Act: The Armenian Genocide and the Question of Turkish Responsibility;* Ben Kiernan's *Blood and Soil: Genocide and Extermination in World History from Carthage to Darfur;* Guenter Lewy's *The Armenian Massacres in Ottoman Turkey: A Disputed Genocide;* Robert Melson's *Revolution and Genocide: On the Origins of the Armenian Genocide and the Holocaust;* Norman Naimark's *Fires of Hatred: Ethnic Cleansing in the 20th Century;* and *Dictionary of Genocide*, edited by Samuel Totten, Paul Robert Bartrop, and Steven L. Jacobs.

"Literally in flames," "massacres everywhere," "gradually annihilating the Christian element," "giving the Kurdish chieftains carte blanche to do whatever they please, to enrich themselves at the Christians' expense and to satisfy their men's whims."—Sébastien de Courtois, *The Forgotten Genocide: The Eastern Christians, the Last Arameans*, pp. 106, 110, 138.

"A man of dangerously unpredictable moods, friendly one moment, ferociously hostile the next, capable of treacherous brutality."—Christopher J. Walker, *Armenia: The Survival of a Nation*, p. 206.

"The measures taken shall be realized justly; and should there be any arrests after the thorough investigations of the documents the criminals shall be sent to the military courts immediately."—Taner Akçam, *A Shameful Act: The Armenian Genocide and the Question of Turkish Responsibility*, pp. 186–87.

"Although the extermination of the Armenians had been decided upon earlier than this, circumstances did not permit us to carry out this sacred intention. Now that all obstacles are removed, it is urgently recommended that you should not be moved for feelings of pity on seeing their miserable plight, but by putting an end to them all, try with all your might for obliterate the very name 'Armenia' from Turkey."—Naim Bey, *The Memoirs of Naim Bey: Turkish Official Documents Relating to the Deportation and the Massacres of Armenians, Compiled by Aram Andonian*, p. 1.

"A deliberate preconceived decision of the Turkish government."—Bernard Lewis, "Distinguishing the Armenian Case from the Holocaust," Assembly of Turkish American Associations, April 14, 2002.

"As bloodstained Gloucester stood by the body of his slain king. He begged of the widow, as they beg of you, 'Say I slew them not.' If you are to say of these men that they are not guilty, it would be as true to say that there has been no war, there are no slain, there has been no crime."—William Manchester, *The Arms of Krupp 1557–1968*, p. 604.

CHAPTER 8—EL AURENS

The starting point for any recounting of T. E. Lawrence's military career is, of course, his own account, *Seven Pillars of Wisdom*. Yet for genuinely factual accounts of the Arab Revolt, Lawrence's own part in it, and its significance to the overall Allied planning and strategy, a researcher has to turn elsewhere. The overall strategic situation in late 1916 can be found, once again, in the First World War histories by Keegan, Ferguson, and Gilbert; each author has his own way of presenting the "big picture" and each succeeds. The precarious situation that existed between the Arabs and the Ottoman Turks is examined in Eugene Rogan's *The Arabs: A History*, as well as in *Arabs and Young Turks: Ottomanism, Arabism, and Islamism in the Ottoman Empire, 1908–1918* by Hasan Kayali. Kemal Karpat's *The Politicization of Islam: Reconstructing Identity, State, Faith, and Community in the Late Ottoman State* explores the religious aspects (and their political consequences) of the Turkish overlordship of Islam's holy cities in Arab lands, supplemented by *Ottoman Empire and Islamic Tradition* by Norman Itzkowitz. In *Lawrence and Aaronsohn: T. E. Lawrence, Aaron Aaronsohn, and the Seeds of the Arab-Israeli Conflict*, Ronald Florence creates excellent portraits of both men, though he overemphasizes the friction between them. At the same time, Florence provides a solid perspective for the Balfour Declaration, which is then further developed in *Jews, Turks, Ottomans: A Shared History, Fifteenth to the Twentieth Century*, edited by Avigdor Levy. Great Britain's goals for the declaration are well presented in Lowe and Dockrill's *The Mirage of Power: Volume Two: British Foreign Policy 1914-22*.

"Desired the downfall of the state" and "would not forgo the smallest opportunity to cooperate with the enemy if there was a hostile attack against the Red Sea coast."—Hasan Kayali, *Arabs and Young Turks*, p. 184.

"The Holy War is doctrinally incompatible with an aggressive war, and absurd with a Christian ally, namely Germany."—T. E. Lawrence, *Seven Pillars of Wisdom,* p. 50.

"There is no national feeling among them. Their idea of nationality is the independence of tribes and parishes, and their idea of national union is episodic combined resistance to an intruder."—Ronald Florence, *Lawrence and Aaronsohn*, p. 20.

"A little snot" and "overbearing."—Florence, *Lawrence and Aaronsohn*, p. 413.

Balfour declaration source.—Doreen Ingrams, *Palestine Papers 1917–1922*, p. 16.

"To carry on extremely useful propaganda in Russia and America."—Ingrams, *Palestine Papers 1917–1922*, p. 16.

CHAPTER NINE—THE ROAD TO DAMASCUS

The collapse of the Ottoman war effort is admirably and comprehensively recounted in *The Turks in World History* by Carter Findley, *The Making of Modern Turkey* by Feroz Ahmad, *Ordered to Die* by Edward J. Erickson, and *The War of the World* by Niall Ferguson, while David Fromkin's *A Peace to End All Peace* fills in the details of the Allied political situation as the Ottoman Empire unraveled. The story of the British campaign in Palestine and the drive to Syria are found in Lawrence James's *Imperial Warrior: The Life and Times of Field Marshal Viscount Allenby 1861–1936*. Although much older, *Allenby of Armageddon: A Record of the Career and Campaigns of Field-Marshal Viscount Allenby*, by Raymond Savage, adds a tremendous amount of contemporary detail, both in tone and in attitude. For the Turks' decision to seek an armistice, see the First World War histories by Gilbert and Keegan.

"To the Inhabitants of Jerusalem the Blessed and the People Dwelling in Its Vicinity. . . ."—Charles Francis Horne, ed., *Source Records of the Great War*, vol. 5, p. 208.

CHAPTER 10—THE FALL OF THE SULTAN'S REALM

The demise of the Ottoman Empire is comprehensively presented in Donald Quataert's *The Ottoman Empire, 1700–1922*, Stanford J. and Ezel Kural Shaw's *History of the Ottoman Empire and Modern Turkey Volume 2, Reform, Revolution, and Republic: The Rise of Modern Turkey 1808–1975*, and Bernard Lewis's *The Emergence of Modern Turkey*. The methods by which the partition of the empire was decided and accomplished is laid out in *From Paris to Sèvres: The Partition of the Ottoman Empire at the Peace Conference of 1919–1920*, by Paul C. Helmreich, while the story of the entire fiasco of the Treaty of Sèvres and its consequences can be found in Lowe and Dockrill's *The Mirage of Power: Volume Two: British Foreign*

Policy 1914–22. How the Turks under Mustafa Kemal reorganized themselves and drove the Allies, the Armenians, and the Greeks out of Anatolia is recounted in Emil Lengyel's *They Called Him Atatürk*, Patrick Kinross's *Atatürk: The Rebirth of a Nation*, and *Modernization in the Middle East: The Ottoman Empire and Its Afro-Asian Successors* by Cyril E. Black and L. Carl Brown. The tragedy of the forcible relocation of Greeks and Turks is made very real in Giles Milton's *Paradise Lost— Smyrna 1922: The Destruction of a Christian City in the Islamic World.*

"Mired in an unending chain of bloodthirstiness, plunder and abuses . . . by a recourse to a number of vile tricks and deceitful means." Their indictment also declared that "the massacre and destruction of the Armenians were the result of decisions by the Central Committee" to "pile up fortunes for themselves" through "the pillage and plunder."—Taner Akçam, *A Shameful Act: The Armenian Genocide and the Question of Turkish Responsibility*, pp. 323–24.

"Its findings cannot be held of any account at all."—Akçam, *A Shameful Act*, p. 480.

"Against whom would these resources be employed?"—Emil Lengyel, *They Called Him Atatürk*, p. 87.

"Being seated between Jesus Christ and Napoleon."—Peter Rowland, *David Lloyd George: A Biography*, p. 578.

"The Entente Powers are determined that the Arab race shall be given full opportunity of once again forming a nation in the world. This can only be achieved by the Arabs themselves uniting, and Great Britain and her Allies will pursue a policy with this ultimate unity in view."—Hasan Kayali, *Arabs and Young Turks: Ottomanism, Arabism, and Islamism in the Ottoman Empire, 1908–1918*, p. 328.

"Barbarous and illegitimate methods of warfare . . . [including] offenses against the laws and customs of war and the principles of humanity."—Charles Francis Horne, ed., *Source Records of the Great War*, vol. 7, p. 214.

"It is the nation's iron fist that writes the Nation's Oath which is the main principle of our independence to the annals of history."—Patrick Kinross, *Atatürk*, p. 246. "In order to develop in every field, the country should be independent and free; all restrictions on political, judicial and financial development will be removed." —Kinross, *Atatürk*, p. 250.

"The unity of the motherland and national independence are in danger. The Constantinople government is unable to carry out its responsibilities. It is only through the nation's effort and determination that national independence will be won. It is necessary to establish a national committee, free from all external influences and control, that will review the national situation and make known to the world the people's desires for justice. It has been decided to hold immediately a National Congress in Sivas, the most secure place in Anatolia. Three representatives from each province should be sent immediately to the Sivas Congress. To be prepared for every eventuality, this subject should be kept a national secret. There will be a congress for the Eastern Provinces on July 1. The delegation from the Erzurum Congress will depart to join to the general meeting in Sivas."—Andrew Mango, *Ataturk*, pp. 389–90.

Bibliography

Ahmad, Feroz. *The Making of Modern Turkey*. London: Routledge, 1993.

———. *The Young Turks: The Committee of Union and Progress in Turkish Politics, 1908–1914*. London: C. Hurst and Co., 1969.

Akçam, Taner. *A Shameful Act: The Armenian Genocide and the Question of Turkish Responsibility*. New York: Metropolitan Books, 2006.

Albertini, Luigi. *The Origins of the War of 1914*, 3 vols. Oxford, UK: Oxford University Press, 1952–57.

Ãzkirimli, Umut, and Spyros Sofos. *Tormented by History: Nationalism in Greece and Turkey*. Irvington, NY: Columbia University Press, 2007.

Barber, Noel. *Lords of the Golden Horn: From Suleiman the Magnificent to Kemal Ataturk*. London: Macmillan, 1973.

Barkey, Karen. *Empire of Difference: The Ottomans in Comparative Perspective*. Cambridge, UK: Cambridge University Press, 2008.

Berend, Tibor Iván. *History Derailed: Central and Eastern Europe in the Long Nineteenth Century*. London: University of California Press, 2003.

Berridge, G. R. *Gerald Fitzmaurice (1865–1939), Chief Dragoman of the British Embassy in Turkey*. Lieden, the Netherlands: Martinus Nijhoff, 2007.

Black, Cyril E., and L. Carl Brown. *Modernization in the Middle East: The Ottoman Empire and Its Afro-Asian Successors*. Princeton, NJ: Darwin Press, 1992.

Carlyon, Les. *Gallipoli*. New York: Doubleday, 2001.

Cleveland, William L. *A History of the Modern Middle East*. Boulder, CO: Westview Press, 2004.

Creasy, Sir Edward Shepherd. *History of the Ottoman Turks: From the Beginning of Their Empire to the Present Time*. London: R. Bentley and Son, 1877.

De Courtois, Sébastien. *The Forgotten Genocide: The Eastern Christians, the Last Arameans*. Piscataway, NJ: Gorgias Press, 2004.

Djemal, Ahmed. *Memoires of a Turkish Statesman: 1913–1919*. New York: George H. Doran Company, 1922.

Easterly, William. *The White Man's Burden: Why the West's Efforts to Aid the Rest Have Done So Much Ill and So Little Good*. New York: Penguin, 2007.

Erickson, Edward J. *Ordered to Die: A History of the Ottoman Army in the First World War*. Westport, CT: Greenwood Publishing, 2001.

Faroqhi, Suraiya. *Subjects of the Sultan: Culture and Daily Life in the Ottoman Empire*. London: I. B. Tauris, 2000.

Feener, R. Michael, and Terenjit Sevea. *Islamic Connections: Muslim Societies in South and Southeast Asia*. Singapore: Institute of Southeast Asian Studies, 2009.

Ferguson, Niall. *The War of the World: Twentieth-Century Conflict and the Descent of the West*. New York: Penguin Press, 2006

Fewster, Kevin. *Gallipoli: The Turkish Story*. London: Allen and Unwin, 2003.

Findley, Carter. *The Turks in World History*. New York: Oxford University Press, 2004.

Finkel, Caroline. *Osman's Dream: The Story of the Ottoman Empire, 1300–1923*. London: Hodder Headline, 2005.

Florence, Ronald. *Lawrence and Aaronsohn: T. E. Lawrence, Aaron Aaronsohn, and the Seeds of the Arab-Israeli Conflict*. New York: Viking Adult, 2007.

Fortna, Benjamin C. *Imperial Classroom: Islam, the State, and Education in the Late Ottoman Empire*. New York: Oxford University Press, 2002.

Freely, John. *Istanbul: The Imperial City*. New York: Penguin, 1998.

Fromkin, David. *A Peace to End All Peace: The Fall of the Ottoman Empire and the Creation of the Modern Middle East*. New York: Avon Books, 1990.

Gilbert, Martin. *The First World War: A Complete History*. New York: Henry Holt and Co., 2004.

Göçek, Fatma Müge. *Rise of the Bourgeoisie, Demise of Empire: Ottoman Westernization and Social Change*. New York: Oxford University Press, 1996.

Goodwin, Jason. *Lords of the Horizons: A History of the Ottoman Empire.* New York: Picador, 2003.

Grey, Viscount of Fallodon (Sir Edward Grey). *Twenty-Five Years,* 2 vols. London: Hodder & Stoughton, 1925.

Hale, William. *Turkish Foreign Policy, 1774–2000.* London: Routledge, 2000.

Hanioglu, M. Sükrü. *A Brief History of the Late Ottoman Empire.* Princeton, NJ: Princeton University Press, 2008.

———. *Preparation for a Revolution: The Young Turks, 1902–1908.* Oxford University Press, 2001.

Haythornthwaite, Philip J. *Gallipoli 1915, Frontal Assault on Turkey.* Campaign Series #8. London: Osprey, 1991.

———. *The World War One Sourcebook.* London: Arms and Armour Press, 1992.

Helmreich, Paul C. *From Paris to Sèvres: The Partition of the Ottoman Empire at the Peace Conference of 1919–1920.* Columbus: Ohio University Press, 1974.

Heywood, Colin. *Writing Ottoman History: Documents and Interpretations.* Farnham, UK: Ashgate, 2002.

Hinsely, Francis Harry. *British Foreign Policy under Sir Edward Grey.* Cambridge, UK: Cambridge University Press, 1977.

Horne, Charles F., ed. *Source Records of the Great War,* 7 vols. No location given: National Alumni, 1923.

Imber, Colin. *The Ottoman Empire, 1300–1650: The Structure of Power.* New York: Palgrave Macmillan, 2002.

Inalcik, Halil, Suraiya Faroqhi, Bruce McGowan, and Donald Quataert, eds. *An Economic and Social History of the Ottoman Empire, 1300–1914.* Cambridge, UK: Cambridge University Press, 1997.

Ingrams, Doreen. *Palestine Papers 1917-1922.* London: Eland Books, 2010.

Itzkowitz, Norman. *Ottoman Empire and Islamic Tradition.* Chicago: Chicago University Press, 1980.

James, Lawrence. *Imperial Warrior: The Life and Times of Field Marshal Viscount Allenby 1861–1936.* London: Weidenfeld & Nicolson, 1993.

James, Robert Rhodes. *Gallipoli: A British Historian's View.* Parkville, Victoria: University of Melbourne, 1995.

Jelavich, Barbara. *History of the Balkans: Eighteenth and Nineteenth Centuries.* Cambridge, UK: Cambridge University Press, 1983.

Kantowicz, Edward R. *The Rage of Nations* (*The World in the Twentieth Century, Vol. 1*). Grand Rapids, MI: William B. Eerdmans, 1999.

Karpat, Kemal H. *Ottoman Population, 1830–1914: Demographic and Social Characteristics.* Madison: University of Wisconsin Press, 1985.

———. *The Politicization of Islam: Reconstructing Identity, State, Faith, and Community in the Late Ottoman State.* New York: Oxford University Press, 2001.

Kayali, Hasan. *Arabs and Young Turks: Ottomanism, Arabism, and Islamism in the Ottoman Empire, 1908–1918.* Berkeley: University of California Press, 1997.

Keegan, John. *The First World War.* New York: Hutchinson, 1998.

Kiernan, Ben. *Blood and Soil: Genocide and Extermination in World History from Carthage to Darfur.* New Haven, CT: Yale University Press, 2007.

Kinross, Patrick. *The Ottoman Centuries: The Rise and Fall of the Turkish Empire.* New York: Morrow, 1979.

———. *Atatürk: The Rebirth of a Nation.* London: Phoenix Press, 2003.

Kinzer, Stephen. *Crescent and Star: Turkey between Two Worlds.* New York: Farrar, Straus and Giroux, 2001.

Kushner, David. *The Rise of Turkish Nationalism, 1876–1908.* London: Routledge, 1977.

Lawrence, T. E. *Seven Pillars of Wisdom.* London: Doubleday, Doran, and Co., 1935.

Lengyel, Emil. *They Called Him Atatürk.* New York: John Day Co., 1962.

Lepsius, Johannes. *Deutschland und Armenien 1914–1918, Sammlung diplomatischer Aktenstücke* (*Germany and Armenia 1914–1918, Diplomatic Document Collection*) (reprint). Bremen: Donat & Temmen Verlag, 1986.

Levy, Avigdor, ed. *Jews, Turks, Ottomans: A Shared History, Fifteenth to the Twentieth Century.* Syracuse, NY: Syracuse University Press, 2002.

Lewis, Bernard. *The Emergence of Modern Turkey*, 3rd ed. New York: Oxford University Press, 2001.

Lewy, Guenter. *The Armenian Massacres in Ottoman Turkey: A Disputed Genocide.* Salt Lake City: University of Utah Press, 2005.

Lowe, Cedric James, and Michael L. Dockrill. *The Mirage of Power: Volume Two: British Foreign Policy 1914–22.* London: Routledge and Kegan Paul, 1972.

Lowe, John. *The Great Powers, Imperialism, and the German Problem, 1865–1925.* London: Routledge, 1994.

Manchester, William. *The Arms of Krupp 1587–1968.* New York: Little Brown and Co., 1968.

————. *The Last Lion, Winston Spencer Churchill, Volume I, Visions of Glory*. New York: Little Brown and Co., 1983.

Mango, Andrew. *Ataturk: The Biography of the Founder of Modern Turkey*. Woodstock, NY: Overlook Press, 2000.

Mansel, Philip. *Istanbul: City of the World's Desire, 1453–1924*. London: John Murray, 2006.

Massie, Robert K. *Castles of Steel: Britain, Germany, and the Winning of the Great War at Sea*. New York: Ballantine, 2004.

McCarthy, Justin. *The Ottoman Peoples and the End of Empire*. London: Hodder Arnold, 2001.

Melson, Robert. *Revolution and Genocide: On the Origins of the Armenian Genocide and the Holocaust*. Chicago: University of Chicago Press, 1996.

Milton, Giles. *Paradise Lost—Smyrna 1922: The Destruction of a Christian City in the Islamic World*. New York: Basic Books, 2008.

Moorehead, Alan. *Gallipoli*. New York: New English Library, 1968.

Morgenthau, Henry Sr. *Ambassador Morgenthau's Story*. Garden City, NY: Doubleday, 1918.

————. *The Murder of a Nation*. With a preface by W. N. Medlicott. New York: Armenian General Benevolent Union of America, 1974.

Naim Bey. *The Memoirs of Naim Bey: Turkish Official Documents Relating to the Deportation and the Massacres of Armenians, Compiled by Aram Andonian*. London: Hodder and Stoughton, ca. 1920.

Naimark, Norman. *Fires of Hatred: Ethnic Cleansing in the 20th Century*. Cambridge, UK: Harvard University Press, 2001.

Owen, Roger. *The Middle East in the World Economy, 1800–1914*. London: I. B. Tauris, 1993.

Paris, Timothy J. *Britain, the Hashemites and Arab Rule, 1920–1925: The Sherifian Solution*. London: Routledge, 2003.

Quataert, Donald. *The Ottoman Empire, 1700–1922*. Cambridge, UK: Cambridge University Press, 2005.

Rogan, Eugene. *The Arabs: A History*. London: Allen Lane, 2009.

Rowland, Peter. *David Lloyd George: A Biography*. New York: Macmillan, 1976.

Savage, Raymond. *Allenby of Armageddon: A Record of the Career and Campaigns of Field-Marshal Viscount Allenby*. London: Hodder & Stoughton, 1925.

Schwanitz, Wolfgang G., ed. *Germany and the Middle East, 1871–1945*. Princeton, NJ: Markus Wiener Publishers, 2004.

Shaw, Stanford J., and Ezel Kural Shaw. *History of the Ottoman Empire and Modern Turkey Volume 2, Reform, Revolution, and Republic: The Rise of Modern Turkey 1808–1975*. Cambridge, UK: Cambridge University Press, 1977.

Somel, Selcuk Aksin. *Historical Dictionary of the Ottoman Empire*. Lanham, MD: Scarecrow Press, 2003.

Totten, Samuel, Paul Robert Bartrop, and Steven L. Jacobs, eds. *Dictionary of Genocide*. New York: Greenwood Publishing Group, 2008.

Tuchman, Barbara. *The Guns of August*. New York: Macmillan, 1962.

Uyar, Mesut. *A Military History of the Ottomans: From Osman to Atatürk*. New York: Praeger Security International, 2009.

Walker, Christopher J. *Armenia: The Survival of a Nation*. London: Palgrave Macmillan, 1980.

Yapp, M. E. *The Making of the Modern Near East, 1792–1923*. London: Longman, 1987.

INDEX

Aaronsohn, Aaron, 173–75; and NILI, 174–75
Aaronsohn, Sarah, 174
Abbas, Mohammed, 35
Abdul-Hamid II, Sultan, x, 21–25, 26–27, 33, 46, 49, 54, 59, 64; and Armenian Massacres, 21–22, 150, 151, 155; and Countercoup, 36–37; deposed 37; and German influence, 22, 23, 46, 58–59; and Revolution of 1908, 29, 30–31
Adrianople, 43, 47, 50, 52, 54, 226
Adriatic Sea, 13–14, 70
Aegean islands, 40, 73–74, 75, 216, 226
Aegean Sea, 14, 42–43, 64, 65, 73, 105, 107, 111–12, 115, 119, 120, 126, 156, 216, 227
Ahmet I, Sultan, 15
Albania (Albanians), 6, 27, 31, 43, 46
Aleppo, 167, 181, 203
Alexander II, Tsar of Russia, 149
Alexander III, Tsar of Russia, 149–50
Allenby, Lt. Gen. Sir Edmund, x, 173, 175, 188–89, 193, 194, 199, 200–202, 203, 228; breaks Gaza Line, 190–91; captures Damascus, 202–3; captures Jerusalem, 191–92; proclamation to citizens of Jersualem, 192
Allies, ix, x–xi, 53, 70, 81, 83–84, 85, 88–89, 90, 96, 98–99, 100, 135–36, 140, 151, 157, 163–65, 168, 169, 172, 177–78, 180, 193, 196, 199–200, 212, 216, 217, 219–20, 223, 226, 234; armistice with Ottoman Empire, 203–4, 205, 207, 208–9, 210–11; and Gallipoli Campaign, 110, 111, 112, 113, 115, 117–18, 124, 127, 130 ; peace treaties between Ottoman Empire and, 212–13, 217, 218, 224, 229–31; opportunity to make peace with Ottoman Empire, 142–45
the Amasya Circular, 221–22
Amara, 101, 102–3, 104–5
Anatolia, 1–4, 6, 21, 24, 38, 110, 113, 150, 151, 152–57, 159, 160, 161, 176, 197, 204, 207, 208, 212, 216–17, 219, 221, 222–23, 224, 226–27, 228, 229
Andonian, Aram, 158
Angora, 219, 221, 222, 223, 227, 229, 233, 235
Ankara, 219, 235
Aqaba, 172–73, 182

About the Author

Daniel Allen Butler is a bestselling author and a maritime and military historian. Some of his previous works include *"Unsinkable": The Full Story of RMS Titanic*; *Distant Victory: The Battle of Jutland and the Allied Triumph in the First World War*; and *The First Jihad: The Battle for Khartoum and the Dawn of Militant Islam*.

Educated at Hope College, Grand Valley State University, and the University of Erlangen, Butler served in the U.S. Army before becoming a full-time author. He is currently at work on two new projects: *The Field Marshal*, a biography of Erwin Rommel, and *Waterloo: The Last Field of Glory*, a history of the Hundred Days. A self-proclaimed "professional beach bum," Butler divides what little time he spends away from his writing between his love of woodworking, his passion for British sports cars, and his fascination with building model ships. He currently lives in Culver City, California.